NICARAGUA:

Past, Present and Future;

A DESCRIPTION OF

Its Inhabitants, Customs, Mines, Minerals, Early History, Modern Fillibusterism, Proposed Inter-Oceanic Canal and Manifest Destiny.

By PETER F. STOUT, Esq.

LATE UNITED STATES VICE CONSUL.

Bella Nicaragua! El Paraiso de las Indias.

PHILADELPHIA:

PHILADELPHIA:
JOHN E. POTTER AND COMPANY,
617 Sansom Street.

TO THE

HON. CHARLES F. MAYER,

Baltimore.

MY DEAR SIR:—

I discharge an agreeable duty in dedicating this Volume to you, for, believe me, your commendations alone have drawn the Manuscript from seclusion.

May I trust that the hopes now fanned into flame may prove other than ashes, and that the work *may* receive the distinction which you have so flatteringly predicted for its future?

Very sincerely, yours,

PETER F. STOUT.

NICARAGUA:

PAST, PRESENT AND FUTURE.

What the Press says of It.

With a beautiful climate, a soil of unsurpassed fertility, and mines of wondrous wealth, this interesting country occupies a prominent position in the eyes of the whole civilized world—but especially so to the people of these United States. She is the key to our Pacific possessions; and with a government of proverbial instability, the lives and property of vast numbers of our citizens annually passing through her borders are placed in jeopardy. All these, with other great points of interest will be found fully covered by this volume. How acceptable it has already provedto the American people, may be gathered from the notices annexed.

"The work is printed on beautiful paper, in a clear type, and well bound. We have read Squiers' Central America, but were more interested with the narrative of Mr. Stout. The work pursues a natural order—overlooking nothing of interest—giving glowing accounts of the country, its scenery and resources—doing justice to the history of the country and its revolution and leaders, and present inhabitants. It gives, in compact style, the history of Kinney's and Walker's expeditions, and results. Altogether, the book is very interesting both for its own merits, and the knowledge it throws upon matters of growing importance in our great future."—*Independent Civilian.*

"Mr. Stout believes that 'manifest destiny' will one day incorporate Nicaragua with the United States. His book is full of interest, and evidently written with great knowledge of its subject."—*Philadelphia Press.*

"The book is replete with interest not only intrinsic, but from the manner in which the subject to which it relates is treated."—*New Orleans Delta.*

"It is a work of about four hundred pages, and embraces more information on the subjects which the author treats of, than any other work of the kind." —*Democratic Age.*

"It is written in a clear, easy style, carrying on its very face, the appearance of truth—no exaggeration of facts or coloring of events, for effect."—*Baltimore Patriot.*

"It treats of one of the most important topics of the political world—is well written—full of pleasant sketches—and takes the reader into a beautiful, and to a great extent, unknown country. Altogether, we highly recommend the reading of this book."—*Evening Journal.*

"It contains a vast deal of useful information about a country which at present occupies a large share of public attention; is written in a pleasant off-hand, readable style, and apart from value as a work of reference, is eminently worthy of attentive perusal as an entertaining book."—*Transcript.*

"During the fillibustering career of Walker, he was a resident of Nicaragua, and saw many of the movements of the belligerents. His information is copious and thorough. The style is clear and lively, and the reader finds no difficulty in taking in the scenes described, and the events related. Whoever is interested in the affairs of Nicaragua, will find this book an indispensable necessity."—*Philadelphia Dispatch.*

"He is an easy and graceful writer, and his style lends many charms to his subject. We commend it to our readers, assuring them of its interest."—*Darlington (S. C.) Flag.*

"It is well got up, and is a book which should find its way into every library."—*People's (Miss.) Press.*

"All who desire to become fully posted in the history of Nicaragua, and spend pleasant moments in its perusal, are advised to purchase this volume." —*American (Md.) Sentinel.*

"One of the most agreeably written books of travel we have met with in a long time. Its style is simple without poverty of expression, and elegant without ostentation; and while it presents its pictures in a soft, romantic light, it is filled with valuable and accurate information."—*Porter's Spirit of the Times.*

"The work is worthy of attentive perusal; and we feel satisfied that the time thus spent will be amply repaid in the knowledge obtained of the Central American States."—*Baltimore Republican.*

"Will be read with much interest at the present time."—*Salisbury (N. C.) Banner.*

"The interest that attaches to every thing relating to Nicaragua, cannot fail to secure for this book a large sale."—*New Church Herald.*

"It is a valuable treatise, and imparts much information in regard to the climate, soil, productions, habits, and customs of the inhabitants; and will, no doubt, be the means of directing the attention of enterprising men to that country."—*Athens (Ala.) Herald.*

"The pages are written in an impartial spirit; is gotten up in capital style —as regards type and paper—and it merits what the trade terms a 'run.'"—*Pennsylvania Inquirer.*

"This is one of those rare books of travel, calculated to instruct as well as entertain the reader. For a number of years past, no portion of the globe has engrossed more of public interest than Nicaragua, arising not only from the fact that it has been the focus of fillibustering, but because across its territory, either by railroad or canal, is afforded the most eligible route for the commerce of the world to pass between the Atlantic and Pacific oceans. To those who wish a treatise on this interesting portion of America, we commend the volume before us as possessing all the general reader can desire."—*Easton (Md.) Star.*

PREFACE.

I HAVE written a current History of Nicaragua, a Guide Book, and furnished in a succinct form, information, Geographical, Topographical, and Statistical. My residence in the country afforded me great facilities for comparing and verifying the authorities consulted, and the results of my observations and deductions are comprised in the present volume.

The Past of every Province of the Spanish Americas, abounds with interest to the student as well as the general reader; and "El Paraiso de Mahoma" has a present historic importance, which renders aught orthodox upon the country desirable and attractive.

I have penned my pages with a view solely to merit the *respect* of the Public, having neither varnished nor tarnished a subject, at present vital to my own country; and I feel assured, that I have not been led astray by the garbled statements of those, whose interests may have suffered from causes, which have not exercised, in the remotest degree, an atom of influence upon me.

PETER F. STOUT.

PHILADELPHIA, February, 1859.

CONTENTS.

CHAPTER I.

CHAPTER II.

CHAPTER III.

CHAPTER IV.

CHAPTER V.

CHAPTER VI.

CHAPTER VII.

CHAPTER VIII.

CHAPTER IX.

CHAPTER X.

CHAPTER XI.

CHAPTER XII

CHAPTER XIII.

CHAPTER XIV.

CHAPTER XV.

CHAPTER XVI.

CHAPTER XVII.

CHAPTER XVIII.

CHAPTER XIX.

CHAPTER XX.

CHAPTER XXI.

CHAPTER XXII.

CHAPTER XXIII.

CHAPTER XXIV.

CHAPTER XXV.

CHAPTER XXVI.

CHAPTER XXVII.

CHAPTER XXVIII.

CHAPTER XXIX.

CHAPTER XXX.

CHAPTER XXXI.

CHAPTER XXXII.

NICARAGUA.

PAST, PRESENT, AND FUTURE.

CHAPTER I.

EXTENT—GEOGRAPHICAL POSITION—VOLCANOES—LAKES—MANAGUA AND NICARAGUA—RIVERS—THE RIO SAN JUAN—TRAILING VINES—ALLIGATORS—MONKEYS—RAPIDS—THE CASTILLO AND MACHUCA—CLIMATE—TEMPERATURE—AN INCIDENT.

THE Republic of Nicaragua is embraced entirely between 83° and 88° west longitude from Greenwich, or 6° and 11° west from Washington, and between 9° 30′ and 15° of north latitude, with an area of between fifty and sixty thousand square miles, being about seven times the extent of Massachusetts. It is bounded by the Caribbean Sea on the east; on the west by the Pacific Ocean; north, by the river Vanks, or Segovia, and partly by the river Roman; and south by Costa Rica—or, as this is a mooted point, we may add, its southern boundary, separating it from Costa Rica, runs in a right line from the mouth of the river Salto de Nicoya to the lower mouth of the Rio San Juan. Its geographical position, having a fine harbor, the town of Greytown, or San Juan, on the Atlantic, and other fine harbors on the Pacific, fully entitles this small State to the consideration of statesmen and the mercantile world, and has won for it its motto "*The vast gate of the twin sea.*" The great chain of Cordilleras diverges in two ranges, and all the streams upon the southern side fall into the lakes Managua and Nicaragua, or into the Rio San Juan. The Pacific range, in volcanic cones, follows the general direction of the coast, gradually settling to low hills and plains. The principal cones are Momotombo, Momobacho, Ometepec, Madeira, with those of Viejo, Santa Clara, Axusco, Orosi, Abogado, together with others less remarkable, yet known not alone as landmarks, and as beautiful natural structures, but as being the traditional depots of great hidden wealth.

There are two remarkable and beautiful inland lakes: that of Managua, erroneously called Leon, and Nicaragua; the former being about fifty-five miles long by thirty-five in width, ranging from two to thirty-five fathoms deep. The mountains of Matagalpa, rich with silver, gold, lead, and other minerals, on the northern and eastern shores, margin with wondrous beauty this quiet basin, while Momotombo, from whose lofty peak I watched thin clouds of smoke wreathing upward, relieved by the dark gray morning sky, rises, grandly, in its bosom; Momotombita, a fit companion, stands in bold relief, so beautifully artistic in design and character, that it wins an involuntary exclamation from us as, on the beach, we gaze far up its shaggy ascent.

The Lake Nicaragua is about one hundred and ten miles long by thirty-five to sixty miles in breadth, and every variety of depth may here be fathomed. This sheet of water is the most beautiful of any I ever saw; and yet within its depths the rapacious shark fins his way along, and the timid mariner witnesses waterspouts, and experiences the most sudden, dangerous squalls met with in any water on the globe. Its sole outlet is the Rio San Juan. During the months of October, November, December, and January, the prevailing winds are from the northeast, and the waves of the lake scud angrily upon the beach, dashing the spray, broadcast, in refreshing showers. At such seasons, travelers, desirous of journeying from the south, experience much difficulty in getting off in the small schooners heretofore exclusively used between Granada and the ports south of it—San Jorge and Virgin Bay. Indeed, I have known parties who have been delayed two weeks, yet endeavoring, perhaps frequently during the day, to launch their boats, but ere their sails would fill, the breakers, rushing shoreward, would drive the boats high and dry upon the beach. It was formerly supposed from this, that there was an ebb and flow to the lake, and judging at such seasons, a stranger would be convinced that it was no dream, but an actual reality. The streams known as the San Carlos and Serapaqui, flow into the Rio San Juan, with numerous others bordering it. This river is from one hundred yards to a quarter of a mile wide, from one to twenty-five feet deep, and about ninety-one miles long, margined by heavy underbrush and fine timber; while the bank on either side is so heavily screened with trailing vines, that at various places it is impenetrable to the eye. I have seen a single one, climbing up a gigantic Trumpet-tree, wreathe round its top, cover it, then falling gracefully in myriads of clusters resembling the various jets of a fountain, reach terra firma, then clasp another tree, and so on until one would almost imagine the Banyan before him. Upon its shores, and on the many sand islets, is seen reposing, in fancied and blest security, like a fat millionaire, the swarthy alligator; and leaping from tree to tree, and shriekingly from vine to vine, are countless monkeys—some short-tailed, others long, ring-tailed, others no-tailed, cropped off short, regular bob-tails.

For calm, quiet beauty, the Rio San Juan is pre-eminent, and will retain numberless charms for the tourist's eye, even should the axe of the settler ring through the wilderness on its banks. There are various rapids in the ascent, viz.: the Machucha, the Castillo, the Tauro, the Cow, and the Calf. The Machucha Rapids take their name from Captain Diego Machuca, who, in 1529, explored the river. They are by no means entitled to the name, but may better be designated as an eddy, for here the river bends, and the current is swift, indeed very swift, yet navigable for stern-wheel boats without much difficulty. The Castillo Rapids—where the old castle frowns from its height of one hundred feet or more above, are truly such, yet far from equaling those on the St. Lawrence River, and others elsewhere. They appear to have been formed by art, rather than Nature. Large loose stones obstruct the river, and the swift current roars through the interstices, seeming at a short distance to be indeed very formidable; yet I, with others, in 1850, endeavored to haul a stern-wheel iron steamer up them, and should have succeeded, had the banks been firm, or had we had a stump around which to trail our hawsers. Our feet slipped, the current swept the boat down—down over the rapids. Being of iron, she bounded from rock to rock, and after sweeping perhaps one hundred yards down the current, ran safely ashore on the opposite bank.

It requires but little valor to brave these rapids; and the heart of a sailor throbs lightly and easily under his jacket, as he steers his craft into the stream, and mounts the noisy little bubbles. Fort St. Juan, called also the Castle of Neustra Senora, surmounts the hill at the Castillo Rapids, on the left in ascending the river. It is now in a state of decay; but in its earlier days it had a small battery, mounted with thirty-six guns, whose platform was level with the water, the whole enclosed on the land side by a ditch and rampart. The garrison consisted of one hundred infantry, sixteen artillery-men, and sixty militia, and was also provided with guard-boats, which were rowed up and down the river every night. The fort was provisioned from Granada; and six months stores were always stowed away in the capacious under-ground garners.

There is a variety of climate in Nicaragua, the heat being less on the Pacific than the Atlantic coast. On the former, the rainy season sets in in the early part of May; and with the exception or intervention of fifteen or twenty days in July and the beginning of August, continues till October, and in some sections till November. During the remainder of the year an occasional shower refreshes the heated air, sufficient only to glaze the parched leaves—yet in this dry season, fine fruits are in abundance; and although the crisp grass and wilted leaves evidence drought, or in fact, correspond to our winter, yet with the difference in mid-day, there is no great change in the temperature. The interior is cooler than the coast by about 14° Fahrenheit. On the Atlantic, rains fall throughout the year with considerable uncertainty; the driest season is from June to October; the wettest from that to May.

From daybreak to 10 A. M., in this country, is always pleasant, and a ride on horseback is enjoyed; from 10 A. M. to 4 P. M. the heat is intense, so much so, that the population are generally swinging in their casas in their hammocks, save the mariners and washer-women, who are sprinkled over the lake beach at Managua and Granada; from 4 P. M. the temperature is modified by the coming on of night. There seems scarcely a pause between the bright glare of the sun and the mellow rays of the moon: twilight being a dream, or mayhap a memory of a far-distant land.

The evenings are delightfully agreeable, and the air pure, so much so, that a party conversing in the usual key, may be interpreted at the distance of a square, and I have frequently been able to follow the air of some serenader, distant at least three-fourths of a mile.

The rainy season is the most pleasant, the thermometer ranging from 78° to 88°, rarely below 72° in the night, and rising to 90° in the afternoon. At Granada, in June, 82°; in Leon, in July, August and September, 83°; and a strong breeze sweeps from the lake, rendering the nights just such as guarantee refreshing sleep. In the dry season, in January, the temperature is less occasionally cool; every thing is filled with dust; clouds of grasshoppers sweep over the forests, devour the leaves of the trees and vines, and leave a ghostly picture of desolation and aridity behind. I remember, during a ride from the little Indian village of Nindiri to Managua, in company with several friends, meeting a host of these rapacious banditti. We were in the midst of a forest; a cloud seemed to hang over our heads; a rattling among the dried leaves of the trees attracted our attention, resembling sand thrown on blotting-paper, though louder. Wherever we turned, there this living cloud extended. We found, upon reaching the outskirt of the woods, that an immense body of grasshoppers were winging past us, leaving leafless bushes, trees, and a trail of barren, poverty-stricken herbage. We pushed forward, in a fast walk, and judging by the time occupied, we estimated this moving mass to have been *at least* four miles long by three miles in breadth. This is not an uncommon visit, nor do I over-estimate the extent of this described party of insects.

Years agone, their devastation was so great, that prayers were offered up in all the churches of the State. The towns were filled with them—the yards, rooms, barracks, and churches; wherever there was a void, there they went. Prayers were unavailing, useless, till one morn, at daybreak, a mighty rushing was heard overhead. A terrible crash, a battling, as it were, of wings, mingled with cries and shrieks.

On came the heavy cloud, and far above, clad in angelic armor, San Miguel was seen driving the enemy back, and at every blow massacring myriads. As the sun rose fully up, the scene on Nature's canvas grew fainter, the cries less distinct, yet the sword of the patron saint was seen still battling. The enemy was routed; the country safe. So runs the story.

These same insects, or their progeny, returned there during my stay in the country, and seemed to have all the fun to themselves. However, they did not settle there, but only paid a flying visit, leaving ample room for other adventurers, whose patron saints were strong arms, whose advent was sure, and whose dispersion was at least uncertain.

CHAPTER II.

DISTRICTS, POPULATION—TOWNS, POPULATION—GRANADA, ITS ARCHITECTURE, CHURCHES, STREETS, CARTS, WASHING AND WASHER-WOMEN—SAN CARLOS, THE COMMANDANTE'S HOUSE, THE OLD FORT, THE CUSTOM HOUSE—LAKE NICARAGUA—RIO FRIO—LA BOQUETA—ISLANDS—VIRGIN BAY AND THE ADJACENT COUNTRY—SAN MIGUELITA—SAN JORGE, ITS PAROCHIAL CHURCH—ROAD TO RIVAS.

THERE are six districts in this State: viz., Rivas; Chontales, Granada, Massaya, and Managua; Leon and Chinandega; Matagalpa; Segovia; and Guanacaste. From a late census return, the combined population amounts to two hundred and sixty-four thousand:—Rivas, twenty thousand; Chontales, Granada, Massaya, and Managua, ninety-five thousand; Leon and Chinandega, ninety thousand; Matagalpa, forty thousand; Segovia, twelve thousand; and Guanacaste, seven thousand. There are about twenty towns, varying in population from five hundred to thirty thousand. Rivas, or ancient Nicaragua, has about eleven thousand; Granada, fifteen thousand; Massaya, fifteen thousand; Managua, eleven thousand; Leon, twenty-five thousand to thirty thousand; and Chinandega, about twelve thousand.

Granada, lying on Lake Nicaragua, occupies the site of the ancient Indian town "Salteba." Its buildings are of adobes roofed with tiles, while its principal edifices, with domes and towers, are of a strange medley of Moresque architecture. The windows are bird-cages on a large scale; the houses are one story in height, and are about sixteen or eighteen feet from the pavement to the eaves of the roofs, which project beyond the walls, and serve to wanderers as coverings from the rain. The pavements are raised, leaving the streets about two feet or more below; and as the town is built on terraces, during the rainy season floods of water rush down this channel with great velocity, rendering it any thing but an easy task to cross from side to side. The streets are narrow, though ample for convenience and beauty. They are unpaved, and in dry weather dusty; yet better sheltered by the overhanging roofs from the tropical sun than those of North America. The churches are generally in a state of decay, and present little remarkable to the eye.

Riding on horseback is the principal mode of traveling. There are mule paths throughout the entire State, but few roads are passable for a cart or wagon, not many of which are used. The carters with their loaded vehicles often afford a rich treat to the observer, though doubtless vexatious enough to themselves. With one wheel perhaps in a deep wash, the other on a rock, it requires assiduous attentions on the part of the driver to ever reach a market with his cargo in safety. The wheels screech, for grease is never used, but instead of it a bush, called the soap-bush, also used for washing; this, for a time, eases the thirsty axle, but, anon, as the wheel rolls on, its plaintive cries for more soap grate harshly on the ear. It is said this custom of non-greasing is deemed politically expedient, for no enemy can thus approach a town without giving due notice.

Taken altogether, the city of Granada is situated beautifully, and is a truly delightful residence. It was founded in 1522, by Francisco Hernandez de Cordova, who built a fort for its protection on the lake beach, which is now much dilapidated, or was, prior to Gen. Walker's entering it. Its gray walls, and its sentry-box, which may once have resounded with martial music, are now deserted, save where the humming washer-woman hangs the banner of her profession—a shirt, or its accompaniments—on the bulwarks, to bleach in the sun. These ladies do a vast deal of thumping. Your clothes are sent to be washed, say at seventy-five cents per dozen; it must be stated, definitely, starching and ironing, or there will be extras in the bill. They take the clothes to the lake, place them between two large stones, (similar to the iron stone,) rub them with the soap-bush, and then beat them till in a foam; then a rinse in the lake; soap them again, and another beating upon the stone, in so vigorous manner, as only to be fully appreciated by the poor fellow gazing on, and questioning himself as to where he shall get buttons to replace those now flying off; and who is to do the sewing. A clean shirt is a luxury; but even a clean one without buttons, is sadly vexatious.

Having ascended the Rio San Juan to Lake Nicaragua, let us pause at this spot, and survey, on either hand, the outspread panorama. To the right, on an eminence, stands the house of the Commandante of San Carlos, protected by a single gun, loaded to the muzzle probably for ten years past, and over whose touch-hole lies a piece of broken crockery. Here also is the Custom House, a regular frame barn, supported on posts some sixteen feet high, and under which goods are piled in indiscriminate confusion. The place was dedicated to the State, but dogs, pigs, and cows here meet on equal terms, and litter and repose in perfect security. The Old Fort lies back on a higher point, decayed, and covered with gross herbage. Its position commands the Lake and the mouth of the San Juan. Here also are piled up a great quantity of balls; and fine cannon, of exquisite mould, lie half hidden in the grass. The town consists of a few cane huts.

The Lake is before us—a wondrous, beautiful sheet—

studded with islands, covered with fruits and valuable woods, while, from its bosom rise Ometepec and Madeira, giant sentries o'er the wide and waving waste. To the left, flows the Rio Frio, whose sources are in the mountains of Costa Rica, from whence is derived the coolest and most refreshing water in the State; and although it has a depth of two fathoms, or more, for fifty miles above its mouth, and, consequently, is navigable for small stern-wheel steamers, yet its history is sealed, naught being, as yet, known concerning it, save from the unfriendly Guatosos Indians, who inhabit its banks, and who deny all entrance there. From some of these, glowing accounts of gold, silver, and opals have been received.

The islands of La Boqueta swarm near Granada, resembling the floating gardens of ancient Mexico. Solentiname, Zapatero, Cubi, the Corales, and numberless smaller ones, all dot the lake, a full account of which we are compelled to forego in our general history, though all are worthy of attention and of a visit. Across the lake is Virgin Bay, the landing point for passengers who have left the United States for California. It is on rising ground. The site will never answer for a town of any importance, although a pier has been constructed at great expense, for the landing of passengers. Its harbor is any thing but safe, the bottom being hard and sandy. Prior to the introduction of steamers on the Lake, vessels anchored at certain seasons, one mile and a half from the shore, to prevent dragging their anchors when the wind was high.

The country around it is rich and fertile, though grown up with rank vegetation and underbrush; and until the axe and plow are generally introduced here, and the hardy Anglo-Saxon dares its privations, malarias will abound, and the stories of Nicaragua's natural wealth and incomparable beauties will be received with suspicion, or listened to as were the traditionary legends of the ancient Incas of Peru.

San Miguelito is on the little bay of the same name, twenty miles above San Carlos. The country around is generally uninviting, though good grazing ground. Beyond, lie the volcanic mountains of Chontales. The shores are low and undulating. Those desirous of visiting what is generally termed Nicaragua, push across to the west side of the Lake where the outlined hills present a more favorable prospect. Beyond the black, volcanic masses, the mind imagines green fields, luxurious savannahs, and other scenes refreshing and pleasant to dwell upon. We shall speak of Chontales elsewhere in our volume.

A few miles north of Virgin Bay, on the opposite shore from San Carlos, stands, on rising ground, the little village of San Jorge, the port of Rivas. It is a pretty spot; almost every house surrounded with the coyal palm, the banana, plantain, and the cocoa. In its little plaza stands its parochial church, built in the uniform Moresque style, and dedicated to San Jorge. It is quite large, and contains twelve or thirteen altars, exclusive of the main one, covering the back part entire. It has few relics, nor is it richly ornamented, but answers that for which it was intended—a house of God. The padre I met acted as my cicerone; and after showing me the church and village, invited me to his house, where he regaled me with a good cigar, some good wine, and his blessing. I sprang into the stirrup, and after promising to deliver certain letters for him, as well as to call again, returned to the main road, and pushed forward to Rivas.

The road verges greatly—its length, probably about three miles, though one may think it five or six. Scattered along the route are ranchos hidden in orange and lemon groves, while, lining the path, the mango, to me the handsomest tree in the world, woos the weary traveler to a siesta. He is tempted to rest; the cocoa-nut hangs bewitchingly from its eyrie above, while the rattle of its milk within, appeals strongly to his tastes. He seizes a full one, leaps from his mule, and for a time forgets absence from those beloved in a distant clime.

CHAPTER III.

RIVAS—THE PLAZA—MARKET—SENORITAS—EARLY HISTORY—GIL GONZALES DE AVILA—THE ARRIVAL OF THE SPANIARDS—NICARAGUA—RODRIGO DE CONTRERAS—HERNANDEZ—THE CAPTURE OF THE COUNTRY—COUNTRY ABOUT RIVAS—BUSINESS—SAMOZA, THE REBEL CHIEF—HOTEL AND EATING—CHURCH OF SAN FRANCISCO—BUST OF WASHINGTON—HENRY CLAY—PRICE OF LAND—STORES AND TRADE—LIVING, BEEF, ETC.—MANNER OF COOKING—STOVES—WOOD.

OUR way is over a rolling country, well covered with fruits, where are numerous sites for beautiful homes. Rivas, the capital of the district, is entered by a broad road leading to the plaza, found in every Spanish settlement. Upon it is located the Cathedral, Government Houses, and shops, while the ground itself is occupied daily by the country people, who here sell their marketing—corn, beans, onions, oranges, lemons, pine-apples, jocotes, coffee, tobacco, sugar, cheese—in fine, everything from the haciendas to tempt the appetite and appease it. The señorita, with her dark olive skin well washed for the occasion, in her nice camisa, not reaching to her waist, and with a skirt independent of any contact above, smokes her cigarita, and laughs with the bargainer, while her sparkling eye entices the unwary foreigner to purchase at an exorbitant rate.

The dark-eyed daughters of Seville, and the nut-brown lasses of Nicaragua, have the same origin ; their language, mayhap, is partially changed, yet their spirits, their souls, are identical, and he who stays his steps beside the little saleswoman, will purchase. Smiles have a common origin, and sweet ones wreathe the pouting lips of Nicaragua's daughters, sufficient to bewilder any poor devil who, for the first time, dallies by their side.

The city of Rivas occupies the site of the aboriginal town. The first Spaniard who visited it was Gil Gonzales de Avila, who sailed from Panama in 1522. This noble landed upon the shores of the Gulf of Nicoya, with four horses and one hundred men. After experiencing many hardships, he entered the domain of the chief, Nicoya, who gave the Spaniards valuable presents, and in turn received from them glass toys and other pretty articles. Gonzales, learning that many miles northward, another chief had his territory, pushed forward, and reached the old town of Nicaragua, now Rivas, the subject of our present chapter. After some difficulties, battles ensued between them. The Spanish horse, an object of terror to these Indians, as well as to the early Mexicans and Peruvians, saved the utter destruction of the Spanish party; and they returned to Panama, with mighty accounts of the country, its resources, and its people.

Pedro de Arias thereupon determined to found a colony there, and dispatched Francisco Hernandez de Cordova for that purpose. Leon and Granada were built; but Pedro de Arias dying, his son-in-law, Rodrigo de Contreras, succeeded him. The orders of the crown, denying him, or any of the officers, holding the Indians as property, were disregarded. Provoked by petty and private jealousies, assassinations occurred. Rodrigo sought Spain to vindicate himself; and in his absence, Hernandez openly revolted, took possession of the country, and then embarked for Panama, which he captured; met with various mishaps, and finally sickened and died. In time it became a province in the Captain-generalcy of Guatemala, and so remained until 1823, when a spirit of republicanism drove monarchy from the country. Such is the history of Rivas.

The country immediately around, is just such as might be rendered all that man could desire. Three good crops may be raised annually. Corn will average fifty to seventy bushels to the acre. Indigo grows luxuriantly; fine woods; and the best-flavored and strongest coffee I ever drank—to my taste, superior to the Mocha. At one time Rivas occupied the prominent position for commerce; its port, San Jorge, being forty-five miles nearer the Rio San Juan than Granada, and the immediate lands about San Jorge being well cultivated and high; but the connection now fully established through from the Pacific, has deprived it of all importance, and Granada must become at some time the favorite locality in the State. Prior to the connection above-mentioned, passengers touching at Realejo, on the Pacific, traveled on mules across the country, and arriving at Granada, would there take bungoes, at whatever rates could be agreed on, for Greytown. This of itself has aided Granada greatly. Impressed with its delightful situation, its bathing, its fine fruits, and the high order of intellect of its inhabitants, many remained there for months. Some intermarried, and thus business connections were formed, which eventuated in Granada becoming the favorite among all classes of foreigners.

To me, however, Rivas is a grand old place. There is something in the ruined cathedral on its plaza, the marks of devastation everywhere to be found, the remnants of antique statues seen in old rubbish, and in the songs of the people, which remind one of some old legend, read in the palmy days of youth. I passed hours sitting on a broken wall, endeavoring to image fully to myself the primal condition of this edifice, of this statue, or of that cathedral. Amid so much fallen grandeur, such general wreck, what lessons have been taught, and what have been learned!

War is common among all the Central States. The leaders think little of an engine which conveys death to the mass; politics are their footballs, and the people the levers, the tools whereby their ends are to be attained. One morn, after a long walk about the suburbs, on reaching a corner, I observed a gibbet before me. I asked a muchacho standing by, what it meant. He told me the famous Samoza, a rebel chief, had been hung there. I took out my knife, and cutting off a piece, put it in my pocket, much to the boy's surprise.

The hotel I lodged in had every comfort—good beds, mattrasses, a good table, and every edible well-cooked, and, to to my surprise, every thing, even to the towels in my room, were white and clean: these luxuries cost two dollars and a half per day. Above the hotel stood the Church of San Francisco. I had been in it frequently; but one day, seated on the steps, and casting my eyes upward, to my great surprise, I marked the bust of General Washington, in a niche over the door. Amazed, I inquired of a man passing, what that bust was called. He replied: "Saint Francis." "Oh, no!" I retorted, "'tis an American, the great General Washington" The poor hómbre raised his hat, crossed his hands on his breast, muttered something I supposed to be a prayer, and then replied: "Ah, señor, he is loved very much by Nicaragua—and Henry Clay, too." Two tributes from a poor Nicaraguan to the memories of great men of my country. I took his arm, walked home with him, and spent several delightful hours in his humble house.

The price of land in and about this city is very moderate, at a short distance from town being only from five to seven dollars per acre. There are many delightful private residences, and the rent of a house, in good order, can be had for from eight to twelve dollars per month; so that on a trifling annuity, a foreigner could live as happily as heart need desire. The business habits of the people are simple; and judging by the ease with which every matter of business is characterized, it would lead to the supposition that they were unaccustomed to trade, yet such is far from the truth. They bargain well; are, in fact, inveterate Jews, whether the amount bargaining for be a dollar's worth or a dime's. The store is one corner of a front room, opening on the street, cooped off, and resembling an old-fashioned corner cupboard. Here are stowed laces, ruffles, calicoes, prints, and other commodities; pins are generally scarce articles. As a general thing, there is much to amuse one among the shop-keepers. A pound of cheese is wanted. The pound cannot be got in a lump—it being the custom to cut it into small square pieces about the size of a sugar-cracker, and in this way one must take it. One wants to purchase chickens, beans, hides, or any thing else at wholesale. The retail price for chickens is, say, twenty cents per pair. By the quantity it will more than likely be thirty or forty cents, for the simple reason that you want them, and therefore must pay. Beef, good and fat, cannot be purchased at any price; the oxen are worked till they nearly drop, then they are penned up, without regard to fatness, until it suits the butcher to kill. The beef is cut into strips, like coarse shoe-strings, and then dried in the air for use. Whatever of fat is found, is converted into candles.

This beef with corn-cake, sugar and cheese, a sprinkle of onions and a heavy dash of garlic from the larder, is the general dish, although at an American hotel a splendid meal can be had. We give, however, the kitchen arrangements of the inhabitants of Nicaragua. The culinary department is remarkably simple—Adam and Eve might have used the same apparatus; it answers pretty well for fries and stews, but it is to be hoped that some kind of a machine may be introduced or invented by which a broil may also be had. Two round stones, on which a pot is placed, is the stove; fire is kindled underneath, and from this results your meal. In regard to wood, one sees no loads brought into town; a small bundle of short sticks is sold for ten cents, and it is very difficult to procure a large supply at any price. It is generally porous and soft, and burns with difficulty; and in many cases is a source of great annoyance. A vast amount is taken on board the Lake steamers, and yet but little steam can be generated from it. These boats run probably six to seven miles per hour; while upon our waters, with our wood, the same vessels could easily make from sixteen to seventeen.

CHAPTER IV.

OLD STATUES—THE OLD CONVENT—THE PAROCHIAL—THE BODY OF THE VIRGIN—THE PADRE AND THE CALIFORNIAN—A WAGER—THE RESULT—LA MERCEDES—SAN JUAN DE DIOS—THE GOVERNMENT HOUSE—HOTELS AND PRICES OF BOARD—THE CUARTEL—THE TROOPS—THE BAND—THE MUSIC—FUNERALS—GRAVE-YARD—BURNING BONES—INSTRUMENTS OF MUSIC—DRESS—PRICES OF CLOTHING—HATS—SHOES—RENTS OF HOUSES—THE GOOD OLD RULE.

In and about Granada are some few things worthy of note, to which we recur prior to commencing our journey toward the Pacific. On the corner of one of the streets in the upper portion of the city—the Jalteva—stands an old relic called "The Stone of the Mouth," which projects about two and a half feet above the ground, and is some two feet broad by the same in thickness. It was brought from one of the islands by a sailor, and is a strange old head. The mouth being open, seems to express "Oh! oh!" At one corner of the plaza, stands a statue of black basalt, representing a human figure with jaws open and tongue protruding, on the head of which rests a cat or panther.

The old Convent of San Francisco must have been an elegant edifice in its day, for even yet it retains a massive grandeur with the paint and varnish of young years effaced. It faces a broad avenue, raised at least ten or twelve feet above the level of the street. Its plaza front occupies an entire square, with steps on either side leading to the level of the street below. The architecture is yet almost intact, and the entire building might be renovated at a trifling cost. It would answer well for a first-class hotel, a school, or government house—by far preferable for the latter to the one now in use. At the corner of this convent stands another curiosity, called "The Whistler," a broken fragment of an antique.

The parochial church is a very ancient structure, containing the bones of some of the early bishops of Managua, some prints and paintings of very indifferent merit, and also, if rumor be true, the body of the Virgin. The story runs thus: This body—which heretics pronounce wooden—was washed ashore one windy night, and found by one of the padres on the Lake beach. It was in a box. Upon opening this, the body was discovered, together with an inscription to the effect, that no harm should ever visit the church so long as this body should be kept inviolate within its walls. The story gained publicity, until finally it reached a doubting Californian's ears. He applied to a padre for the facts, who told him It was true.

"Well," said the Californian, "I'll bet my pile it's not so." The padre's eyes glistened as he replied, "You shall judge for yourself. The body is discolored, having been in the water so long; but you may paint it white, or any color desired, and by to-morrow morning the paint will have vanished." "Agreed!" said our friend of El Dorado. The evening came, and the Californian, with his gold in his pocket, and his pot and brush in hand, went to paint the statue. The padre did not flinch. "Now," said our friend, placing his money on the floor of the church, "there's my bet; and look you, padre, I shall sit here all night after I daub this: and remember, here are two Colt's revolvers, and if you dare to touch the body after I've painted it, I'll shoot you." The padre's heart failed him. He thought the Californian would trust to the sacred character of the church; but the ruse failed, and the matter becoming public, a laugh ensued. Whether the joke hurt the padre or the Californian most, I did not learn.

In the interior of the city stands the Church of La Mercedes, which is truly an imposing building It is situated similar to the Convent of San Francisco, and although it cannot boast of a gilded interior, costly altars, or choice paintings, still its exterior commands attention. About this church the private houses are of the first order, and within a stone's throw chiefly reside the elite of the city. The street leading to the Jalteva runs by La Mercedes to the south side of the plaza, immediately in front of the unfinished Church of San Juan de Dios. The façade of this church is quite elaborate and elegantly designed; it fronts north, however, which, as I learned, was considered ill-omened, or unpropitious, and it is consequently left to decay.

The Government House is a shabby saloon, thirty feet long by twenty wide, and furnished with long desks and benches, made of Madeira wood—a species of cedar—like those used in country school-houses. There are several fine hotels in Granada, the best, if it still exists, being the Irving House. Price, one dollar and a half a day, or thirty-one dollars a month. It is located on a street leading east from the plaza, and immediately in the rear of the parochial church.

Upon the northeastern side of the plaza, stands the cuartel, a long, one-story building, roughly built, serving as barracks, magazine, armory, drilling-room, and prison. From this celebrated depot the troops are trotted out at 12 M. every sunny day. The drummers beat very well, and a march is taken around the plaza and the principal streets. The band generally consists of two violins, two clarionets, one flute, two or three brass instruments, and a drum and fife. They really perform remarkably well; though, for their very lives, they cannot play "Yankee Doodle" properly. The music in church is usually good. The orchestra is larger than the band, and there is generally a good second tenor voice of considerable compass and sweetness.

Funerals are attended by any and every body. After the anointing with almond oil, the body is placed on a bier; the bearers take their posts, and the procession moves on, headed by the priests, singing. Should the funeral be that of a child's, the corpse is neatly dressed, the little hands crossed on the breast, the eyes sometimes closed, and wreaths or bunches of flowers cast over it and placed about the head. Three or four musicians are kept fiddling and singing, and boys are firing off rockets, squibs, and crackers incessantly, and thus they march to the final resting-place. To become accustomed to such scenes greatly reduces the horror, the unknown, indescribable feeling occasioned by sudden or familiar approach to death. Yet it is trying to one's nerves; and I kept my eyes about me to avoid scenes repulsive to me, brace myself as I would. The grave-yard is about one hundred feet square, enclosed with a high fence. They commence at the gate, and bury in a circle; and when the entire ground is covered, which, I am told, is about once a year, they then dig up the bones, collect them under a slab placed for the purpose, and on a certain fixed day burn them all. So we go: dust we are, but to thin air we vanish.

All the feast days in the calendar are kept sacred. Every

one bestows his time upon them, and holy week and all other holidays are hailed with great pleasure. The bells are so constantly ringing, that one grows accustomed to their ding-dong, and feels ill at ease when wandering in some secluded spot, with nothing but the songs and chirps of birds to break the monotonous silence.

The instruments of music are quite numerous. I have heard, on a serenade, the overture to the Caliph of Bagdad, overture to Lucia, with various masses and anthems, by the old masters, performed in much better style, and in more perfect time, than in my own city, where so much respect is paid to musical education. The guitar is pre-eminent in all Spanish countries and provinces, and will ever remain so, for as an accompaniment to the voice, it cannot be surpassed. The flute and clarionet are also heard. Many of their compositions I have listened to with great pleasure, and regret that I can only remember or recognize an occasional link in the chain of the melody.

The masses dress neatly; the legislators usually in black, with black silk hats. The public, as a class, wear white coats, white pants, and a scarf of scarlet or yellow silk, as a sash, about their waists. This, with the jaunty, easy, graceful panama, completes the costume, which is agreeably convenient in such a climate. Clothing is dear. They have a French tailor in Granada who cuts well. Shoes can be bought for about one dollar and twenty cents a pair. Hats at various prices. Rent is very low. For eight dollars per month, I took a house in the centre of the city, nearly adjoining the Church of La Mercedes, containing three large rooms, with a kitchen, an immense yard, and large stable attached. I deemed this very reasonable, but my friends thought it more than sufficient.

The customs are extremely primeval, and I was never offended by any rudeness or incivility. I found the old rule always brought me out right in the end—Do as you would be done by. And yet I have heard of extreme cases of duplicity, particularly toward foreigners, by those in power. There is little for outsiders to hope for, when a nation is wanting in faith to its own.

CHAPTER V.

RIVAS—THE HOMBRE—LEONEZE—AZTECS—THEIR MONUMENTS—BETWEEN RIVAS AND GRANADA—OBRAJE—GIL GONZALES—A LUXURY—SNAKES—HINTS FOR THOSE GOING TO NICARAGUA—BOA CONSTRICTORS—TIGRES—TIGRE NEGRO—MOUNTAIN CATS—COYOTE—BATS—THE CALIFORNIAN'S PURCHASE—THE CHAMORRO ESTATE—TROOPS—MUSKETS—COLT'S REVOLVERS—ENROLLING SOLDIERS—MONOPOLIES—INCIDENT IN MANAGUA—A FLOGGING.

RIVAS was once the seat of a Mexican colony, governed by a Cazique, Niquira. The dirty hómbre, who bears prodigious burdens of corn upon his back, and who hesitates at nothing for a little money, can readily be traced to this origin. Indeed, in the various districts of Nicaragua, the inhabitants differ greatly, not only in physiognomy but in manner. Those of Leon, and the interior generally, bear themselves with greater ease, are more enlightened and refined, and evince a studious neatness in their apparel. Upon the volcano of Ometepec, in the midst of the Lake, are the descendants of the Aztecs with some of their monuments still remaining, though both are in a decaying state. The early padres who accompanied the Soldiers of the Cross, evinced any thing but forbearance toward these dumb statues, from which we might now gather so much. Even those remaining have, in many cases, been hidden by the natives, who yet hold them in reverence.

Within two leagues of Rivas, is a greater population than is found to the same extent in any other portion of the State. The land is well cultivated; between the road to Granada and the Lake, a perfect garden; to the left, voluptuously rolling, at times rising to a little hill, yet every acre capable of cultivation. Its many beautiful sites for haciendas has frequently attracted my attention. Three leagues from Rivas is the large, long town of Obraje, truly an aboriginal production. It is one of several around Rivas, and is a pretty fair sample of them all. Beyond Obraje stretch luxuriant fields, carpeted with waving grass, inviting one to slip from the saddle for a roll; but the sun beats fiercely there, and we jog on through rows of papaya trees heavy with fruit, beautiful gardens well trimmed, and fields of maize rich in promise of an abundant harvest. We ford a stream, where my mule stops to drink and I to rest. This is the Gil Gonzales, so named after the adventurer of whom we have already given an account. Water is appreciated here, for though a mountainous country, streams are scarce. The volcanoes, thirsty fellows, seem to have swallowed them up.

On a bush, by the roadside, hangs something resembling a cart-lash, striped like a barber's pole, and which I am told—to use an English word—is a barber snake, and very venomous. Taking the hint, I give the gentleman a wide margin and pass on. These reptiles are sometimes found where least expected. In Central America the houses rarely have any ceiling to the rooms, and they sometimes hide away in the thatched roofs; occasionally falling upon persons underneath. Those visiting this country should take calico with them for ceilings as well as for canopies to bedsteads. They should also provide themselves with mattrasses, musquito nets, blankets, India-rubber clothing, hats, strong boots and shoes, knives, pins, percussion caps, and mercurial ointment wherewith to oil the locks and barrels of their guns and pistols.

A stray boa constrictor may also be found on these gorgeous savannahs. At Virgin Bay I saw a very fine specimen, and felt particularly relieved when I learned it was dead. By the roadside I saw two panthers, called tigres or tigers. They are the jaguars or ounces of South America, and are quite numerous here. They are of a tawny color, breast and belly almost white, while the body is variegated with black oblong spots; are from four to five feet in length, and immensely powerful. They attack animals, but rarely man. The tigre negro, or black tiger, is larger, fiercer, and no doubt more powerful; it is of the same species, but scarce.

There are mountain cats, varieties of the tiger species, constantly roaming after fowl and other domestic attachès; but they prove annoyances only, and are not to be dreaded. The coyote, or wild dog, is very scarce, though they exist in the mountain districts. They are said to be descendants of the Spanish bloodhounds, and are sometimes caught, but rarely, or never, tamed or domesticated. The bat is said by some to partake largely of the vampire. Many stories are told of them, drawing strongly on the marvelous. They are great enemies to horses, and worried mine much. He was a good-looking pony when I bought him; but a sorrier-looking animal when sold, I never wish to see. "Oh! agates and sassafras, stranger," said the sanguine Californian who made the purchase, "what a face! It is made of patchwork! He's the ugliest critter I ever see'd, and by thunder, I'll buy him for a specimen;" and so he did.

In the stirrup again, and after a brisk dash, a clearing is reached, in which an air of comfort reigns, strongly reminding me of some quiet nook in my own native land. It is a fine old estate belonging to the family of Gen. Chamorro, late President of Nicaragua. It commands a beautiful view of the surrounding country, and is just such a retreat as a statesman or warrior would be likely to seek after retiring from the cares of state. Here the outside world could be forgotten. Chamorro, sprung from an ancient and aristocratic family, was a prime mover in all public matters, and the Commander-in-chief of the forces during the revolution of 1850, and other wars since. He resided in the city of Granada. During my stay there, the troops were regularly reviewed upon the plaza by him, and instructed in military drills.

To an American eye, these troops presented a queer medley. No plumes waving, no gay banners, no brilliant uniforms, but a heterogeneous collection of shirts, bare legs, blanketed Indians from the hills of Matagalpa and Segovia, all banded together under their respective leaders, and as seemingly unconscious of what was to be done, or to be expected, as they were regardless of exposing their natural beauties. Standing on the elevated places, and glancing along the line, reminded one of a worm-fence; here protruded a knee; there squatted a poor Indian, with bow in hand and arrows over his shoulders or by his side. Poor fellow! From the harangues of Rocha, the minister of war, he heard abundance as to "human rights," but his experiences were only hardships, privations, and ceaseless labors.

The veterans were as illy accoutred, and were armed with condemned English muskets, about as dangerous at one end as the other. Besides being bad shots, their muskets were loaded with a cartridge six to seven inches long, so that the chances for life for the poor fellow who carried it, seemed to be increased in proportion to the fewer number of times he had to fire. Upon a march from place to place they presented a strange appearance, as they came up a hill, or went plunging through a ditch. Still, they are generally true to their leaders, and armed with their heavy scythe blades, are dangerous opponents. The horror of these gentry are the Colt's revolvers. They can witness a crack shot from a rifle with tolerable composure, but cannot stand the consecutive firing of these dread engines of war.

During these revolutions, resort is had to every means for the enrolment of soldiers. The market-people are taken unceremoniously from their wares, the sailors from their bongoes, the laboring classes from the ranchos and fields, and a general embargo is laid upon every man capable of shouldering or lifting a musket. Those owning mules hide them, that their property may not be sacrificed for their country's good. Promises are made for payment, yet the issuing of State scrip has been so extensively carried on, that credit is at a low ebb. In perilous times, monopolies of tobacco, liquors, &c., are sold to the highest bidder; but not unfrequently, should the war continue for a length of time, the State deems the consideration money insufficient, and extra sums are demanded.

Punishments are summarily inflicted in the army. One morning in Managua, as I strolled to the Lake beach, I observed an unusual crowd concentrating in the plaza. I asked what was going on, and was told that some thieves were to be publicly punished. The soldiery, probably five hundred in number, marshalled in due form, the files were opened, and the General-in-chief appeared, heralded with trumpets and drums, and supported by his staff. The criminals were brought from the cuartel, their hands bound behind them, and they were placed in a conspicuous position, to be seen by their comrades. A superior officer, after much drum-beating, read the charge and condemnation in a loud tone. Charge: "Stealing money and knives from certain persons."

Two or three soldiers, at a signal, stepped from the ranks, and took off the shirts of the criminals. "Ground arms!" or its equivalent, "Drop!" "Draw ramrods!" and certain other soldiers advanced. A temporary post was fixed firmly in the ground, to which the thieves were tied alternately, and the whippers commenced their exercise. The blows fell heavily, and the cries of the poor fellows smote upon my heart. Their crime merited punishment, yet the whip, in my opinion, is not the proper instructor, whereby a moral and lasting result is to be attained.

CHAPTER VI.

RIO OCHOMOGO—OLD STRUCTURE—ADOBE BUILDINGS: THEIR STRENGTH—OLD INDIGO PLANTATION—NANDYME—HORSEFLESH—PRICES—GAITS—HORSEMANSHIP—MOMOBACHO—ITS ASCENT—GOLD MINE—LAKE ON THE SUMMIT—FRUITS ON THE ROAD-SIDE—DIRIOMO—OLD STATUE—LANDMARKS—CORN ESTATES—ANCIENT INDIGO PLANTATIONS—FIELDS OF VOLCANIC MATTER—GRANADA—THE ALERTE—MUSICAL ANALYSIS—SYMPATHY—THE SALVE REGINA—THE TRANSPARENCY—STRANGE EFFECT—HOME AND A HAMMOCK.

ANOTHER stream, washing the sandy road ahead; our nag scents the water, and reinvigorated, quickens his pace. This is the Rio Ochomogo, beyond which, on a hill-side, is a dilapidated old adobe structure, square in form, with open sides and tiled roof. It is used by the muleteers as a stopping-place, and is surrounded with dense forest trees, finer, as a body, than any we have yet seen. These adobe buildings will stand firm in a tropical climate, for many, many years, though time weighs heavily upon all things else. The rich earth producing immense crops of weeds and spontaneous vegetation, greatly changes the appearance of a rancho in a very short time. A vine creeps over a high wall in a week, and in damp corners a vegetable mould will form so thick in two or three years, as to warrant a stranger in supposing it the work of half a century. I have read wonderful stories of Central America; of estimates formed and deductions drawn relative to the age of a building, a temple, or a wall, from the immense mass of this mould collected thereon A residence for a little time in this country will satisfy any observing man that too much care cannot be taken in weighing such a matter.

An old indigo plantation is before us, now vacant, though the vats yet remain. The unsettled condition of the country has caused this, together with the great amount of expense and labor involved in raising so precious an article. Still on, is a plain with calabash and forest trees margining the road, and at intervals screening a lovely landscape from the view. Beyond is the Indian village of Nandyme. Large outskirts flank the town, and the generality of the houses are of medium appearance. The land is more clayey, and at times slippery even during the dry season; but in the wet, it is a breakneck ride to trot a mule over this road. Though mounted on a very fair animal, I met frequent mishaps in the way of slidings, stumblings, and fallings. Horseflesh here is valued pretty much according to gait; a fine trotter can be purchased for twenty to forty dollars; while a pony that racks, paces or canters, will command one hundred.

The Spaniard of Nicaragua is probably as much attached to his steed, as was the Castilian of yore. Their animals possess wind and bottom, and are remarkably strong, but slow; and few can excel in speed the fourth-rate horses of New York or Philadelphia. I had heard much of the horsemanship of these people, but saw little to boast of. The Nicaraguan can "stick" to a horse well enough, but there is many a country lad of fifteen with us who can beat him.

For endurance, these horsės are unexcelled; they are small, compact and reliable, but a great majority of them sprung in the knees, rendering them unsafe as hackneys. The mules are well-bred, and preserve their gait better than the horses; they are small and can safely be trusted with the rein over the craggiest or most slippery camino real. The precision of his step in descending a hill-side is wonderful. Where no man could walk without slipping, the mule jogs easily along, his head bent down, and his long ears flapping to and fro, a perfect picture of easy carelessness. His foot once planted, give him the rein and trust to him. He lives upon scanty allowance, braves all weathers, endures any amount of privations, sleeps well, works well, and is ready for his burden and his journey at the appointed hour. The cruel muleteer spurs him up with a spike, fixed in the end of a long spear.

On our left rises the defunct volcano of Momobacho, lined with dark masses of mould-covered lava; its side bare of trees, and exposing a tremendous orifice. There is said to be a small lake on its side, and one on its summit, each studded with gold fish. The ascent of this volcano, from a distance seems gradual and easy, but is found on trial to be almost impracticable. In 1849, a few Americans tried it, and after much toil and severe privations, planted the "Stars and stripes" upon its very summit. On the inland side, years past, it is said, was a valuable gold mine, yielding bountifully; but during a volcanic eruption it was buried, and so remains. I was told by old inhabitants, that Momobacho formerly had but one peak; now there are two points of elevation, joined by an intervening mass. The Lake on its summit is said to be a quarter of a mile long and half a mile wide. Momobacho looms grandly up, and can be seen in clear weather even from the Jalteva of Granada.

The country through which our road leads us becomes more rolling, and huts, corn-fields, plantain and mango groves increase. Palm and orange trees appear in quick succession. The lemon fills the air with its fragrance; fruits of various descriptions hang from the overladen boughs; while the tall cocoa, running spirelike into the blue ether, is relieved by floating clouds.

Diriomo, an Indian pueblo, lies three leagues from Granada.

It is a pretty spot: its cane huts with thatched roofs peer out from amid the graceful though dense foliage of the orange and banana trees, while on either side extends a lot of ground sufficient to afford fruits and vegetables for the entire family. Near by stands a stone figure, browned with age and neglect, probably used as a boundary between municipalities. These landmarks are religiously respected; and as a general thing, the definition of "meum and teum" is understood and appreciated, though if we credit the reports of travelers, thefts and robberies here are of frequent occurrence.

Corn estates are principally relied on now, though from the remains of indigo plantations adjoining Granada, considerable quantities of this article must have been produced at a former period. The native article of Nicaragua is very valuable, and commands a high price. It is generally purchased by foreign merchants, at the annual fair of San Miguel, and forwarded to Europe. Again we meet vast fields of volcanic matter; in some places pulverized and yielding, in others, loose, hard, and rolling under our horse's feet.

We strike the road entering into the plaza of Granada at an early evening hour, and answer the challenge of the stirring and watchful sentinels. The voices of the people seem strange, comparing somewhat with a parrot's notes. The tones are drawn out or prolonged, and the word of three syllables has a finale not pleasing to the ear. The sentry's "alerté," or cry, rings distinctly on the air, and is as musical as the chirp of the mocking-bird in the moonlit eves of a northern clime. It is composed of notes designated in melodic order, as the third, the eighth, and the fifth of the common major chord. There seems to exist a certain chain of sympathy between people of the same caste, in widely separated climes. Recall to memory the old cry of the watchman in our country villages of the United States. When the snow lay clustering upon the roof-tops, and mantled all nature with its spotless shroud, how clear, cheerful, and distinct did the cry of the patrol break upon the ear, "Ten," or "Twelve o'clock!" Analyze it; it commences on the fifth, ascending to the tenth, or third above the octave, and ends on the eighth of the common major chord. And so the rosy strawberry woman at the door, basket in hand, for whose song the maid stops to listen. You hear her silvery tones pervading your sanctum, "Straw-ber-ries!" It commences on the key note, and the last syllable ends with crescendo, and diminuendo on its octave or eighth. The "attenta la guardia," of the Italian sentinel has its peculiar sweetness; and we might instance a variety of others, all logically leading us to a sympathetic affinity between such public characters in every clime.

"Alerté" was always grateful to my ears; it was indefinite, not conclusive; swinging in my hammock, puffing a native cigar, it was an ever ending to begin again, an expectation of a resolution never resolved.

The heavy buzzards slept cozily on the tiled roofs of La Mercedes, as I threw off my philosophical mantle, and leaving musical matters at home, attracted by sweet sounds, I strolled far down the street. Approaching, I found several musicians accompanied by their violins, chanting the beautiful "Salve Regina." An hómbre carried a transparency, upon which was rudely limned the image of the infant Saviour resting in the Virgin's lap. At the door of the house before which they stood, were men, women, and children, kneeling and devoutly counting their rosaries. A mother raising her little child toward the imaged Creator, muttered a prayer in unison with the common melody, and quietly dropped a tribute into the hand of a collector who accompanied them. This custom is general, and shows how strongly exist the elements of music in this strange, eventful, but neglected land. A spirit of harmony pervades all nature, and a master's touch would educe from discord, strife, and jealousies, twin-born love, peace and good-will toward man.

I turned homeward, threw myself into a hammock, and blew out the light; the world outside grew dimmer and dimmer, images and fancies less distinct; memories became confused, and the pall of Somnus gathered heavily over my senses. Good-night to all. The cool air took possession of my room, and I sank into temporary oblivion.

CHAPTER VII.

THE HOUSES OF NICARAGUA—SIZE—APPEARANCE—ADOBES—SIZE—FORM—MATERIAL—CEMENT—WELLS—WATER—MONEY, VALUE OF—TRADE—BONGOES—NATIONAL VESSELS—THE ORUS AND DIRECTOR STEAMERS—MANNERS AND CUSTOMS—BELFRY OF LA MERCEDES—THE SHARPSHOOTER—HIS DEATH—SANDOVAL'S ESTATE—INDIGO PLANTATION—THE LAKE—ORANGES AND MANGOES—CORN—SACATE—PINE-APPLES—JOCOTES—A BEAUTIFUL ESTATE—COST—INTEMPERANCE—VIRTUES—CLOTHS—SOCKS—SICKNESS—PHYSIC AND LAW.

THE edifices of Nicaragua merit more than a passing notice; to me they were entirely novel; the architecture, though possessing its own peculiar character, partakes of the Moresque. They are built round a hollow square, and are only of one story in height, as elsewhere observed. The tiled roofs sloping to the street, are inwardly supported by posts, sometimes of polished iron, mahogany or other wood. At the inside corners of the roof, gutters are formed for conducting the rain water into tanks, placed in the yard. This is by far the best agua to be had in the country. The apartments open upon this hollow-patio, and are lighted by large barred-windows, which project, and in which two or three persons may sit and chat very cosily. Entirely independent of the main house, is the kitchen, which adjoins the stable. Neither of these are enclosed, and the fodder, corn, and manure, lie in threatening proximity to the comestibles preparing for the table. The houses are built of adobes. These are formed into blocks about twenty-two inches long, nine thick, and nine wide, made of a tenacious earth or clay, mixed with fine reeds, tough grass, or straw, which possesses durability against the tropical rains and storms. Some of the poorer houses thus constructed, are considered entirely finished; but those of the wealthier classes are plastered with a close mould, resembling a clayey-marl, soft and yielding, which, upon receiving several coats of white paint, resembles marble. I can describe it, perhaps, more satisfactorily, by calling it mineral-mortar. Such a cement was discovered by the conquerors of Peru. Many of the dwellings in the latter country seem to have been constructed without cement; and therefore it has been contended by some writers, that mortar, or cement of any kind, was unknown to them. But such a mould as above described, mixed with lime, may sometimes be found filling up the interstices of the granite, brick, or porphyry structures; and in others, where the blocks fitted precisely, and left no vacancy for this coarser material, the eye of the antiquary detects a fine glue, bituminous in its character, as hard as the rock itself. Humboldt, who analyzed the cement of the ancient structures at Cannar, says that it is a true mortar, formed of a mixture of pebbles and a clayey-marl; and Father Velasco is in raptures with "an almost imperceptible cement," made of lime and a bituminous substance resembling glue, which incorporated stones so as to hold them firmly together, like one solid mass, leaving nothing visible to the eye of the common observer. This glutinous composition, mixed with pebbles, was used for macadamized roads, much prized by the Incas, as hard and almost as smooth as marble.

The houses differ as much in appearance as in size. Many of them are at least seventy feet front, and more, and probably one hundred and fifty feet deep. Wells, now almost dry, are found in the courts, of immense depths. The one in the yard of the house I resided in, was at least one hundred feet deep, and I have seen others exceeding this. Whether they were of yore rigged with the windlass, I could not determine, yet I found no notches in the well-wall to justify any such belief; and I have always seen a rope used, which was drawn up and lowered by hand. Water, as a beverage, is an extra in every town in the State. It is brought from the Lake by the muchachas, in large jars, who indeed move very gracefully along, bearing their cantaros and tinajas upon their heads. The price for a certain number of these daily, is ten cents, or probably twenty-five cents per week. Two dimes are equal to twenty-five cents, as in the Southern States of America; and at times American gold can be purchased, reckoning eight dimes to the dollar. This is the currency from the Lake to the Pacific, but not at Greytown or San Juan del Norte. Merchants from the interior purchasing from, or trading with those at Greytown, stipulate the currency to be used, and thus avoid breaches of contract and other annoying mishaps.

Trade is carried on in bongos, a rude boat, made out of a large log; though small-sized canal boats have been built, which are not safer or swifter, but are more capacious. Lake Nicaragua is far from being a placid sheet of water. Squalls, violent and sudden, sweep from Ometepec's heights, and for a moment every thing is in confusion. I have been in a bongo, during one of these changes, and have seen two water-spouts, each of which threatened to engulf us. The natives are swimmers—not sailors; their oars are not long, but have only small paddles at the extremities, instead of the usual oar-blades, so requisite for speed and power. Yet the progress made against tide with such aids, is at times very remarkable. There are also sailing bongos, but these are not managed with skill; and whenever the mariners find that safety depends upon "lightening" their crafts, they plunge overboard, and cling and swim alternately, till the elements have calmed. The first steamboat which was introduced upon the waters of Nicaragua, was

5

the Orus; she was wrecked on the Machuca Rapids. The second was the Director, and the Company owning it, succeeded in warping her over the Rapids. Subsequently it plied upon the Lake, and for years was the sole transport for the passengers from San Carlos to Virgin Bay. The increase of the business of the Transit Company, however, induced the exportation from New York of the "Central America," and other steam vessels.

But to return. The buildings are comfortable, and require ceilings only to render them all that could be desired as retreats from the rain or sun. They are the coolest I ever lived in; while one avoids that abominable nuisance, the climbing up flights of steps. The wood-work is stanch; every house being a fortress *per se*, though not in every instance impervious to a musket ball, for the casa in which the American minister resided, while in Leon, had been riddled by those of the revolutionists a short time prior to his arrival. In the early part of the present revolution, the belfry of the church of La Mercedes was used by a celebrated sharpshooter, of Chamorro, who from this eyrie singled out, *ad libitum*, the Americans encamped in the suburbs of the city. A diversion having been made, however, by the forces under General Muñoz, for the ostensible purpose of intercepting a party conveying powder and provisions to the town, the antagonists met suddenly on neutral ground; and the wretch who had been assassinating his friends and countrymen, fell, pierced with avenging bullets. His funeral was solemnized with all the pomp of the church—the army attended "en masse," and the deepest sorrow pervaded the city. The death of this notorious villain brought matters to a climax; battle succeeded battle, until General Muñoz was shot at Masaya, with other brave fellows. Then followed Chamorro's death, and a new regime.

Passing out of the plaza, upon the South, is a good road over a rolling and gradually ascending country; a mile's ride brings you to a gate. Dismount! A lane leads to a casa perched on a beautiful eminence, commanding a view of the Lake, Granada, and the country for many miles around. It is Sandoval's estate, an old indigo plantation. The vats are dry, but yet remain in good order. From the mansion in front, are seen fields of luxuriant, wild indigo. Upon the rear is a deep ravine, leading to level ground which margins the Lake. We descend slowly. Here, stretch beautiful lemon groves; there, nod the grateful orange trees, filling the air with suffocating fragrance, while the arched mangoes, heavy with golden fruit, complete as sweet a picture as the heart of the most romantic could desire. Fields of corn are rustling beyond. The fodder, or sacate, is bundled up and taken on mules tc the city, where a dime is charged for a small sheaf.

This fodder, under certain circumstances, is the best crop, as it commands a good price and ready sale.

Pine-apples and other fruits are abundant, the white and the yellow; I must not overlook the jocote, a species of apricot, without its sweetness. It is peculiar in flavor, and the taste is to be acquired; for I could not eat one at first, but after a time always had my pockets full. They are sold at five cents per small basket. The beautiful estate alluded to I could have purchased for about twelve hundred dollars. There were three hundred acres, well cultivated, with good barn and other buildings, indigo vats included. But there was one misfortune—securing operatives to till it regularly, for natives are not always to be depended upon. Their wages are only ten cents per day, and after they have received a dollar or two, great difficulty is experienced in inducing them to remain. Remember, a piece of cheese, a lump of brown sugar, and a corn-cake compose the larder of these hómbres; and what a pile a dollar would purchase! The vice of intemperance is not indigenous. It is an imported article; and a shame it is, that on such soil should have been sown the curses of wine-bibbing, with so many other unmanly vices, and that so few of the virtues have as yet been introduced. I do not believe the race to be entirely lost, as some others profess to do. I have found much talent, and many virtues there—much good old-fashioned common sense, and have experienced many kindnesses from those strangers to me; and where a single good seed has taken root, I will not condemn a nation for private wrongs or private prejudices.

There can be found in Granada, almost every thing desired. Clothes are dearer than in the United States. Cloths at a very moderate figure, looser in the web than ours, having been manufactured expressly for this market, and are both cooler and more elastic. Socks, shirtings, &c., are plentiful, but far from cheap. Medicines are dear, fruits cheap. Lawyers are abundant, and must be well and frequently fee'd. This is a co-relative of other civilized nations; and those who go often to the Forum will learn, at least, many of the ways, if at all attentive and cute, by which living is made easy in a few lessons.

As a general thing, physic is not in much repute, save in slight cases of fever, cold, and other minor diseases. Travelers will eat and drink immoderately, or expose themselves at night or mid-day, either of which are equally injudicious; they then upbraid the climate, and neglect to call folly by its right name; but not to do that would be consistent, and inconsistency consists in being consistent so far as affects our desires or appetites. Then we can afford to grumble and revile a country, generous in its pleasures, and gentle in reproofs. Were foreigners to care for themselves and guard against changes and seasons as they do when at home, a residence in Nicaragua would prove beneficial to many who are now feeding young apothecaries, and who are emptying box after box of some patent vegetable vermifuge, or new-fangled elixir, which robs us of the little stomach that fast living at home leaves many of us at thirty years of age.

CHAPTER VIII.

RELIGIOUS FESTIVALS—ST. JAMES' DAY—SAN IGNATIUS DE LOYOLA—TRANSIT OF THE VIRGIN—THE CORPUS—ST. PETER AND THE HOLY KEYS—IMAGES—SANTA THERESA—COCHINEAL PLANTATIONS—MODE OF CULTURE AND PREPARATION OF IT FOR MARKET—COFFEE—ITS CULTIVATION—SUGAR—INDIGO—AMOUNT OF HARVEST—TOBACCO—AMOUNT RAISED—PROFITS—GUNPOWDER AND OTHER GOVERNMENT MONOPOLIES—ARTICLES OF MANUFACTURE—ARTIFICERS IN GOLD AND SILVER—OPPOSITE GRANADA—CATTLE ESTATES—CATCHING CATTLE—THE PETA-HUIJA—FIGS AND OLIVES—A HINT.

It would be an almost hopeless task to properly describe the many religious festivals of the people of this country. I entered some of the "occasions," however, in my Diary, which were new to me, and may be of interest to the reader. St. Iago, or St. James, is the patron saint of the Americas, as also of Gallicia, in Spain; and on this day, July 26th, all the shops are closed. He drove out the Moors from Gallicia, tradition says, appearing on a white horse before the armics of the Christian. The celebration of the feast of San Ignatius de Loyola, the founder of the Jesuit Order, is upon the 30th day of July. The altar is dressed with artificial flowers, and on this the image of the founder is placed. August 13th is the celebration of the Transit of the Virgin. In every house an altar is erected in the sala or parlor, and recitations are performed from three to four in the afternoon. Upon a cushion, covered with gold lace and spangles, lies the image of the dead Virgin. She is clothed in gold and spangles; prayers are recited to her before the image, and two waxen candles are kept burning, in silver candlesticks, though sometimes brass or glass is used. This altar is to be illuminated for fifteen successive nights; and in addition to the prayers already named, others are said every night at eight o'clock.

The Corpus, which takes place in June, is, however, the most remarkable, and of course all business is suspended. About ten in the morning, a cavalcade moves from the church. A troop of military, with funereal measure, leads the way, who are followed by six girls, fancifully dressed, bearing large wax candles, and accompanied by the "big drum," borne on the back of a grotesquely-accoutred Indian, and beaten by two others. Then follow men with wooden platforms on their shoulders, on which are images of saints. Then, representations of beatified cardinals and bishops, escorted by angels with spread wings. Then, an immense statue of St. Peter, supported on both sides by angels, bearing the holy keys. Then other images in succession precede the Host, which is carried under a gorgeous canopy, accompanied by the bishop and clergy. Other groups still follow; the military bringing up the rear. Passing round the plaza, the procession stops at every corner, where altars are erected, covered with artificial flowers, wax candles, and looking-glasses, while the spectators kneel on either side. Sky-rockets signal the setting out from and return to the church, and the houses by which the Host passes are hung with red silk or cloth. As in all Spanish and Catholic countries, images are much venerated. At Viejo, near Leon, is one of the Virgin, which is visited on a particular day in February. It is traditioned as being the gift of the Immaculate Virgin, Santa Theresa.

We had intended to add a few more particulars relative to the productions of this State, as well as to notice those of States adjoining, for the products of all are similar. The nopaleras, or cochineal plantations of Nicaragua, have dwindled into insignificance; but there are still small tracts in many haciendas which are given to the cultivation of this article. A piece of ground is carefully fenced in with parallel rows of prickly pear, the cactus cochinillifer, or common Indian fig. Immediately after the rains have ceased, the cactus, an insect, is sown upon the plant. Twelve of these are collected with a feather, from the parent, enclosed all together in a small bag of the maize leaf, left open, and pinned with a thorn to the leaf of the cactus. Seven or eight bags are placed on different leaves of the same plant. In a short time the insects begin to breed in the bags, and the young ones crawl out upon the plant. As they grow, they gradually cover themselves with a mantle of white paste, which protects them from the weather, and in the course of three months they are ready for gathering. This is done by scraping the leaf; and after a sufficient number have been reserved for seed, the rest are either placed upon tins in a large oven, or thrown into hot water. When dried, they assume the appearance of small grains, and are ready for market. A second crop is then sown, and in three months another harvest is reaped, after which the seed is preserved, by covering the plant till the rainy season is passed. After four or five years, from the great quantity of nourishment extracted by these insects, the cactus decays. It is then rooted up, and a new plant succeeds. The female of this insect is the true cochineal, though there are two other species in the market. Dried, pounded, and prepared, it is sold under the name of carmine.

Coffee is cultivated to no very great extent, though the crop of Guatemala has produced one million of dollars in a single year. If the land be properly drained, the coffee-tree lives to an old age. It begins to bear at three years, and is in its prime at seven. At five, the top branches are pruned off. Every branch droops downward. In Brazil, the tree bears two crops annually: the largest in spring, the smallest in fall. The first is picked when the berry is red; the second, generally small, is allowed to remain until fully dry and ripe. This crop cured in the husk is very superior in quality, and is called "pearl coffee," the blossom being small and tender. It remains three or four days on the tree. If the weather be warm and showery during these few days, the crop is sure, but if cool at night, it often fails. The berry being carried home, is taken to the millhouse. The mill consists of three small rollers. The berry is put into a hopper, and a constant stream of water falls on the rollers during the time the mill is in operation. By this process the outside hull is taken off and separated from the berry. The coffee falls into a brick tank, where, after being washed and perfectly cleaned, it is put away, and covered with tile or brick raised in the centre for the water to drain. It is then taken to the curing-loft, where it is turned four times per day, until the hull is dry and crisp. When it is fanned, the inside hull comes off, and the berry is ready for market.

The principal source of the early prosperity of Guatemala was the cultivation of cocoa, which was produced in immense quantities, and of superior quality. The province of Nicaragua is said to have exclusively supplied San Salvador and Comayagua. About the beginning of the seventeenth century, however, the shores of Central America were devastated by the repeated incursions of the Buccaneers, who massacred the inhabitants, destroyed the plantations, and compelled the proprietors to seek shelter in the interior. This, together with the excessive duties imposed by the Spanish government, and the expense and difficulties of land carriage, has caused a vast diminution in the production of the article.

The cultivation of sugar shared the same fate, as also indigo, notwithstanding their acknowledged superior qualities. During the interval from 1790 to 1818 inclusive, the Central American States produced 13,346,640 pounds of sugar; and it will be borne in mind that in 1791–2–3, alone, 3,304,250 pounds were harvested. Cochineal, the cultivation of which was unknown till 1821, yields an immense revenue. Guatemala produces larger amounts than any other State in the Confederation, reaching, in 1826, to 90,000 pounds.

Tobacco is raised, but little except for home consumption; though in San Salvador 70,000 pounds have been exported in a single year, and from 80,000 to 100,000 from Honduras. The clear profit to the nation, from 1815 to 1819 inclusive, was $1,594,447.

Cotton is raised in great quantities, and is superior in quality, supplying home wants, and also leaving a margin for exportation to the provinces of Mexico.

Gunpowder, saltpetre, tobacco, lead, shot, and liquors, are

all government monopolies. Hats, shoes, saddlery, jewelry, fancy articles, earthenware, and pottery, are manufactured, though not to a very great extent. The artificers in gold and silver in Nicaragua are extremely ingenious and skillful, and exhibit great taste and experience in the manufacture of ornaments.

A visit to the cattle estates, on the opposite shore of the Lake from Granada, will richly repay the traveler. Over the fine, fertile pasture lands of a single hacienda, roam a thousand cattle, and an equal number of horses and mules, though generally inferior in quality. When a sale has been effected, the major-domo summons his men to "lazo" the chosen stock.

The horses are saddled, and one end of the lazo—made of twisted thongs of hide—is bound round the tail of each horse, care being first taken to prevent the flesh from becoming lacerated by subsequent friction. The rider gathers the loose end of the cord in his hand. He approaches the bull, who, finding himself singled out, starts away at full speed, but the horse, accustomed to the game, runs as though aware of every winding the bull may make. Coming within the desired distance, the lazo is whirled with great dexterity over the bull's horns, and on the instant the horse wheels, and the bull, starting rapidly off, is thus thrown upon his haunches. Should he prove fractious, he is turned on his back and firmly tied. At times, however, the enraged bull, driven to extremities, lowers his head, as though aware of the object of his pursuer, and retreats to a close place, from whence suddenly wheeling he makes battle. These estates are immense, and very frequently the cattle and horses exceed the number here given, though during the few past years every thing has shared the same eventful fate—neglect.

Among the countless fruits is one I have never seen described, but which is by no means common; and why it should not be more extensively cultivated, I cannot imagine. It is called the peta-huija. It grows upon a bush about the size of the pine-apple plant. The fruit is nearly as large as an ordinary ruta-baga turnip, in form like the strawberry, having a complete covering of leaves or folds, which overlap each other like the different pieces of a coat of mail. It is a deep carmine in color, full of small, black, round seeds, when cut open. The meat of the fruit is sweet and soft, and in taste resembles the flavor of the raspberry. When sliced, sugared, and baked with wine, it is extremely luscious. It is held in great esteem, though I never met with it but once during my stay in the country, and this was at Granada.

Figs and olives would flourish here to perfection, as well as the grape; and there is no reason why wines should not be manufactured fully equal to the superior article of Peru and Chili. The first olive was carried from Andalusia to Peru in 1560, by Antonio de Ribera, of Lima. The jocotes, referred to among the different fruits, are said by writers generally to be a species of plum, but I rather class it as an olive in color, meat, texture, size, and in some instances in similarity of taste. Our present limits will not permit us more extended latitude amid the fruits and productions, which subject we leave for the present with regret.

CHAPTER IX.

THE MALACCAS—CULTIVATION OF THE CACAO—DESCRIPTION OF A CACAO ESTATE—AN UGLY FISSURE OUTSIDE GRANADA—A SHOCK OF AN EARTHQUAKE—SPECULATIONS IN CASE OF EMERGENCY—LAKE POYO—DELIGHTFUL JAUNT—A LAKE COMO—A CUP OF TISTE—ITS USE—PRODUCTIONS OF THE COUNTRY—CIGARS—MAIZE—AGUARDIENTE—EFFECTS OF NOT TO BE MISTAKEN—WHEAT—MINERALS—GOLD, SILVER, AND COPPER MINES OF DEPILTA—THE CHONTALES MINING DISTRICTS—MATAGALPA—PAYNTER—THE CENTRAL STATES—THEIR MINES—ACCOUNT OF HONDURAS AND SAN SALVADOR—COSTA RICA—COAL—WANT OF MACHINERY, MEANS, AND ENTERPRISE.

FIVE miles from Granada is a cacao estate known as "The Malaccas." The ride from the city is over a level country, studded with white cacti and flowering shrubs. This plantation may be considered a fair sample of that which proper culture and industry may accomplish. The cacao is cultivated extensively, but is very rarely exported. That of this State is considered very superior, and is worth three times the price of that raised at Guyaquil. The tree is delicate, and requires great attention, though it repays every expense lavished upon it. It bears in seven years, produces two crops annually, and its yield is perfect in its fifteenth season. It grows to the height of twenty feet, its leaves are large and pointed, and it bears a small red flower. The pod contains about fifty beans. The shoots are planted fourteen feet apart, and are shaded by the plantain and the coral tree; the latter is called "The Mother of the Cacao," and shields the nursling from the glowing sun-rays. The cacao drops its bright crimson leaves about the beginning of April. It is indigenous; one laborer will attend one thousand trees, which will yield an annual income of three hundred dollars. Its beans are in circulation in the absence of smaller pieces of money than the media, and are of the value of one cent. A visit to the Malaccas is full of information. Its graveled roads are margined with mango groves, laden with golden fruit; and being perfectly free from weeds or underbrush, resemble a public square in Philadelphia.

Beyond the limits of Granada, upon the right, there is a large chasm, where a bridge spans the Camino real. It is the result of an eruption of the volcano of Masaya, in 1529, more of which we will give in another place. Your head grows giddy as you stand on its brink, gazing far down the dark abyss. The stones thrown within this yawning gulf bounded from crag to crag, while from far below came the echoes, faint and fainter, till they ceased. I should judge its width to be from twelve to fifteen feet, and probably one hundred yards or more in length.

One eve, while lying in my hammock, and about sinking into a pleasant slumber, I felt myself bumping against my neighbor, and turned, thinking he desired to attract my attention. Again, while talking, the motion was repeated. Mutually we sprang for the candle. Hearing a bustle in the street, we opened the door, to find the inhabitants abroad, and expecting a grand crash. Here was a dilemma. Señoritas in distress, with dishevelled hair and terrified appearance, appealing for aid, and yet none could be rendered. The shocks, however, soon ceased, and we gladly returned to our hammocks.

About the same distance from the city, a road winds through a forest of trees of most beautiful symmetry, and arched groves of mango, to an eminence visible through a cluster of palms, whence the path leads to an indefinite conclusion. The eye cannot pierce the heavy shroud of dense foliage ahead or on either hand. Carefully our horses tread this shelving inclination, reminding one of "Old Putnam's" riding scene in the melo-drama. The loose stones, becoming detached under the horse's feet, rattle down the precipice to the right. We hear a splash; another moment, and the gorgeous Lake Poyo bursts upon us, fully equaling those of the fairy tales in appearance.

This sheet of water is oblong, about three miles in length by two in width, the banks inclining around it. The air is heavy with the incense of countless flowers, mingled with the orange and lemon, while playing over our heads are gay-winged parrots, paroquets, and the really magnificent macaw. The water is very clear, and impregnated with sulphur. Not a hut is to be seen. It has an exit in a small stream on the left border, and is an inviting solitude for a bath.

The lake is full of gold fish, which we can see distinctly finning along, their gleaming scales relieved by the white sandy bottom. Oh, what a paradise is here before us! As fair a picture as e'er was tinted on an easel. There, rise soft hills, voluptuously falling to the water's edge, and in the ascent flowing to a graceful height, margining a sheet of wondrous beauty. The whispering leaves breathe happiness; the birds skimming the rippling-basin seem ignorant of the world beyond, and wing close to us, as though they feel we are strangers, and come to welcome us to their sweet retreat. Such is Lake Poyo, calm, clear, truly beautiful—the embodiment, the realization of Bulwer's "Lake of Como," where every floating cloudlet hath its mirror, and every wind hies to kiss its surface. I gaze back as I mount into the saddle, reluctant to quit it; and now, seen through an interval of time, I still deem it one of the loveliest of my foreign memories.

We breast the hill and gain the plain, turn through another path to a glade of brown-leaved trees, and reach a rancho embowered in a quiet, cosy niche, removed from the glare of the angry sun. Here, on either side, are pine-apples in abundance. The bush whereon they grow is only about four feet high, guarded by sharp leaves, which punish a hasty intrusion. A cup of tiste is prepared for us, and we wander back to the house. Tiste is composed of roasted or parched corn, ground sugar, and cacao, and is rolled in long sticks like pomatum. This is carried about by the marineros and travelers; for by putting it into a tin cup, adding water, and stirring with a spoon, a delicious and cool beverage is instantly at hand. In cases of dysentery it is very beneficial; and this, with the milk of the young cocoa-nut, is generally used, and found highly beneficial.

We may now notice more particularly some of the productions of Nicaragua. Coffee has been but little cultivated, though in Costa Rica it forms a prominent source of wealth, and the return has been as high as one million dollars per annum; the necessary expenses for labor being but nominal—from a dime to two dimes per day. Indigo has also been neglected lately. The plant is said to be indigenous, though there is a cultivated species, and the quality is unsurpassed.

Tobacco is cultivated; and that which is raised upon Ometepec, in Lake Nicaragua, is said to rival fully the

Havana, though I was not very favorably impressed upon my arrival, with either the make or flavor of their cigars. I found them loosely rolled, and the tobacco very imperfectly cured; but "homeward-bound" Californians have taught the natives how a better article can be manufactured. Prime cigarros can now be purchased, though at advanced rates. Maize flourishes very abundantly.

The native species of sugar-cane is very different from that cultivated elsewhere. It contains more saccharine matter. Two crops are grown annually, and it requires replanting only once in fourteen years. From this is manufactured the great drink of the country, "aguardiente," which is strong as Hercules, and like lightning in its effect. If you desire to have a friendly tipple upon it, there is no mistaking your position for the morrow. You are certain to be "tight" enough, and equally certain that your friend will be as "oblivious" as yourself.

Cotton is raised to a considerable extent, but is generally manufactured for home consumption. Some years past it formed an article of export. Rice is also cultivated, but not exported. Wheat is grown in the Segovia district, where the climate resembles that of the Middle States of America. These are the principal articles of value, though it possesses an enormous wealth of cabinet and dye-woods, mines of precious metals, rivers of considerable extent, whose banks require only willing arms to reclaim them from entire neglect; and I cannot believe that the far-seeing, thrifty American who has partially scanned this hitherto sealed book, will not refer to some of its bright pages when he shall have returned to his home, and ere many years shall have circled, I predict that many listeners to his strange truths will emigrate to this rude Eden, prepared for labor. Its minerals are gold, silver, copper, and iron; lead, nearly virginal, has been found, fully ninety per cent., and the residue silver. The district of Segovia is famed for its mineral wealth. Rich washings have been worked by the Indians at Matagalpa, as also copper mines, which latter yield from thirty-three to forty per cent. of metal.

In the district of Nicoya, many evidences of wealth exist, and gold has been brought to Granada and other cities from there, by the Indians and traders. The silver mines are numerous, the veins broad but irregular, and yield from twenty-five to ninety per cent. Those of Depilta, in the north, have been worked to advantage, though the ores average not more than two per cent., and yet the returns in one year, and that, too, under all the disadvantages of opening the mines, sinking shafts, &c., were about six thousand pounds of silver. The gold is of fine quality; the washings are more than fair, on an average, even to a Californian, who has been led to expect heavy results, and I accept his testimony without any hesitation, for he had only to pull up stakes if dissatisfied, and journey on to the land of promise—Home.

Many miners have crossed the Lake, and entered the Chontales district. In its almost unexplored streams, they have found abundant evidences of wealth; but illy provided with tools, provisions, and boats, they conld not give that time to the matter which probably will be bestowed hereafter. I piloted a party across and waited for them three days; and upon their return, saw the gold, a portion of which I afterward brought to the United States, where it was pronounced to be fully equal to the best Californian.

An Englishman, by the name of Paynter, resided many years near Matagalpa, where, in conjunction with a native, he carried on the crushing of ore, which paid him handsomely. He told me his machinery was primitive: a rude, rough hammer, worked by water power, for the crushing of the rock, which, when broken, fell into a solid basin. He used immense pestles, and in this way he said he made as good a living as he desired. He could at any time have as much money as he wanted; only increase the number of workmen, and this result was certain. Machinery could not be had at any price, nor could travelers be even favorably impressed with the facts as to this golden but rugged country; and he added: "As I am old, and shall never again return to

England, I am content with little to do, and that little satisfies all my desires."

Poor honest Paynter! he died shortly after. A better companion or truer friend never lived. He was a nobleman of Nature, with a soul extensive enough to feel for a world of friends, with not a selfish feeling, nor an ignoble principle. His bones rest far from his rock-bound island home, and there are many hearts, no doubt, which throb in unison with mine, as I repeat, Poor Paynter!

The mineral wealth of the United Central States is immense, each province boasting of numerous mines, washings of gold, and veins of silver. In the plain of Lepaguare, in Honduras, there rises a hill about eight hundred feet high, called Cerro Gordo, full of silver veins. Santa Lucia, a half day's ride northeast from Tegucigalpa, Mina Grande, San Martin, the Gatal, El Chimbo, a mass of copper dust two leagues from Tegucigalpa, De la Plata, San Juan de Cantaranos, La Mineral de Guascaran, silver; De Plomo, Villa Nueva, and other mines adjoining, Tuscaran or Yuscaran, and nine other mines, one of which, the Guyavilla, is very celebrated, the Veta Azul, Mairena, the Corpus, Cedios, Santa Barbara, San Antonio, Las Animas, the Malacate, and Encuentros: these form the principal mines of Honduras.

Near Cape Gracias à Dios are found fine opals in abundance. I have many in my possession, a few of which are considered fully equal to the finest Hungarian. One in particular, is large and full of fire. They are found in a bluish rock, rich flinty quartz, which is with great difficulty even perforated with a drill. They are seen peering from their rock-beds like the eyes of a bull, round, as large, and very frequently much larger. Again, they run in veins in a milk-blue rock. The stone then assumes a brilliant mother-of-pearl appearance, being striated, and not so transparent. An old Frenchman has been for years engaged in their exportation to France, and owns a specimen the size of an ordinary sickle pear. I had a very valuable one, but it was broken, through the want of skill of a lapidary in New York. The Indians are engaged in collecting them, and on the mountains their value is esteemed very inconsiderable. In San Salvador, at the village of Zatapa, about nine leagues from Santa Ana, there are iron and also several good yielding silver mines; and within five leagues of San Miguel there are numerous deposits of gold and silver, the principal of which are Tabanco, Macuelizo, La Baca, El Cuyal, La Carolina, and Merendon.

I have witnessed various interesting experiments by the savans of the mineral regions, to discover what kind of metal was in an unknown ore, from the color it imparted to glasses. The ores were pulverized and placed in a covered vessel, over a fire strong enough to create a moderate red heat. A few grains of the powdered residue was mixed with an ounce of crystalline glass, reduced to a powder also. Care was observed that nothing metallic, or aught else which might tinge glass, should mix with it. After being over the fire in fusion for some hours, the vessel was taken out, and after it grew cold, was broken. From the color of the fragments, they then endeavored to discover what metal or metallic earth was contained in the ore: as, for example, from the whitish or milky, that it contained tin; from the green, copper; and from the rusty green, iron. In an old Latin work upon Docimasia, I have found a highly interesting note, which I shall add:—"Precious stones are supposed, in their natural state, to be originally of two classes—the adamantine and the crystalline. If they are found in their matrixes untainted by any metallic substance, they remain pure diamonds, of the clearest, finest water, or crystals perfectly transparent; but if a diamond is tinged with lead, it appears yellow; if with copper and iron, it becomes green; and if with cinnabar, it makes a most beautiful red, and then changes its name to a ruby, and loses of its hardness in proportion to the mixture of the metal in it. A crystal, tinged with iron, becomes a garnate; with copper and an alkali, a sapphire; with copper and an acid, an emerald; with lead, a topaz and a jacinth; with gold, a chrysolite; with copper and iron, an aquamarine; and so on in many varieties; and each of these may be imitated by mixing preparations of metals with the finest white flint glass, by which method all sorts of gems being counterfeited, are called pastes, and are used to take off impressions of antique intaglios and caméos."

In a country whose mineralogy is so imperfectly known, little can be said; and I only add here the result of my own observations, with such information as I could gain in various portions of the State from miners and those who were interested in mineral development. I have noticed schistus, slate, mica, talc, asbestus, interspersed with stratified sand-rock, while superimposed on this conglomerate were veins of trachytic or basaltic rock. Those of the calcareous, more especially, I observed, were marbles, calcareous spars, gypsums, and limestones, the latter very compact, and in color white, red, blue, and gray. The marbles are white, gray, black, and green, and like those of Chili, are susceptible of a fine polish. The varieties of spars are infinite, and I have seen them crossed in various directions by very fine golden filaments.

Quarries of gypsum, the parallelopipedal, rhomboidal, and striated, are numerous. That of a light blue, very brittle, is found in a semi-calcined state in the vicinity of volcanoes; of this latter, a highly useful and beautiful plaster for walls might be made. There are various kinds of the sandstone, viz.: the flint, whetstone, quartz, and rock crystal. Of the plain jaspers, I discovered the fine red, the gray, green, white, and the lapis lazuli, and also the gray spotted with black, the white interspersed with blue and yellow, and the yellow, variegated with blue, gray, and red spots.

I also found quantities of colored crystals, supposed by the inhabitants to be precious stones, as they resembled in appearance rubies, jacinths, diamonds, &c. Among the quantities of quartz in the mountain districts, I purchased for a trifle several beautiful specimens of agate; and along the western shore of Lake Nicaragua, have seen the blood-stone. In the Department Septentrional of Matagalpa, amethysts have been found which were enclosed in a gray quartz. Had those who discovered the specimens shown to me, dug deeper, the stones would have proven more valuable. They varied in color, some of a pure violet, others tinged with the deepest tint of purple.

I have been shown, also, several turquoises, greenish-blue in hue, and others which were very hard, of a deep blue. According to Abbe Molina, "these stones ought, with propriety, to be classed among the concretions, as they are only the petrified teeth or bones of animals, colored by metallic vapors." ("History of Chili:" Vol. i., pp. 64, 65.) Being but imperfectly acquainted with mineralogy, and in fact, not having expected to meet with so much of an interesting character, I had not at hand a "vade mecum," by which I could at once gain a transient intimacy with the quality and value of these stones, and not being in a country where I could gain reliable or satisfactory replies to my queries, I have given here the ultimatum of my information, although I thought in some instances that colored spar was received by the natives as emeralds, topazes, and sapphires. I am aware, now, that my latter suggestion is fully endorsed by those intimate with the subject; but in the instances given, I may have been mistaken.

In Prescott's Peru, Vol. i., p. 321, by reference, is found, that the conquerors having reached a town in the province of Coaque, they rushed into the deserted dwellings, and found there "a large quantity of gold and silver, wrought into clumsy ornaments, together with many precious stones; for this was the region of the esmeraldas, or emeralds, where that valuable gem was most abundant. One of these jewels that fell into the hands of Pizarro, in this neighborhood, was as large as a pigeon's egg. Unluckily, his rude followers did not know the value of their prize, and they broke many of them in pieces by pounding them with hammers. They were led to this extraordinary proceeding, it is said, by one of the Dominican missionaries, Fray Reginaldo de Pedraza, who assured them that this was the way to prove the true emerald, which could not be broken! It was observed that the good father did not subject his own jewels to this wise experiment; but as the stones, in consequence of it, fell in value, being regarded merely as colored glass, he carried back a considerable store of them to Panama."

It was subsequent to the capture of this province, that Pizarro continued his march along the coast, when a " strange epidemic broke out in the little army." The Spaniards, exhausted by fatigue and disease, "and grievously disappointed at the poverty of the land, which now offered no compensation for their toils, cursed the hour in which they had enlisted under his standard; and the *men of Nicaragua*, in particular, says the old chronicler, calling to mind their pleasant quarters in their luxurious land, sighed only to return to their Mohammedan Paradise."

The topazes shown to me were mostly imperfect, and full of flaws; but I saw not one with double pyramid. I was informed that sometimes these gems were found in quartz crystals, and that in some instances they were green. I doubted this, believing that if any substance of that color resembling the topaz, did occur, it was most probably euclase, which may be and has been mistaken for it.

In the mountains of Aguacate, near Cartago, in Costa Rica, there are several gold mines; and the neighborhood of Olancho is famous for its fine ore, which is said to have been collected in the sands of the river Guyape, in its course through the valley.

Many writers have given statistical accounts of the revenue of said mines; but never having seen an official statement, I shall make no estimates of my own. A few months labor to a party possessing a knowledge of mining, and the proper machinery, would be ample for the amassing of a fortune. Coal has been found in Costa Rica, upon the shores of Lake Nicaragua, and upon the Mosquito coast.

With such evidences of wealth, there can be little doubt of the early explorations of these provinces by the hardy and experienced miners of the United States. Their arrival would be hailed with enthusiasm by a people who venerate our government, and love its citizens for their intelligence, sociability, and enterprise.

CHAPTER X.

BEYOND GRANADA—A VIEW—INDIAN MOTHER AND HER LOAD—THE CONQUERORS—MY OPINION—MASAYA—THE PLAZA—THE CHURCH—STORES AND MANUFACTURES—FINE HATS, PRICES—HAMMOCKS—PROVISIONS—EXTENT OF THE TOWN—DOGS AND BUZZARDS—COUNTRY BEYOND THE TOWN—NINDIRI—ITS CHURCH—COOL SHADE—ITS ORANGES—ANOTHER FINE VIEW—MAL PAIS, A ROAD OF LAVA—RIO TIPITAPA AND THE LAKES—SOMETHING FROM OVIEDO—AN OASIS—A DRINK, AND A SWING IN A HAMMOCK—ENTRANCE INTO MANAGUA—WHOM WE MET—CITY BY MOONLIGHT—NIHAPA—INDIAN TEMPLE—A SELL—DIFFERENCE OF OPINIONS ABOUT IT—OTHER LAKES—WASHER-WOMEN AGAIN—ANCIENT HISTORY—SENORITAS.

BEYOND the city the palm is seen waving on either hand. The roads are bad enough, but every one should lay in a supply of good humor when traveling, especially in this country. Through dark and dense ravines, draperied with bush and brier, we hold to the mule path, while myriads of macaws, parrots, and other birds, flit across the almost arched trees above us. The lake lies on our right, and from the eminence now gained, seems like a fine thread of silver tracing the distance. From the summit of this ridge we have a glorious prospect. There lies Lake Nicaragua; and there, like a tail to a silver kite, runs the Tipitapa. In the background are the mountains of Matagalpa and Segovia. A slope, covered with forest, sweeps between us and the outlined picture. The road is narrow and much worn. Far down to the left, a line of smoke wreathes palely up from some hidden hacienda, while the hills seem to chase one another in graceful flow, far back to a blank horizon. The Indian woman approaching has her load of corn, a bushel or two, in a net bag, suspended from her forehead and resting on her back. I have seen, too, besides this heavy burden, a strapping child of six years of age sitting philosophically on her hip, perfectly resigned to the slavish condition of the toiling parent. This custom, however, is the result of the brutalizing treatment of the early Spaniards, the tormentors of these poor Indians. Gladly would I forget that the Spanish conquerors introduced neither civilization, peace, nor plenty, but wars, rapine, and discord; sowed dissensions; and after robbing their prostrate victims of vitality, left them poverty-stricken and enfeebled. Spain's day of reckoning must arrive. He whose Cross has witnessed so many inhuman outrages, whose symbol has been profaned, whose people have been wronged and betrayed, will not forget the untutored Indian, whose hearth has been desecrated, and whose home and hopes have been defiled.

We enter Masaya. On either hand are fruit trees, amid cool cane huts. As we advance, a better class of houses, with tile roofs, are seen; and still on, for a considerable distance, we reach the plaza. In the centre stands a large church, about which are gathered a vast number of market people; and, piled on the pave, are quantities of fruits and various articles of domestic manufacture. I was surprised to find abundance of cordage, hammocks, cotton cloth, saddles, and mats of numerous descriptions, exposed for sale in the stores surrounding the plaza; but learned, upon subsequent inquiry, that Masaya was celebrated particularly for its manufactures. I saw some beautiful hammocks, very fine, exhibiting considerable taste in the blending and arrangement of colors, adorned with tassels, all of which were offered at reasonable prices. For an American dollar I purchased a very good one; and for two dollars and a half, one of the finest among them. There is a nack in sitting or lolling in one of these airy cradles; and two persons, reclining midway in one, upon different sides, will thus find a grand improvement in their siestas. For warm eves, give me the grass hammock. I can rock myself to sleep, or remain torpid *ad libitum*.

Upon the left hand of the plaza you reach a posada, or hotel, where you find plenty of room, beans, corn-cakes, sweet cakes, dulces, preserves and candies, hard-boiled eggs, and fried chickens. The town covers a square league; though, we must say, that it would be impossible to estimate the extent of any of the towns of Nicaragua, or the number of their inhabitants, without allowing a margin for guess-work. None of the cities are very extensive—that is, the adobe or finely-built portion; but the precincts, or suburbs, are immense. After riding through the principal streets, until you fancy every estimate made by travelers wide of the mark, a gap in the foliage will reveal cane and mud huts on the brink of some ravine, completely embowered in orange and lemon trees; or you will strike a winding foot-path, leading far into a hidden depth of bananas and palms, which leads you to a populous community of plebeians. These are a distinct body, save on holy days, when the masses assemble to witness the fireworks, or to welcome the entrée of a conqueror, or a dictator.

Dogs and buzzards are abundant in and about all the towns. The former throng the streets, snarl, bark, growl, and run where they are sure to be in the way; while the latter, on outstretched inky pinions, settle upon the tiled roofs of the convents and churches, as though they were part and parcel thereof. They are universal appurtenances; and the former mar a quiet stroll through the shady suburbs, while the latter break upon the landscape just as your imagination is about to lend enchantment to some vine-twined ruin, and blot out the fair proportions of some imaginary airy structure.

Masaya is a sweet retreat, and is celebrated for its industrial populace. Passing through the outskirts one morn, I saw in a hut several men making hats. I entered, and found some shaping and manufacturing, while others were slitting into fine shreds, a species of palm, which forms the fencing about the country generally, and which grows only about four feet high. The leaf is long, slender, remarkably strong, and is of a dark-green color—though when dried, it becomes very light indeed. These were the finest hats I ever saw, and I ordered one for twelve dollars, which was to have been delivered to me in ten days. The only reply, however, to my frequent messages for it, was "Poco tiempo," which has passed into a national proverb. Every thing is conducted on the "in a little time" style; and although it at first disarranges all your plans, and puts you to numerous inconveniences, yet you become accustomed to it, and in a little while adopt it also, in self-defense.

The country beyond the city is very luxuriant; and following the broadest road, we pass through a deep cut in a volcanic rock, about mid-distance to Nindiri. Indian women, with only skirts on, and children refreshingly naked, are seen moving about in the orange-arcades on either hand; while the latter, noisy as all are and should be everywhere, are found propagated in immense quantities. To the right of the road is a plaza, on which stands a cosy church. Fruits of every variety are found here in perfection—among others, excellent oranges, hanging from the tree, large, thick-skinned, juicy and firm. Passing out toward Managua, which lies twelve leagues from Masaya, we soon rode into the forest, and reached elevated and volcanic ground, whence the view of the country was complete. The Lake, plain, hills, mountains, valley, and forest, all lay far out on Nature's easel, fresh and fair.

Beyond this point we passed a miserable piece of road, called by the natives, "Mal pais,"—bad country—; and certainly it richly merits the title. It is an immense body of lava, ejected from the volcano of Masaya on the left, which was in full blast about 1670, and of which some strange stories were told by the early chroniclers. It is a vast mass of hard, grating, unyielding, bluish-black—a useless waste of matter collected by terrific force. It has flooded the country for miles; and, as has been conjectured, blocked up the Lake; for in olden times it was supposed the Lakes Managua and Nicaragua were one, as the Rio Tipitapa is supposed to be all remaining of the lakes in their former unity. The adjacent country is full of accumulated pummice. On the right, toward the Lake, is truly a desolate picture. Trees buried; others just projecting above this mass; rocks toasted, half covered, or overturned; valleys filled with it; and our nag's tramp sounding hollow beneath—all this lends any thing but enchantment to as drear a landscape as I ever wish to see. Oviedo, an old chronicler, who visited it while in a state of eruption, in 1529, says, that neither Vesuvius nor Etna were to be compared with "the Hell of Masaya," as it was called. It is said that tigers and pumas are numerous in the vicinity. The mountain, at the base, is about three leagues in circumference, and rises to the height of a league from the foot to the summit. He also adds, "Some assert that the light caused by the eruption is sufficient to read by at the distance of three leagues. The whole country is illuminated by the flame of the volcano." The crater is about five hundred feet in depth; and owing to its regular ascent, the width diminishes as it descends. The bottom of the crater is at least two hundred feet in circumference. The country immediately surrounding is barren and desolate—an occasional blighted tree still standing, a melancholy sentinel over this desert of scoriaceous mass.

After a pause sufficient to fully satisfy us, we resumed our saddles, and over a rough, wild, hollow, rumbling road, reached a lovely and rolling country, a grateful relief to the eye and feelings. Hard by, on our right, we espied a hut; and not having found a stream where we might refresh ourselves and our jaded animals, we turned from the beaten path, and rode to the open door. Here we found several Indians of the Chorotegan race, who furnished us with lemonade, cakes, candies, and eggs, and we lolled in the ever-ready hammocks until the sun began to decline, when again springing into the stirrup, we hastened to Managua. The entrance to the city is agreeable, the road being lined with trees; the cane huts, whitewashed or painted, pitched gracefully upon the side of a hill, or stuck jauntily upon its summit, surrounded by heavily-laden orange and lemon trees. The effect was indeed the more striking, as we had just left the black fields of Masaya, and turned from our halt in the broiling sun to a delightful repose.

The army of the Grenadinos was quartered in Managua, and our posada was the headquarters of General Chamorro and suite, and consequently we fared better, probably, than those travelers who arrived in town a few hours later. The drums were beating, troops were marshalling in the distance, and the guards were about being relieved, as we strolled out to survey the city by moonlight, after sipping a cup of tiste. The people were sitting at their doors, smoking and chatting over some imaginary entrée of General Muñoz, who, it was currently reported, was to attack the town that night. As we advanced, the challenge of the sentry on every corner announced our approach to the plaza. The moon rose beautifully over the towering coyal palms in the distance, and illumined a large sheet of water beyond us, which we subsequently discovered was Lake Managua.

Lake Nihapa lies about nine miles from the city, and occupies the crater of an extinct volcano. Here we found masses of black lava, partially covered with patches of grass, while before us were small huts. Beyond, flowing in harmonious swells, were mountains, crowned with graceful foliage; and far beyond stretched Lake Managua, gemmed with islands, gleaming like a huge burnished mirror. We descended to a position of safety, and gazed far down the depth of the crater, where we saw a variety of uncouth, red-painted figures, concerning which I had no time to gather any thing, and probably saved my labor, for queries are to but little purpose in Nicaragua. "Quien sabe?"—Who knows?—is a fit companion for the everlasting "Poco tiempo;" and between the two you derive as little satisfaction as from any sources imaginable. There is said to exist here the remains of an Indian temple. If it does, I did not see it; but I found an arched cave, which, to an inexperienced eye, aided by a fertile and superstitious imagination, might prove a temple as well as any thing else. The choice is altogether a matter of taste, and I suppose the inhabitants delight in believing that which tradition has handed to them.

There are various other lakes in the neighborhood of the city, all of volcanic formation and origin. The Salt Lake is one of them, the water being brackish. The descent to it is steep, and overgrown with underbrush and briers. Another, the name of which I cannot recall, is reached by a path margined with cacti. The water is very cool, the sun is felt but little, and it is the favorite resort of the washer-women of the city Managua, in ancient times, after the expedition of Cordova, was said to be nine miles long, contained forty thousand inhabitants, and the country generally might be said to swarm with population. It is now a quiet place, celebrated only for its neighboring lakes, a few old statues, and for the exceeding grace of its nut-brown señoritas.

CHAPTER XI.

MANAGUA—ITS INHABITANTS—SERVILES AND LIBERALS—HISTORICAL INTERLUDES—EDUCATION—THE FATHERS OF ELD—BIGOTRY—ECCLESIASTICS—AN ANCIENT CARVING—PADRE VIGIL—RELIGOUS CEREMONIES—THE INDIANS—SQUIER'S ASSERTIONS RELATIVE TO THE MOSQUITO INDIANS—HISTORY AGAIN—IDEAS ABOUT MIGRATION—ANTIQUE STONES (PIEDRAS ANTIGUAS)—THE CONFESSORS OF THE CONQUEST.

MANAGUA is the seat of the meeting of the Legislature. Its inhabitants are deemed stanch and loyal citizens; and there being continual jealousies and strifes between Leon and Granada, here, on neutral ground, the opposing cliques eventually meet, arrayed in the "panoply of war," to battle, fortune deciding in turns for either party. These intestine broils are waged with acrimony; families are arrayed against their own; kin forget, or forsake kindred ties, and bury in the preparation for strife every ancient feeling of love and reciprocal friendship. Events of long standing are causes for animosities, which only require a breath to fan into a flame. The embers of discord are smouldering, a blaze arises, intercourse ceases, appeals to arms ensue, and the already poverty-enfeebled country groans under new taxes and fresh imposts. The Englishman, too, has been busy, sowing the seed of dissension, that he might reap a golden harvest; and in its troubles he fattens upon the vitals of the helmless State.

There are two factions, viz., the Serviles—the aristocrats or monarchists—and the Liberals or Republicans. Prior to the independence of Nicaragua from her confederated articles with Honduras, Costa Rica, and other states, the Serviles favored a monarchy, of which the Emperor of Mexico was to have been the head. The Liberals of Guatemala and Nicaragua united and opposed these suicidal schemes, and lost or gained, at different times, till in 1829, Gen. Morazan discovering that the church was intriguing also against liberal views, seized the prelate and marched him out of the country, forbidding his return, under penalty of death. Monks and friars were summarily expelled. The convents and monasteries were consequently deserted; and the State of Guatemala passed a decree forbidding the "taking of the veil," suppressing monastic establishments, and confiscating to the State's support these wealthy garners of exclusive church monopolies. Papal bulls were not permitted to be promulgated; church dignitaries were to be appointed by the President of the Republic, and the sale of papal dispensations proceeded from the Federal Government.

Honduras legalized the marriages of the priests, and legitimated the children resulting from their union. The confederacy dissolved, and the Serviles being in the ascendency, convents were reopened in Guatemala; but the other States maintained their prohibitions. The taxes upon property have greatly enriched the church coffers notwithstanding. These liens accumulated rapidly, and encumbered the largest estates of the country; but the Legislature of Nicaragua, in 1850, abolished ten per cent. of these, except such as were applied to education.

Nicaragua and Costa Rica constitute one Diocess, dating back to 1526. Education is at a low ebb. On the outskirts of Masaya, to the left, we passed an adobe school-house. I peeped in and saw about sixty muchachos and muchachitas busily engaged in poring over their books. They recite in one class, and sing their lessons. The rod is known here, too, and is measured by no stingy rule; but how to detect, in such an universal method of recitation, the delinquent student, I could not arrive at; but suppose the ear becomes accustomed to the scholastic melodies, and readily discovers a false note, or an inharmonious tone. Mr. Squier's correspondent observes, that "in the University of Granada, are taught the following branches: Latin and Spanish grammar; Philosophy,

Civil and Canonical Law, also Theology, English and French. In mathematics there is a void. The time devoted to Spanish, Grammar, and Latin, is two and a half years—to Philosophy, two years—Civil, and Canonical Law, and Theology, three years; and that many, wanting the patience, skip and skim over them, to secure their titles;" and there are priests who have read so little, that they may be dignified as self-taught. Salaries of professors do not exceed two hundred dollars per year.

Liberal inducements have been offered in Central America for the establishment of schools of every grade. The Government House, after business hours, is used for school purposes. Education, in a country where Catholic influences were always prominent, in fact universal from the conquest, has been but lightly regarded. It could not be that the Fathers of the Church were illiterate. It could not be that education should be considered a disqualification, an incubus upon progress. Why, then, has it stood still, since the introduction of Christianity? Has the precept of our Saviour been carried out, "Suffer little children to come unto me"? or have the holy padres used the temples of the Most High for other purposes more holy? Has this not occurred wherever the Cross has been planted by force, as in South America, Peru, Mexico, Guatemala, and upon the ruined shrines of the Incas and Aztecs?

If civilization does not contain the germ of educational purposes, what shall we find within it? Nought save a painted, treacherous nuncio, a promise worse than a positive denial, because unfulfilled. And calmly reviewing the conquest, we find no spirit of enterprise inculcated by the church. Blind obedience, slavish submission, unnatural exactions, jaundiced expectations, faithless pledges—these only are the results of the incoming of these Soldiers of the Faith. These provinces, instead of even remaining as pure in principle, and honest in sentiment as the holy fathers found them, are degraded by moral and intellectual prostitution, where, amid the just shooting germs of natural hopes and religious feelings, the Cross of the Crusade trembles upon a tottering foundation.

It has been contended by some, that bigotry is universal. I must differ from those who probably have had no superior advantages of self judging. An apathy pervades the community in general, I admit. There is a want of decision among the higher classes—a void of sentiment—a laxity of discipline; but I have found abundant evidences of moral worth and common sense, which are guarantees of substantiality. The night of fanaticism is fast waning; the dawn of moral and physical independence is already breaking; and in the dayspring of Nicaragua, a future of greatness and prosperity is shadowed, which will forever close against the Church of the Conquest the hopes of a revival of its past absolute sovereignty, and merciless control.

Amid the body of ecclesiastics, nevertheless, I have met with many men whose unexceptionable demeanor attracted not alone, attention, but inspired reverence and respect; men who were capable of friendship unalloyed, and who reciprocated those many little minutiæ, which form a pleasing whole. Padre Vigil, the curate of the parochial in Granada, is of this class, a man of genuine sterling virtue, a friend of the oppressed in heart and deed. I remember a sermon delivered by him in 1850, in which he noticed a want of proper feeling among the natives toward the Americans, who, instead of kneeling as the Host passed by, raised their hats in respect. Difficulties have occurred in Catholic countries where natives have deemed the omission of kneeling an insult to their religion; we may mention Mexico, Peru, Italy, and many other states. This ecclesiastic subsequently represented Nicaragua as Minister to the United States.

Having heard that there was a carving of considerable merit in a small hut, in a remote portion of the city, I hastened to examine it, anxious to incorporate in my "notes" a description of it. It proved to be a representation of a cavalier on horseback, almost of life-size; the costume and arms were of the fifteenth century, in his upraised right hand he clasped a straight-bladed sword, and in the left, a long cross. The figure itself, was designed with a great deal of spirit; the long hair and flowing beard, the cap, upon the side of which was represented a feather, the sash about the waist, and the spur upon the right heel, all corresponded with the paintings of the Indians subsequent to the conquest. The eyes of the cavalier are raised, and his entire attitude denotes the moment of his embarking upon some enterprise, such as the advancement of the Holy Cross into new lands. The horse is executed with a boldness seldom seen in the engravings or paintings of the early Mexicans or Indians. The carving occupies the entire side of the cane hut; and the reply to my query, as to whom it was supposed to represent, was, "Hernando Cortez." As to its history, they knew nothing more than it had been in their family for many years. The panels encompassing it are filled with dim, and nearly obliterated tracings. They represent armed white men, with long beards, battling with nude Indians with primitive weapons; while interspersed, are seen dogs with open mouths, rushing upon the terrified natives.

In the court of our posada, I saw a large brass bell, which had rung the tocsin of a revolution in Spain, the name of which I have forgotten. I was told it was brought here by the Spaniards, but for what purpose was not known. The casting was superb, and the metal equal to the matchless cannon of Chagres Fort and those lying on the lake-side at San Carlos.

The Indians of this country were, we learn from the early chroniclers, divided into "two distinct families, corresponding with the sections of the Provinces. The Caribs maintained a precarious living on the Atlantic coast, with a peculiar religion." Squiers remarks: "A portion of their descendants, still further debased by the introduction of negro blood, may still be found in the wretched Mosquitos, who, by a brazen fraud, are attempted to be passed off on the world as a sovereign nation, comprehending the duties, and capable of fulfilling the requirements of government." It is not our province, nor our intention here, to dilate upon the title of the Mosquito king to that part of the country, known as the "Mosquito Territory," and inhabited by the Moscos or Mosquitos, Valientes, Wawas, and other tribes on the shores of the Caribbean Sea, from the ninth to the fifteenth degree of north latitude. We shall speak of it hereafter, and furnish the titles of the claimants in juxtaposition, and draw our inferences.

On the river San Juan, are the few Melchoras of Carib stock, and the same is said to be true of the Woolwas, Poyas, Ramas, Toacas, and the Bravos to the southward on the Atlantic coast, toward Chiriqui Lagoon. In the interior, the natives partook of the characteristics of the Mexicans, and were divided into distinct governments. They appear to have been one people, with the exception of those living on the small isthmus between the Pacific and Lake Nicaragua. These latter spoke the language of the ancient Mexicans, and possessed their customs and religion. The other races, called

Dirians, occupied Masaya, Managua, Tipitapa, Diriomo, and Diriamba. Oviedo says, "they were true Chorotegans." The Nagrandans occupied the plain of Leon between the northern extreme of Lake Managua and the Pacific. The Orotinians settled the country south of Lake Nicaragua around the Gulf Nicoya. The Cholutecans, occupied the districts north of the Nagrandans, extending along the Gulf of Fonseca into what is now Honduras territory. The Chontals covered Chontales, northward of Lake Nicaragua, and lying between the tribes already given, and those on the Caribbean Sea. That these tribes should have migrated is no great wonder, for migrations greater occurred prior; that they should be remnants, or entire tribes from Mexico, is not at all strange—for after the conquest of Mexico, various tribes sought safety from the swords of the conquerors; and that Nicaragua should have been the home of their exile should not be as strange, as to know positively that the language of Mexico is spoken by some of them, and yet, not to believe them hereditary descendants of the Aztecs.

Many statues, or "antique stones" have been discovered, either too much broken to be entirely recovered, too bulky for the means of present transportation, or too difficult of access; and there can be but little doubt that numbers have been hidden by the Indians, who yet retain a distinct remembrance of their traditional virtues. Could these senseless blocks speak, with what eloquence would they tell the wrongs of their worshippers, and how depict the fanaticism of the holy fathers, who waged a long crusade against them and their venerators! Yet some of them remain, pure as when chiseled, while the Confessors of the Conquest sleep in dusty chambers, far from the scenes of their rapine, remembered by their atrocities, and revered, certainly not for their advancement of the Holy Cause. Time will weigh each in his balance, and justice will be accorded by Him who "marks the sparrow's fall," the Father of the Fatherless.

CHAPTER XII.

IDOLS—GOOD TEETH—CIGARITAS—UNIVERSAL USE—A PRIMITIVE PEOPLE—A CLEAN BREAST OF SEVERAL MATTERS—A VISIT WITH THE CONSUL-GENERAL OF THE UNITED STATES—AN INTERESTING DOMESTIC GROUP—RECOGNITION OF A WELL-KNOWN VOICE—COMFORTS NOT EXPECTED—COUNTRY ABOUT THE CITY—FRUITS—FIELDS—COOKS—SOCIETY—OUR POSADA—BIOGRAPHICAL SKETCH OF CHAMORRO—ALSO OF JOSE TRINIDAD MUNOZ—OUTSIDE OF MANAGUA—ON OUR TOUR AGAIN—SCOUTS—NEW ROAD OVER THE MOUNTAIN—NARROW PATH—AN INCIDENT BY THE WAY-SIDE—GLIMPSES OF THE COUNTRY—OUTPOSTS AHEAD, AND OUR PREPARATION.

A NUMBER of statues may be found in this city, though much defaced, and so rude in execution, that for me they possessed but little interest, and probably for the reader less. I of course consider them idols; I could not mistake them for modern statues, for Nicaragua has erected no monuments, that I discovered, to the memory of any of her sages or patriots. Had I been told that these rude stone cuttings portrayed a Sophocles or a Hannibal, I should have questioned the likenesses, and have given the sculptor credit for chiseling the deceased out of that transient respect, which a fair picture of a departed sage or hero receives even from the stranger.

I have said elsewhere that this city was celebrated, among other matters, for the graceful carriage of its females. This is not confined to the wealthier class ; it is a general thing. The señorita, decked in her gayest apparel, possesses the same ease, the same quiet dignity ; while the muchachas, who upon their heads balance the tinajas, sweep past with an eloquent motion which instantly attracts your attention. As a general thing, too good teeth are prevalent; and having heard the learned Professors of Medicine in the United States anathematize the practice of smoking and chewing as injurious to health and teeth, I felt relieved as I observed its universal use here, where from earliest infancy no restraints had been imposed, no Candle lectures from tidy housewifes, no vigorous handling from the hand of an enraged governor, who probably might have set the example to his erring child. Every one enjoys a smoke, old and young, male and female ; and you at first deem it singular, that as you sit tete-a-tete with a smiling señorita, she should in a moment make a paper cigarita, and after lighting it, puff it once or twice, and hand it to you with a smile, that of course overcomes any remnant of antipathy yet lingering as to a "draw."

I might mention some particulars for the curious, and whittling away as I am at facts, not fancies, and as probably some of my readers may take a trip to Nicaragua some time, I may as well make "a clean breast" of that which I feel pressing to my lips and eager to have utterance. Now I wish to be fairly understood. I consider the Nicaraguans a primitive people in many respects—self-taught, self-dependent; rich in many virtues; and wanting only in that which I honestly believe is not solitaire in Spanish countries, but even has status in the United States—*Nationalizing*, and one other element essentially Spanish—*want of self-government.* My premises thus given, I shall be considered properly, I trust. A favorite, to whom your serenade is given, your sonnets improvised, your waltz or polka dedicated, is as shy of a loving embrace, or a warm, rich, ripe kiss, as are some of the blushing and beautiful daughters of my own country, but they do not object to being very scantily clad, and bathing with you. I must confess this want of consistency, or rather this primitive idea of fig-leaf-date, was rather a "stopper in my pipe" at first; though, like other bashful young men, I soon recovered my equanimity, and enjoyed "old-fashions" in old-fashioned style. Altogether, I really believe I prefer them to the many new-fangled notions, under a heavy press of which, propriety is altogether lost sight of, nature checked, and good old common sense reduced to old fogyism, and its relative chances—bad fare and "back seats."

The Hon. W. F. Boone, United States Consul-General, one evening accompanied me to visit several ladies, daughters of an advocate. We entered, and found the mother swinging in a hammock, her daughters sitting at the door. I ushered him in with little ceremony, omitting, of course, his titular appendage. After a few moments we heard what seemed to each of us to be a very familiar noise, and after a careful survey, observed a female pig with her family, in the extreme corner of the room. The father of this pork brood was rooting and grunting away in a very undignified manner, and advanced between the General and our entertainers with a sang froid only equalled by the want of notice of the intrusion upon the part of the ladies. This rather confused the Consul, and he remembers the visit to the advocate's house to this day, and often laughs as he recalls the incident. And yet you pass a pleasant agreeable evening; and it is only in proportion as you enter and indulge in female society everywhere, that a just appreciation of national character may be formed. In other cases, you find many of the comforts enjoyed at home—sofas, bedsteads, carpets, mattrasses, pianos and other articles of luxury. Dress varies in style and arrangement, according to class and age.

The country around Managua is probably as rich and fertile as in any other portion of the State. Fine fruits are abundant, and can be purchased for a trifle; but as a residence, I prefer Granada, or the country about Rivas, probably because at those points more foreigners may have settled, and the public houses generally kept by them afforded every delicacy which could be obtained. The diet of the country is very simple, though you find many Jamaica cooks, or those who have been taught the secrets of the French larder, who may be engaged for from two and a half to three and a half dollars per month, while the Spanish can be had for from one and a half, to two dollars. Prices vary, suddenly and frequently.

From the fact of the meeting of the Legislative Assembly in this city, a great number of the elite reside here, and consequently the society is desirable. At the posada we patronized, General Chamorro and suite were quartered; and as he maintained an elevated position in the estimation of his admirers, and subsequently was elected Supreme Director, we may add our personal recollections of him. In height he was about five feet, six inches; corpulent, possessed the air of a man "well to do in the world," and conscious of his position and his ability. His face was oval, eye large, features regular, and was withal quite prepossessing. His countenance indicated a good-liver, a good feeder; a jovial expression illumed his eye as you approached him; and, to a stranger, he seemed any thing but that which his enemies and rivals would have induced us to believe.

His officers were much attached to him, and he had the utmost confidence of his soldiers. He possessed the secret of swaying the mass with an impromptu manner, that disarmed malice, and which gave a certain recklessness to self, both dazzling and attractive. His enemies vilified him when they proclaimed him a coward. His defense of what he deemed sacred, the Constitution and his country, at Granada, during the revolution, when General Muñoz led the opposing party, which was defeated frequently, and which subsequently was commanded by General Walker, is a recorded denial of this charge; for he spurned quarter, refused truce, and even when the enemy encamped about the city, and nearly starved his rank and file, he did not swerve. He was ubiquitous; he visited every post, inspected the arms, commanded in person foraging parties, and finally fell a victim to his over-exertion. Let me not hear these idle calumnies. If he differed with me, or with the party with whom my countrymen were joined, there should be at least the truth told of our adversary; and I know that the future will be generous to him. He battled for his rights; he defended his countrymen when called to the post of trust and honor; occupied it with ability, and died, mourned and beloved.

And here, leaving the corpse of one of the leading men of the State, with whom history will have much to do, let us turn to another, celebrated as the "Great Captain" for many years, and whose life has been as eventful as chequered, namely, General Jose Trinidad Muñoz. His Excellency had visited the United States, and had been in the Mexican army under General Santa Anna. He possessed a proper appreciation of the Americans, for whom he ever decidedly evinced his preference. He was about five feet eight or nine inches in height, rather spare, had a commanding figure, a fine intellectual head, a full and very expressive eye, a clear voice, a quickness, remarkable in Central America, in forestalling your conclusion, an agreeable smile, and was as courteous and affable in his casa as any man I ever knew. His lady was a rare specimen of Nicaraguan beauty, as also her sister, both of whom I believe were born in Leon. He was a native of Granada. He was an admirer of the great Napoleon, and wore his chapeau, top-boots, and coat, à la Bonaparte. In his saloon, he had engravings of several of the chief battles of that distinguished hero, and evidently desired to imitate him so far as the artists could aid him. He was General-in-Chief of the army for many years; and as war was his profession, when peace settled with healing wings over his own State, he offered his services to others, and thus "kept his hand in." We shall meet with him hereafter, and shall only here record our judgment.

He had a certain dash of talent, and the secret of its being produced at certain times; he possessed also the tact of producing it all at once. He had a certain degree of foresight. He knew, sooner or later, the flag of his country must be succeeded by another, and he had sufficient prudence to communicate this only to those whom he knew also were ready to aid him. He felt the part which England was endeavoring to play in Central America, and had the good sense to nerve his countrymen to oppose her machinations; but the honest, heartfelt patriotism, the pure devotion to his country's welfare, the desire to be great only in the hearts of his countrymen, the disregard of foreign influence, the abandon of self, and the courage, perseverance, and *never-give-up*, *inborn* religious principles of Chamorro—these he never inherited.

Pursuing a well-beaten road over level ground, we passed out of Managua, and pursued our tour, while our refreshed animals gave evidence of renewed pace and spirits. Everywhere we met detachments of troops posted, and moving rapidly from place to place, for an attack from the opposite party, under General Muñoz, was hourly expected. Scouts were stationed at intervals along the camino real, and we halted at the foot of a high eminence—which is the only one between Granada and the Pacific, *via* Leon—to prepare our nags for its ascent. A road also has been constructed around this ridge to the left, so that in the rainy season, when the ground is slippery, the arduous toil of surmounting it may be obviated. It is the work of General Muñoz, who has achieved and deserves great credit for the consummation thereof.

The country spreads before us, refreshingly lovely. The ridge is steep, and the road winding over it very narrow. About half way up, to the right, a wall of masonry guards the traveler from a summersault down a frightful precipice, should his mule stumble; while, on the left, a ridge of apparently loose rocks line the perpendicular immensity overhead. Should horsemen meet in this canalled ravine, there would be some difficulty in passing; and how laden mules would accomplish this I cannot determine, save where the muleteer could find a niche by the way-side, in which he might temporarily house his animal. This wall is not remarkably durable; and there are, at spaces, huge rocks remaining, which are so perfectly balanced that it seemed to us a slight effort on the part of one man would send them thundering down the abyss. This, however, upon trial, we found required our united efforts. After much struggling, we detached a fragment, which swept with the noise of the broadside of a frigate down the craggy depth, crushing the young palm and the tender saplings. A myriad echoes came reverberating from glen, through cove, from rock to rock, from chasm to chasm, till in the far distance a low rumbling faintly told us of the onward rolling of our messenger. Glimpses of a beautiful outlined country are caught through detached groups of distant forests, and the calmly sleeping Lake creeps on the landscape, with its silvery bosom.

The scene on our right, now that we have reached the summit, is immensely grand. Upon the left we mark the serpentine road, creeping over the hills, and threading its course through level stretches, and again lost in a copse of gigantic trees. Upon the extreme right, the picture is framed by outlined eminences; while on the rear, or toward the point of our offset, the forests, vales, and flowering cacti, are margined by the silver setting of Lake Managua. The view repays us for having chosen this mountain passage-way—tinkling bells come swelling gently up from a few straggling mules, laden with corn and fodder. We hasten from the narrow summit-defile, and pass on to the base of the ridge, once more halting 'neath the cool shade of a gigantic Cebia.

Our road is now apparently an easy one, and we jog along at a quiet pace, descrying a few huts ahead, where we will refresh selves and mules, although we have ridden scarce two leagues. Here we are already observed by the outposts, and not knowing whether we will be permitted to pass quietly, inasmuch as our "passport" bears the signet of the General of the opposing faction. There are rumors also floating of Americans having joined the enemy, and consequently we prepare to defend ourselves, and break, if necessary, the blockade ahead.

CHAPTER XIII.

MATEARES—POPULATION—APPEARANCE—THE HOUSE OF OUR HOST—OUR EXIT—OUR PASS—LAKE MANAGUA—A HOT SUN AND AN INFERNAL ROAD—A HUT AT HAND—A FRIEND IN NEED—A STREAM—A HALT—A BATH—NAGAROTE—A POSADA—THE LAND—HOST AND HOSTESS—MUSQUITOES—ATTEMPT TO SLEEP—FARE—FRIJOLES, TORTILLAS, AND AGUARDIENTE—PLEASANT RIDE, AND AN EARLY START—BEAUTIFUL APPEARANCE OF THE COUNTRY—DEER-ROADS—FIELDS OF MAIZE—SUNRISE—COCOA-NUTS—PALMS AND CALABASHES—CANE HUTS AND TRIM GARDENS—FINE CACTUS—PUEBLO NUEVO, AND A POSADA—OUR MEAL—BEYOND THE VILLAGE—FEATURES OF THE COUNTRY—SOIL AND TIMBER—THE PLAIN OF LEON—DITCHES—HUTS—NINE VOLCANOES—GLIMPSE OF THE CATHEDRAL—GUADELUPE—CITY IN THE DISTANCE—EVIDENCES OF AN ANTICIPATED SALLY ON OUR ENTRANCE—OUR POSADA—CUP OF CACAO—INHABITANTS—LEGACIES OF THE CONQUERORS—THE TROOPS—DRAGOONS—RAINY SEASON—OUR HOST.

WE reached the paltry village of Mateares, at the junction of several roads, which in the United States would have borne the title of Mateares cross-roads. It comprises a few huts, and a rather respectable cuartel. The expectations of travelers are not disappointed by the aspect of the place, for it has as little to recommend it as could be found anywhere; while the fare at exorbitant prices corresponds. The people seem to be an intermediate race between the lowest of the Indians in the southern portions of the State, and the imported negro. The population is probably less than one hundred; their occupation any thing which may turn up, from the courier to the assassin; and I am told, that during the frequent visits of the freebooters, in past days, to the State, a plentiful supply of villains could always be relied upon at a moment's notice from this village. Our guide whispered in my ear, to look out for our animals and purses, as the "whole breed were bad, very bad, and the government assassins were all quartered here." The village is hidden for the most part in palm, banana, orange and lemon groves; after a stroll through the dense thickets about the place, I entered the house of our host. Arms were stacked around everywhere; and I really think the natives I met, were the most abandoned-looking set that ever graced the decks of a piratical craft.

We resumed our saddles after a dinner of hard-boiled eggs, corn-cakes, and bad water, tempered bountifully with aguardiente, and without a regret, left the place at a fast gallop, by a road to the right which led down a hill and thence upon a plain of some extent covered with trees. Here, as we emerged from the hot sun into the cool shade of overarching palms, we observed a barrier ahead, and upon the left hand a hut of recent erection, in front of which a strong detachment of soldiers were drawn. We halted, handed to the superior officer our passport, and after many delays were permitted to advance. Beyond this post, we were in the country of the enemy, and we learned that detachments of the opposing parties had met a few miles beyond this in the morning, where a sharp conflict had ensued, in which the Grenadinos lost two men. Vigilance was therefore necessary.

Passing through a copse, we found Lake Managua upon our right, while bare cliffs ran up abruptly on the left. The road was pebbled with colored stones, and the shores of the Lake covered with cranes and ducks, while overhead winged the gaudy parrots and the brilliantly-plumed macaws, mirroring back, resplendently, the fierce rays of the noon sun, which now in full force fell upon us. The heat was indeed intense; the reflection from the vast sheet beside us, and the rocks upon our left, penetrated by the hot, burning glare, only served to increase our uncomfortableness, as we turned in vain from side to side to escape the broiling, or to gain a moment's relief. The road was very sandy as we passed through clusters of a species of thorny or prickly willow, and really I deemed this place could be more distinctly named "a hell," than the "Infierno de Masaya." Upon the left hand, amid a cluster of trees, we observed a thin wreath of smoke slowly rising, and hastening up an ascending path, found a hut, where we soon obtained lemonade, a few dulces, and a swing in a hammock.

The road now wandered from the Lake, running through cool and leafy coverts, and sweeping gradually again to the beach, alternating, till we reached the top of a hill, the foot of which was laved by a fine stream. This was a luxury indeed, a halting-place for travelers, though not a hut is seen. The ground for a little space being cleared, and withal hard and firm, we unbuckled our girths, and lifting off the saddle-bags from the weary animals, refreshed ourselves, and bathed in the limpid rivulet, the first we had met since leaving Granada. Here we remained some time, and then pushed on for Nagarote, where we arrived after a tiresome ride, though the distance from Mateares is but two short leagues.

Nagarote is an ill-looking village, a brother of Mateares, though boasting of probably three or four good houses. We found a posada, where boiled eggs, fried chickens, stale bread, and berries, were prepared for us at fair traveling rates, and I strolled about, vainly endeavoring to find any thing of interest. The land here is a stereotype of that through which we have passed; though the face of the country begins to assume a more level character; the orange and lemon trees are not so prolific, but the cactus seems more exuberant. The village is composed of straggling cane huts, alive with children, and we found here a welcome worthy of our own country. The host and hostess were sensible people, and knew that Americans would pay well, and consequently attended to our table, supplying it bountifully.

After refreshments, we endeavored to take a siesta; but between little lizards crawling about me, musquitoes singing in my ears, and fleas biting me, I cursed the whole race of nuisances, and resolved to walk and nod rather than submit quietly to be thus fed upon. To saddle our nags and accomplish the distance to the next village was not in our power, for we had ridden slowly, and fished in the Lake, and hence were compelled to remain all night. I drew from my cabas several bundles of cigars, and sitting in my hammock, puffed away the thoughts of sleep, leisurely surveying my sleeping companions. One was kicking at an ever-restless flea, another slapping at a vigilant musquito, another cursing the hard-boiled eggs, tortillas, and frijoles, another, the country and the bad aguardiente, until finally awakened by the clouds of smoke emanating from my cigars, they laughed heartily to see me taking the whole affair so philosophically.

A word, now, for aguardiente, tortillas, and frijoles. Aguardiente is the rum of Nicaragua, and is a government monopoly. Sweet Spanish wines and light French wines may be had, as also Champagne, Sherry, Maderia, Cognac, and all the varieties of other countries. The duty is one dollar and twenty-five cents per gallon upon all liquors, and hence there is no reason why a common article should be imported. There is also a liqueur brought from Peru, called Pisco or Italia, which is very fine, though not so gentle in its effects as has been remarked by some writers. Its manufacture is confined to a small amount, though, at Panama and Valparaiso, a spurious article bearing the name can readily be obtained.

The standard, I may add the national dishes, are tortillas or corn-cakes, and frijoles or beans. The first are made of corn, ears of which are carefully selected. The grains are soaked in alkali, to remove the hull or shell, and subsequently allowed to soak for a little while. They are then placed on a grinding stone, called metlatl, and reduced to the proper consistency by being beaten with a long round stone roller or pounder, similar to the whet-stone used in our harvest fields in the United States; a little cheese is added, when Anita or Mercedes beat the batter into flat cakes, and place them in warm earthen pans. When nicely browned upon one side, they are turned, and in a little time we have them on our plates, crisp and smoking. If good butter could be obtained, tortillas would be indeed desirable; but I preferred ship-bread, or crackers.

Frijoles are beans of a different flavor and appearance from those of our latitude. They are small, and in color ranging from white to black. Tortillas, frijoles, and hard-boiled eggs comprise the Bill of Fare of every Nicaraguan posada; and if any of my readers feel their inability to bolt the trio, the sooner he or she cultivates their concerted-acquaintance, the more proficient will he or she be in the science of getting their money's worth in a tour through El Paraiso de Mahoma.

We roused the household, and after a little delay, resaddled our nags and left. The air was cool, the road level, the sun had not yet risen, and it was a delightful beginning to a day which we knew full well would be a "scorcher." As we descended a short curve, we could see, tracing above us on either hand, gigantic towers, turretted battlements, all seemingly real, although but piles of rocks, and we felt as though we were passing through a land of enchantment, so calm was all around. No dust, and not a sound, save as a timid deer, roused by the tramp of our mules, sprang from his covert, dashed past us, and went leaping through the glades. Dimly seen, outlined against the just flickering gray dawn back-ground, rocks, grouped together, appeared like embattled garrisons, and we were struck also with the many narrow defiles which could be so ably defended by a small party against a host, and wondered why such positions had not been occupied by one or the other of the combatting parties.

The road is at times broad, smooth, and free from ruts and heavy washes, and for many miles there would be no difficulty in driving a carriage at a fair speed. It would require, however, but very little outlay to render all the roads in the State reliable; but while its manufactures and productions are sufficient only for home consumption, it would not be policy to incur this heavy expense. At length the road leads us from the depths of dimly-shadowed forests to an open country, where, now that the sun has risen, we see finely cultivated fields of maize, groves of fruits, marañons, jocotes, nisperos, and mamays, while on the right hand the tall, feathery palm, towers grandly up, with the calabash ladened with its golden-colored burden. Beyond again, we find the cocoanut peering out, with its heavy top bathed in the sun's first rays; and a little further on we reach cane huts and trim gardens, that woo us to a hearty breakfast.

The cactus here grows to perfection. The fences are formed of it. It grows to the height of from twenty to twenty-five feet, and in circumference from twenty-five to thirty-six inches. I have seen a variety of birds issuing from their nests in the stalk of a single cactus. From a distance, you are surprised at the singular appearance of these flowering fences. They are so regular, and so closely planted together, that it is impossible for a pig or dog even to find exit through them. This species of the plant is very prevalent; and another, the trailing, or broad-leaved, is equally as singular in its immense size, though it is not so useful. After reaching the summit of the slight ascent before us, we entered the village of Pueblo Nuevo, and sought a posada, where, after a ride of five leagues, we were glad to rest, ere pushing on to Leon. We had accomplished the worst portion of the journey; the rough country was behind, and the fertile plain of Leon before us, covered with forests, through which we determined to travel at our ease, for the day was yet young, and we had no inducement to hasten. Our old friends, chickens, beans, corn-cakes, and tiste, were before us, and we did ample justice to the outspread meal.

The road beyond Pueblo Nuevo is broad and smooth, lined with palm and odoriferous trees. The country assumed the features of having been at one time well cultivated; the forests are far from virginal, and the soil is probably of a more loamy character than any we have yet observed. We are now twenty-four miles from Leon. Ascending a hill some few miles from our point of starting, through occasional breaks in the forest, volcanoes loom up in the distance, broad fields of grass sweep to the outlined mountains, while clumps of the stately palm rise up like landmarks on the vast plain of Leon before us. There is nothing to interrupt the view. The country is all cleared, the road perfectly level, and on either hand are well-made ditches, verifying the suggestion that, at one time, the soil has been cultivated. Numerous huts are seen, and during the warm afternoon you gladly seek therein shelter from the sun, or refresh yourself, after a long ride over a waterless road. Nine volcanoes margin and dot this magnificent plain, among which the most prominent are Viejo, Telica, Momotombo, and Orota.

We rode on, the towers of the Cathedral gleaming not far distant, and our desire to visit the rival of Granada, and learn the particulars of the current Revolution, stimulated us to renewed efforts. Passing through the Indian suburb of Guadelupe, we descended a ravine, and emerged upon a broad, paved street into the city of Leon. Everywhere, as in Managua, we met detachments of troops. After a few halts, and passing numerous barricades, we entered upon the plaza, where at least two thousand soldiers were training and lounging, and where we found evidences in preparation of an anticipated sally upon the enemy. We hastened to the posada, and, after a cup of cacao, received the many friends who thronged to welcome us, and subsequently paid our respects to the American Minister.

The inhabitants differ from those in the Southern Department, being lighter in color, more dignified, and more like the Hidalgos of old Spain. There is, in Leon, an aristocratical air, a settled aversion to Granada, and a distinct selfishness of belief in the superiority of their city, which surprised me. I had never expected to find such nice, invidious distinctions, drawn in this part of the world; yet I found, during my stay, that the Conquerors had left all their vices, and carried with them only their virtues, which, as they were but few, they could stow in a small compass.

The soldiers were drawn up in front of the Cathedral as we returned from our stroll, and I witnessed the evolutions of a small detachment of dragoons—which I subsequently discovered was composed of Americans, and a small body of native artillerists—that would have reflected credit upon more experienced soldiers.

The sun sank, and the rain began to fall heavily. The rainy season had just set in, and we stowed ourselves away in the house, where, in the society of the pleasant family who kept the posada, we passed a very agreeable and delightful eve. From my host I learned much of the city of Leon; and as he reverted to Granada, his eye would brighten, and his thin lip wreathe with disdain, as he drew comparisons, either between the towns or their inhabitants. A jicara of aguardiente as we sought our ox-hide beds, and lulled to repose by the pattering rain on the tiled roof, I soon sank into a state of dreamy and blessed unconsciousness.

CHAPTER XIV.

HISTORICAL INTERLUDE—LOCATION OF LEON—RUINED HOUSES—THE PLAIN—SUBURBS—CANE HUTS—PIRATES IN 1685—REVOLUTIONS—THE CATHEDRAL—ITS SIZE, COST, DESCRIPTION—THE INTERIOR—THE ORGAN—THE GREAT ALTAR—PORTRAITS—CONFESSIONAL CHAIRS—GALLERY—VIEW FROM THE ROOF—COLLEGE OF ST. RAMON—THE EPISCOPAL PALACE—THE CUARTEL—THE GOVERNMENT HOUSE—LA MERCED—CALVARIO—RECOLLECCION—STATUES—SUBTIABA—PLAZA AND CATHEDRAL—ALTARS—MARKET OF LEON—FRUITS—TRADE—STORES AND MERCHANTS—THE BISHOP'S BATHS—PARAISO DE MAHOMA—CLIMATE—THE BISHOP—HIS CARRIAGE—MR. SQUIER—A VIEW FROM THE ROOF OF SAN PEDRO—BAPTISM OF A VOLCANO—PLAIN OF LEON—EARTHQUAKES—A VISIT TO GENERAL MUNOZ—HIS ATTENDANTS—A TETE-A-TETE—A WORD OR TWO—HIS RESIDENCE AND FAMILY.

THIS city was founded by Hernandez de Cordova in 1523. Its original site was near the base of the volcano of Momotombo, which, however, was abandoned in 1610 for the present locality, formerly a large Indian village, Subtiaba, now a municipality of Leon. It is about half way between Lake Managua and the Pacific, and covers a vast area, built upon as in Granada and Managua, though a finer class of houses originally existed here, many of which are now shapeless ruins. A few still remain, and those are not in the best state of preservation. The principal entrances to some of these edifices exhibit considerable taste and skill. Above some of the portal-arches, the arms of the nobler class were placed; and altogether, even in the ruins, a grandeur is perceived not met with elsewhere in the country.

The plain we passed over, described in our last chapter, surrounds the city; the land is fertile and particularly adapted to the culture of sugar-cane and cotton. Upon two sides are ravines, through which fine streams of water flow, whence the inhabitants are supplied; the article being purer and fresher than that to be had in other localities. The suburbs are composed of cane huts, some with mud, others with tiled roofs. The city suffered extensively and frequently from the English pirates, in 1685, who sacked it, burned the cathedral, the convent, and many of the principal edifices. Subsequent to the Declaration of Independence, a war ensued between the Serviles and the Liberals, during which the richest portions of the town were destroyed.

A few of its public buildings are worthy of notice. The Cathedral of St. Peter, on the eastern side of the grand plaza, was commenced in 1706 and finished in 1743, occupying thirty-seven years in its completion, and is deservedly called the finest edifice in Nicaragua. Its cost is said to have been from four to five millions of dollars. Its front occupies the width of the plaza. It is built of cut stone, light in color. There are six or seven immense arches upon the roof; and its strength may be better arrived at when it is said that ten thousand troops have been concentrated upon it at one time, with no less than thirty pieces of artillery. Its ornaments are stucco. The interior is chaste, and almost devoid of ornament.

The great altar, at the easternmost extremity, is composed of silver, handsomely graven, though it has been despoiled in the numerous contests. The side altars are plain and unattractive. Within a side room are many portraits of the bishops, rather rude in execution and harsh in color. Both the front and rear were once ornamented with the Royal arms of old Spain, but these have been removed. The confessional chairs are placed in the northern and southern aisles, but were vacant during my visit. A small gallery extends over the main portal, and there I found an organ. The friend who accompanied me, the father-in-law of General Muñoz, asked me to perform. I touched the keys, but found its voice harsh and discordant. It wanted tuning badly, and had I had even a pair of pincers, should have volunteered my services. At one time the wealth of the cathedral was enormous; but at present it is a massive and elegant edifice, which only at a small expense, could be restored to its primal magnificence. From its roof, the Pacific and nine volcanoes can be seen; the view is the finest that can be obtained of so many remarkable objects at one glance.

The College of St. Ramon, founded in 1675, an university of law and medicine, is to the left, and like many other public buildings grouped below us, it has fallen, though efforts at restoration are being made. Adjoining this is the Episcopal Palace. It is built of adobes, has two balconies, tiled roof, and was at one time a splendid residence.

The cuartel, or barracks of the Government forces, is a large building on the south side of the plaza, where are stationed the troops, constantly on the alert, and in readiness for action. The Government House is opposite, and occupies the entire north side. It has a large, raised corridor along its front, and is higher than other adjacent buildings. It is built of adobe, and beyond this is in no respect remarkable. The churches of La Merced, Calvario, and Recolleccion, are fine structures. The niches in the façade of the Calvario are filled with the statues of saints, and ornamented with panels of scriptural groups. The Merced contains a few paintings, and its altar piece is decidedly good. A convent, formerly attached to this, has been abolished. There are many other churches, though smaller, and more or less in progress of decay. The municipality of Subtiaba contains some good buildings, a fine plaza, and a cathedral second to that of Leon. The interior is tastefully arranged. It has eight altars, four or five chapels, and many columns with gilt capitals. Its proportion is graceful, and altogether I think it the handsomest of any church in the conntry. From a city, Subtiaba has degenerated to a municipality, and it is fast "fading and falling away."

The market of Leon is probably better supplied than that of Granada. Pine-apples, melons, oranges, limes, lemons, papayas, pomegrauntes, plantains, bananas, beans, corn, nisperos, jocotes, and a variety of other edibles, are clustered together upon the northwestern side of the plaza every morning. The city has but little trade beyond a mere supply of home wants, the principal business being carried on at Chinandega, two leagues from Realejo. However, the stores are well stocked, the merchants rich, and its inhabitants generally landed proprietors.

The Bishop's Baths, beyond the ravine, on the western side of the city, is a beautiful spot. There are a number of stone seats and the remnants of pedestals, no doubt upon which statues were once placed, grouped together under arched, leafy trees. The baths were of stone, and I bathed in the pure water at least more perfectly pleased than I did when swimming in the Lake, for here I feared not the shark nor the alligator. There are many beautiful localities of a similar character about the city. The streets are paved, though, unlike those in the United States, they incline to the centre; channels are thus formed for the floods of water which deluge the city during the rainy season, and the side-walks are left perfectly dry. The city was styled by some of the ancient chroniclers, "Mahomet's Paradise," and truly it could be rendered so at very little outlay. The climate seems purer here than in Granada, the sun less broiling, and the evenings cooler. The streets are cleaner, and for a residence, many would prefer it on account of its pure water and general healthfulness.

The bishop I met frequently, in his carriage, returning from a purveying tour. Ensconced behind a load of fodder which completely filled the dasher and the front of the vehicle, you would only hear his snuffle as he approached, or sometimes as he recognized a passing friend. He has been a great man, and once wielded a mighty power in affairs of State, but this influence is passing away. As the Anglo-Saxon advances, the shadow of ideality decreases, and superstition must and will give way to education and commercial intercourse with enlightened nations. I will here leave the City of Leon, for Mr. Squier, during his residence, gathered every information concerning it, and has given it publicity; the reader may rely upon that writer's truthful and graphic description. Mr. Squier was very popular among the inhabitants, and every avenue was opened gladly by the natives to his inspection. He filled his post with honor, and won for every subsequent American traveler a ready and hearty welcome.

Standing on the arched roof, or rather upon an arch on the roof of San Pedro, what an immensity of space recognizable lies within the eye's grasp. This is a truly volcanic vicinity. The volcanoes of Central America margin the Pacific. Those of Nicaragua, active or full of being, with the extinct craters, are as follows: Joltepec, Coseguina, Orota, Telica, Santa Clara, El Viejo (six thousand feet high), Las Pilas, Acosusco, Momotombo (six thousand five hundred feet high), Managua, Nindiri or Masaya, Momobacho, Solentinami, Gunacaure, Gunapepe, Zapatero, Ometepec, Madeira, Orosi, Rincon de la Vieja, Tenerio, Meriballes, Cerro Pelas, and Abogado. There are fourteen volcanoes within one hundred miles, standing singly, and all abound with hot springs and floods of lava, with other evidences of their vitality. It is a well-known fact that new volcanoes are in course of formation not alone in this State, but also in other portions of the globe; and it is not unusual in this country for some dignitary of the church to be called upon to baptize the new mountain, or to stand godfather for it, to bless it, and thus to endeavor at least to keep the invader within proper bounds for the future.

The plain of Leon, at its most elevated point, is from one hundred and eighty to two hundred and ten feet above the sea. Volcanic eruptions are more violent and perhaps I may add more frequent about the first of November and the first of May, these being the entrance and the close of the wet and dry seasons—probably more severe at the former date. As many as sixty shocks in twenty-four hours, continuing too for several days, have occurred, during which the lightning flashed with remarkable brilliancy; these shocks are said to be strongest during the night.

I received a card from General Muñoz, and having determined to call upon him ere leaving Leon, strolled forth one morning for the purpose. I found his house a complete barrack; at least three hundred soldiers were in his garden and about the corridors, and I received a challenge from every sentry, even though within the casa proper. I found him in his drawing-room, seated, studying a chart of the country. As I approached, he rose, and warmly welcomed me. I had ample opportunity—as he was reading a note just handed to him upon my entrance—to study his features. I found them decidedly Mexican. His brow was indicative of deep, rapid thought. There was a certain decision in the thin lip, but a vacillating energy in his nervous glance, which failed to impress me with the greatness of the General, whose prowess seemed to be universally admitted. In person, he was spare, well-formed; in demeanor, gentle, and apparently confiding; but it seemed to me that where his interests were vested, there would he mould himself; there was a strata of cunning in his nature, a want of will, a seeking after, a courting of applause, no matter from what source. It was the title, not the public good he sought; and in his conversation there was a world of leaven. Yet he was beloved by the masses; and the natives of Subtiaba, who had fought and conquered the enemies of the State, followed him, nor murmured at the decisions of fortune. Had he survived the revolution, Nicaragua would, without doubt, have sought admission into our Union ere this, for the General at least listened to some purpose, and could easily see the waning apathy which pervaded all classes of his countrymen.

His lady and her sister were the most beautiful ladies I saw in the country, and yet I could not trace much similarity of feature to the many I had heretofore met. There was more intellectuality in their chiseled features, more decision in the eye, a subdued though accustomed tone of questioning, a suavity and not the gravity of expression of the general class, a rare appreciation of foreign elements, and finally a positive knowledge of the true position of their country, which rendered them to me the most pleasant trio I had met. His house was furnished with a variety of elegancies, and many luxuries, all of which were foreign. The walls were hung with pictures, his book-case filled with rare volumes, his memory stored with valuable information, and there was the cordiality and hospitality of the most polished Southerner. Couriers arriving and departing were ushered into our presence, either to deliver special news, or to receive privately final orders, which in nowise discomposed either of the ladies.

His señora at times partook of his love of excitement, and wished she were a man to aid her husband in furthering his plans for emancipation, and although slender, and apparently fragile, still her deep-hued eye, gleaming with intense fervor, would belie the apparent feebleness of her constitution. The Bishop Don Jorge Viteri Y Ungo, who was appointed in 1849, aided, and openly countenanced Munoz; and naught relating to church privileges throughout the entire State was transacted without the especial permission of his Excellency. An American, whose wife died after a short sojourn in Granada, desired to remove her remains to the United States. He was told by the city authorities that, ere they could grant him permission, he must have the sanction of the bishop. Although the latter was known to favor the enemy, yet his influence was unimpaired in church matters, and the American was compelled to seek Leon, where, with the aid of General Muñoz, he obtained the consent desired. Had he failed, he could not have removed her corpse.

CHAPTER XV.

CITY OF LEON—HISTORY—DECREE OF ANNEXATION TO THE UNITED STATES—CONSTITUTION ADOPTED—ABOLISHMENT OF PAPAL BULLS, MONASTERIES—ABRIDGMENT OF CERTAIN ECCLESIASTICAL PRIVILEGES—THE NATIONAL FLAG—THE BISHOP, ARCHBISHOP, AND HIS HOLINESS THE POPE—VARIOUS WARS—GENERAL MORAZAN—CARRERA—MALESPIN—CAPTURE OF SAN JUAN BY THE ENGLISH—SAMOZA—A KNIGHT—HIS REVOLUTION—CAPTURE AND DEATH—DEATH OF MUNOZ—PRESIDENT PINEDA'S SUMMARY REMOVAL—WALKER—A CHANGE COMES OVER NICARAGUA—THOUGHTS AND SPECULATIONS.

LEON has been the scene of many severe and sanguinary struggles, especially in the wars between the Servile and Liberal factions. The Serviles of the States adjoining Nicaragua determined upon placing the entire country under the sovereignty of Mexico, with Iturbide as emperor. Step by step the battle was fought. Hopes long sustained in secret by the Monarchists, found full vent. The Republicans were aroused first at San Salvador, Guatemala; they adopted measures for defense and resistance, and defeated the army sent by Mexico. Granada was second in the field; San Jose in Costa Rica, third; while in Leon, the bishop who favored the monarchy, opposed republican principles, and advocated, by threats of excommunication, the Mexican scheme. Battle succeeded battle; the imperial forces were soon arrayed; and the Liberals of San Salvador, after a remarkable contest, were forced to submit.

In 1822 the Mexican government was proclaimed in Guatemala, and by an Imperial decree the country was divided into three Captain-Generalcies: the Serviles of course filling every post of emolument, profit, or honor. Though the Liberals were defeated, they remained true to their principles, and the Provisional Congress still remained unbroken. It was during this period of distrust and anarchy, that the country having become truly and purely nationalized, this Congress resolved upon annexation to the United States of America; and by an act dated December 2d, 1822, decreed its incorporation with the American Confederacy; and yet true as this is, how singular that our Government took no action in the matter. The dream of monarchy was soon dispelled. The Serviles were beaten by the recoil of their own magnificently adjusted plans. Iturbide was dead, and without foreign aid, they could not sustain themselves, while the Republicans assumed their prior position. Nicaragua, Costa Rica, Guatemala, San Salvador, and Honduras, determined upon an union of States, declaring themselves independent of Spain, Mexico, and every other power, while Chiapas alone remained subservient to Mexico. This decree is dated July 1st, 1823.

The Constitution of the Confederation was adopted in November, 1824, in which was embodied the guaranties of individual rights, the habeas corpus, the liberty of the press, the representative principle; all of which, however, were combatted by its enemies. Titles and privileges of rank were abolished, the sale of papal bulls prohibited, all foreigners were guaranteed the security of their property, and the title of "The Republic of Central America" was fixed upon, and its national flag bore the device "five volcanoes," and the motto, "Dios, Union, Libertad." By a decree passed April 17th, 1824, slavery and slave-dealing were to be heavily punished. The Constitution, although published December 27th, 1823, was not decreed until November 22d, 1825. Matters swam happily on for a time, yet the Serviles, aided by the bishop, were not forever quieted; and although his party were in the minority, they were men of wealth and influence; after a time civil war again drenched the streets of Leon. For over one hundred days, brother met brother armed for the strife; the richest and choicest portions of the city were burned; one thousand dwellings were consumed by fire in a single night, and this butchery continued until the Liberals received a reinforcement from San Salvador. The church had openly arrayed itself against Republicanism, and the war was one where quarter was neither asked nor granted.

Then from this chaos rose the light, the beginning of better days. Schools were established which were made free. The soldier threw aside his knife and bayonet to hold in his brawny hand the primer; and thus from a confusion of blood-stained cliques arose the Independence of Nicaragua. San Salvador deemed the power vested in the State to choose for herself her religious principles and its expounders, and acting thereon, elected or appointed one of its own citizens Bishop of the State. The Archbishop of course denounced the act, and the Pope himself threatened excommunication, but it fell fruitlessly upon the ear—subsequently Costa Rica followed San Salvador. Years passed away, when the Serviles prepared for war, and the Liberals, taken by surprise, were overpowered. Many of their best men were brutally murdered; finally, after a union of the forces of Nicaragua, Honduras, and Guatemala, affairs were restored, while Costa Rica remained in her mountain fastnesses, a calm spectator of the butchery and assassination of her sworn friends. General Morazan, probably the greatest man of Central America, certainly the man for the times in which he was born and lived, after assuming the leadership of the Republicans, determined to strike a blow at the church, and thereby relieve his oppressed and bleeding country. The Archbishop, and the heads of the monkish orders generally, the Capuchins, Dominicans and Franciscans, were arrested, escorted by a military guard to a distant port, and thence banished. The convents were put to the use of the masses, and some appropriated for prisons, others for schools; while the inmates of the nunneries were free to go where they pleased, and the future taking of the veil was prohibited.

In 1832, all laws recognizing the Catholic creed as the faith of the country were annulled, and freedom to worship the Creator as each desired, was decreed by the several States. From this confederacy, in 1829 or 1830, Costa Rica seceded, and maintained a neutrality; but in 1831, when the Republic was re-established, she re-entered. Various events, similar in character to those described, followed, till in 1838, when a convention assembled in Nicaragua, and then and there declared Nicaragua an independent Republic, and framed its constitution. Honduras followed; each, however, sustaining the idea of nationality, and providing for the resuming of their positions when there should be a confederated reorganization. Years sped, and the changes which marked former times, still followed the successive periods, till Morazan with his two sons was shot at San Jose, in 1842, after a glorious struggle for Republican principles.

Carrera, his rival, thus swayed anew, till Malespin, a former bandit, having conciliated Morazan's friends, was placed in power, but subsequently went to San Salvador, and occupied the command. Then a new emeute occurred, and Malespin invaded Nicaragua, and after a most sanguinary battle at Leon, was nobly defeated by a far inferior party. Nicaragua was again quiet. A local insurrection of not much importance soon transpired; then the English, in 1848, seized San Juan del Norte, and the battle of Serapaqui, on the San Juan River was fought. A rude fortification, of tree trunks, limbs, and boughs, was hastily made, and about one hundred and thirty men determined to contest the passage of the river, their arms, as I have elsewhere remarked, being condemned English muskets and machetes. The English, in number three hundred, well armed, came up in boats, and after a fierce struggle, with the loss of fifteen or twenty men, the Nicaraguans were defeated.

This occurred in February, 1848. Then followed Samoza's insurrection, in 1849. He was a somewhat remarkable man: brave, daring, dashing, full of humor, honor, and talent, and yet singularly balanced. There was a recklessness in his actions, a brilliant gleam of a hidden meteor through out his whole life, a promise of a hero half fulfilled: in fact, he had outlived his fellows. He was a knight, and fought principally with his lance. He dressed dashingly and gayly, sang an excellent song, told a good tale, and seemed ever intent upon dreams of knightly devoir. In truth, he was a most extraordinary lancer. He would leap from his horse while at a full run, and pick up a kerchief, or pierce an orange with his spear, at the same rate of speed. He fenced well, was enamored of the Americans, and raised this revolution in 1849, merely because he had nothing else to do. He was feared by a certain class, yet esteemed by the mass. He was taken in 1850, at the command of General Muñoz, and gibbeted at Rivas.

In 1851, while Pineda was president, occurred that which I elsewhere have written; and from that period Generals Muñoz and Chamorro were adverse leaders in civil dissensions. The former was shot during an assault made by him on or near Chinandega, and Chamorro died in Granada during the siege of that city by the Muñoz forces. General Walker then entered the arena; we shall detail hereafter his adventures. Thus, since the departure of the Conquerors, Mahomet's Paradise has been more like a hell; and the country which furnished Spain with wealth and luxuries, how has she been repaid? Every town has in turn been bathed in gore, every foot of her soil has been the death-bed of some of her children, and the vices of the early Spaniards have frightfully matured.

I have sometimes thought, as I swung in my hammock through the twilight hours, listening to the dark-eyed daughter of Granada, singing, or rather moaning her song, how like a dream all this of the Moriscos, and then I would endeavor to recall their history. They left Spain, dismembered, it seems for ever. Where fled they? Some to Morocco, to Tunis, others—where? I have thought, and breaking the repose of the languor which would ever follow her song, have asked: "Where did you learn that lay of the Cid?" The answer was, "Oh, my mother taught me!" "And where did she learn it?" "Oh, from home!" Perhaps she dreamed of that paradise forever lost to her, when torn from her race by the barbarous hand of Spain.

There are many traits which remind me of the Moors: the arrangement of the hair, of the kerchief round the head, their figures, the proud, stately step, the high cheek-bone, the deep, earnest, piercing eye, the firm, proud lip, all distinct and in no respect alloyed by the grosser, sensual form, mien, or gaze of the Spanish race, or the admixture thereof. Would the impure race dream of a fatherland, and recognize its history in its songs? I have been led to this digression, for I confess many, many times have I thought the matter over, and the more I thought the more my mind became confused. The liquid, minor melodies would find an echo in my soul, and arouse memories of the Alhambra's gardens, her terraced cliffs, her jeweled beauties, her noble, heroic children, and I felt welling o'er my soul a kindred tide of sympathy, while I clasped my guitar, to catch the echoing air, or perhaps only the melancholy murmuring refrain.

CHAPTER XVI.

LEON — SUBTIABA — COUNTRY — QUESALGUAQUE — THE DESCENT — FRUITS— POSULTEGA—CHICHIGALPA—POPULATION—COUNTRY AND FRUITS—A PLEASANT RIDE—A CHOICE ESTATE—CHINANDEGA—ITS COMMERCE AND INHABITANTS—OLD CHINANDEGA—BAD ROAD TO REALEJO—REALEJO—ITS HARBOR—CUSTOM HOUSE—DEPTH OF WATER—DOCKS AND WAREHOUSES—CARDON—SAN JUAN DEL SUR—LOCATION—SIZE—HARBOR IMPROVEMENTS—THE PAPAGAYOS—BRITO—COUNTRY BETWEEN SAN JUAN AND VIRGIN BAY—ROADS IN RAINY SEASON—VIRGIN BAY AGAIN—WHARF—TRANSIT COMPANY—RIO TIPITAPA—PASO CHICO—FALLS OF TIPITAPA—DEPTH OF THE RIVER—RIO GRANDE—SURFACE OF LAKE MANAGUA—DISTANCE FROM REALEJO—CHONTALES—PRODUCTS —MINERALS—WOODS—ANIMALS—LAND—STREAMS —CATTLE—ADVICE AND REFLECTIONS.

LEAVING Leon, our journey leads through the suburbs of Subtiaba, and crossing a stream which runs laughingly through an arched and shady nook, we reach wide-spreading fields of corn. The road winds through open plains, and we reach the woods after a toasting, and seek a ravine whose banks are steep and high. At the foot we find quite a stream, known as Quesalguaque. The descent is circuitous. In succession, as we spur on, fields of pine-apples and corn appear, and we reach a small village called after the stream. Two leagues beyond, the road is broader, the country well wooded, and we find another village, Posultega, which contains a dilapidated church, and probably four or five hundred inhabitants. Two leagues farther, and we halt at Chichigalpa, an ancient Indian pueblo, which although dilapidated, has a population of five thousand. It is a pleasant spot, and just the place for a month's recruit. The country is level, and supplied with fruits. The pine-apples, particularly, are very luscious, the nisperos remarkably fine, and the oranges sweet and cheap. A pleasant ride of seven or eight miles over a well-shaded road brings us to San Antonio. This is a very large and choice estate. It was originally a sugar plantation. The house is commodious, well built, and well constructed, besides having been painted. A foreigner I heard had previously owned it.

A short ride, probably a league, brought us to Chinandega, which, if not so large as Granada, or Leon, is nevertheless the most flourishing city in the State. It contains about sixteen thousand inhabitants, and is truly the commercial emporium of Nicaragua. The houses are generally of a better class than in other towns, although they are built of the universal adobe, but with tiled roofs. Old Chinandega contains a population of about five thousand, and is situated upon a stream which flows through it. It possesses little of interest, save a large old church, standing on a terrace in the plaza. A strange-looking wall margins the terrace edge, and above the flights of steps by which we ascend, are high arches, different from any thing seen in this country. Chinandega is regularly laid out in squares, and although in a level district, is an agreeable residence.

The worst road, in fact the slipperiest, I ever traveled, especially during the wet season, leads to Realejo, two leagues distant. This port is small, the land low, and most probably is very unhealthy. The Custom House is located here. It has a population of about one thousand or fifteen hundred. The town was originally built nearer the water, though on account of the numerous pirates who once frequented the coast, the present site was chosen as being farther removed from speedy visits and instant spoliation. Docks and warehouses, as also depots for coal have been built, and the port is far superior to any on the coast. The entrance to the harbor is protected by the Island of Cardon, which is about a mile and three quarters long, and so situated as to protect it from the boisterous winds and heavy swells which enter the outer bay of Conchagua from the Ocean. The North entrance is about a quarter of a mile wide, free from rocks, and has a mud bottom, and at no point has less thar five fathoms of water. Vessels may enter one of these openings with a leading wind, from any point of the compass. The inside consists of a fine basin not less than four fathoms deep, and two hundred ships at one time may here ride securely at anchor. Merchant vessels lie about a mile from the entrance, in the branch of a creek. Opposite the port there is a fine beach, the water being deep to its very edge. The rise and fall of the tide is eleven feet.

San Juan del Sur was located in 1851, and although its harbor is small, and many speculators discouraged the capitalists from any investment in it in its early days, yet it has acquired a place upon the chart of Nicaragua, and is now one of its most thriving towns. There are a large number of broad streets, some fine hotels, good houses, and altogether it is really North American in its character. The Custom House is located here, and the Californians returning to the United States have considerably augmented its resources; the depth of water two hundred yards out, is about two fathoms. The entrance is about eleven hundred yards, between promontories at least four to five hundred feet high. The land is sandy. There are ten fathoms water at the entrance, and the tide rises fourteen feet. The Papagayos, or revolving winds, drive the sand into our plates as we sit at table, through our clothing, into our eyes and ears, and altogether, aside from its stirring character as a depot, and as the port of exit for travelers by the Transit Route, it is far from being a pleasant residence. Lands are held remarkably high in the immediate vicinity. One mile North there is another port of about the same size, called Brito or Nacascolo. The approach to this portion of the coast for ships is extremely difficult during the season that the revolving winds are in the ascendency.

The country between San Juan del Sur and Virgin Bay is high, well-timbered; and prior to the road now constructed, the path between was in a truly horrible condition. During the rainy season, many mules were killed by over-exertion. The road was of a soft, slippery, clayey character, and very frequently I have seen mules dashing along, their backs covered by the mud, and their heads only visible. Really it was a swim through a muddy sea. Many travelers perished in this short transit. The hotels at Virgin Bay were composed of tents without floors; and for three coarse meals and a sleep in a hammock, strangers were charged four dollars per day, and very frequently, too, were compelled to sleep in the mud all night, or probably for a series of nights, when the steamers did not connect. I have seen many extreme cases of hardships which might have been prevented, had not a grasping monopoly governed all. In its incipient stage, this Transit Company was miserably managed; but shrewd and careful officers succeeded in establishing it firmly. A wharf was constructed at this point, and the landing of passengers is effected with less difficulty than formerly.

In 1852, the steamers would anchor about three-quarters of a mile from shore, where a rope would be passed to the land, and by this an immense launch would reach the vessel and return laden to the shore. The bottom of the Lake here is hard and shelving, and the winds often blow the small schooners ashore, where, after much difficulty they are secured and again launched.

We have thus traveled through and around the State of Nicaragua. We have crossed the country from the Atlantic to the Pacific, have noticed the volcanoes, streams, cities, towns, manners and customs, products, &c., and reaching Realejo, wound round to San Juan del Sur; to complete our circuit, we must reach Granada, whence we started upon our tour.

Between the Lakes of Managua and Nicaragua, sixteen miles intervene, twelve of which is a broad, shallow arm of the former, called the Rio Tipitapa, or Estero de Panoloya, which is from six to twelve feet deep. The banks are low, and the bottom muddy to the head of navigation, about one and a half miles above to Paso Chico; the bed of the river is supplied with streams, and rests on beds of rocks, a mixture of lava, jasper, granite, and other stones. One mile from Lake Managua is the Fall of Tipitapa, opposite which is the little village of the same name. The falls are from twelve to fifteen feet high. The old bed of the river is here about three hundred and fifty feet wide. From this point to the Lake the bed is shallow and covered with rank grass. A very small quantity of water falls over this natural dam even in the rainy season. The alligator lies in the reeds which line the shores, and every thing about looks desolate and forbidding. The Lake here is shallow. The banks of the Tipitapa generally are low, and we pass many large cattle estates; the valuable Brazil wood here is very abundant. The Rio Grande flowing into the Lake does not increase it much, which latter has a surface of about twelve hundred square miles, and its distance from Realejo is about forty-two miles.

The views from the boat as you pass up are very beautiful, and the outlined mountains look charming; the setting sun gilds with magical effect the rugged crests of Momobacho, and lights with subdued grandeur, far upon our left, the hazy outlines of the defunct volcano of Masaya.

Opposite Granada rise the hills of Chontales, a district universally believed to be as rich in mineral wealth as any portion of the known world. Mahogany, India-rubber, and the Ebo, from which a valuable oil is extracted, are found here in abundance. Rose-wood, Satin-wood, Cedar, Braziletto, and the Nicaragua wood, one of the most costly of all dye-woods, as also the Ceiba, or wild Cotton-tree, are all found wonderfully grouped.

Chontales is celebrated as a grazing country. The lands

are fertile, well watered, and are remarkable pasture lands. The climate is cool and invigorating on the hills, while on the plains the thermometer ranges from 64° to 78°. It is also rich in specimens of natural history. Monkeys, tigers, a species of lion, ant-eaters, armadillos, and sloths are frequently found, as also deer in abundance. The mining districts, so long over-looked, are being settled, and there can exist no doubt of the quality and quantity of its silver, gold, copper, and lead. The lands lying upon the streams gradually incline, and thousands of fine cattle are seen roaming on the hills, or heard lowing in the valleys. A most profitable business might be pursued by those who would construct a large craft, and freight the cattle down to Virgin Bay, where they could dispose of the stock at highly remunerative prices. The land in this district is probably more like that of Honduras than in any other department of Nicaragua, and it certainly is healthier than upon the plains of the interior. Chontales invites the stranger, and has abundance of hidden wealth to repay him for his coming.

Standing npon the beach at Granada, the eye comprehends a glorious prospect. The many islands covered with verdure, the towering and majestic Ometepec and Momobacho, with other giants of lesser magnitude, break the monotonous water-view. The breakers rush shoreward with great force, so much so, that it is far from being an easy task to effect a dry landing. Owing to these heavy ground-swells, the steamboats and sail-vessels are anchored about half a mile from shore. There is a constant breeze on the water's edge. Gazing eastward, are seen the rolling heights upon the Chontales shore. I often wondered at so little being known respecting that region, although conjectures were rife as to its numerous deposits of gold and silver. Many streams flow from it into the Lake, all of them apparently accessible for boats drawing two and three feet of water. There are numerous cattle estates, but beyond these, little of a reliable nature can be gathered as to its innate wealth of soil or minerals. The water is cooler, fresher, and decidedly purer than at any other point, except in the single instance of that obtained from the Rio Frio.

Why those glorious valleys and rich savannahs should not tempt the hardy and thrifty Anglo-Saxon, I cannot imagine. A living is certain, for the banana and plantain are indigenous, as also the nutritious and sweet orange. A comfortable cane hut can be soon erected, vegetation is ever-blooming, and the changes of temperature are neither sudden or great. A patch containing two acres, planted with plantains alone, would sustain a settler, and his labor would be rewarded in the vegetables he would easily and speedily raise. The markets of the country are but sparely supplied. The cauliflower, cabbage, melons, lettuce, beats, turnips, radishes, salsify, peas, lima beans, sweet potatoes, cucumbers, and various other classes, grown in our southern climate, would flourish upon the plains of Leon, and in the neighborhoods of Managua, Masaya, Granada, and Rivas.

Nine-tenths of the settlers in new countries neglect certainties, and avariciously seek the mines for the gold, which is obtained only by toil and great privations. Every useful pursuit is neglected, and even comfort, too, in the search for hidden treasures, which, when found, often prove disadvantageous to the mass, by increasing the idleness of the finders. Very few, whether owners or operators, are wealthy, few even comfortable. Those curving shores before us especially invite the agriculturist. In almost every city there are numbers of foreigners, and the vegetables and melons not only would find a profitable market among these, but the natives would also purchase.

The mineral districts of Spain, and of North, South, and Central America, are the poorest. Where one man becomes opulent, fifty are rendered the more wretched. The miners are paid well, consequently they spend the more carelessly; the vice of gambling succeeds, and is established as a pastime. For example, Capon, in Brazil, is celebrated for its topaz mines, Villa Rica, the rich village, the capital of the province of Minas Geraes, is reputed the richest in the country, and the Cerro of San Antonio, is a place famed for diamonds; the country surrounding each of these is fertile, producing the finest woods for cabinet-ware, fruits and vanilla, and possessing plantations of cotton, equal in color and quality to any in the world, yet their inhabitants are degraded. Little can be expected from those who have been reared from infancy to consider labor as degrading; but he who will settle in Nicaragua, willing "to take the chances," may rest assured he holds trumps in the plow, the hoe, and a civil tongue.

CHAPTER XVII.

GREYTOWN—TOPOGRAPHY—EXTENT OF MOSQUITO TERRITORY—INDIAN TRIBES —POPE'S BULL— SPAIN'S CLAIM AND ENGLAND'S, ALSO NICARAGUA'S—WHOSE IS VALID?—CORONATION OF A MOSQUITO KING—HIS DRESS—THE DRESS OF HIS CHIEFS—ENGLISH OFFICERS—THE KING'S DIGNIFIED MANNER OF EXPRESSING HIMSELF—BAPTISM—SUPPER AND FINALE TO THE FARCE—GRANT TO THE SHEPHERDS—THEIR TITLE—CONVEYANCE TO THE CENTRAL AMERICAN COMPANY—ISSUING OF STOCK—OBJECTS OF THE COMPANY.

LEAVING the interior, let us descend the Rio San Juan to Greytown, or San Juan del Norte, where we may glean from floating chronicles and "old inhabitants" something of interest relative to that portion of country known as the Mosquito territory or kingdom. It commences at Cape Honduras, the extreme northwestern part of the territory, and extends thence southwardly to the said coast, including Boca del Toro and Chiriqui Lagoon, to King Buppan Rock, adjoining New Granada, thence southwestwardly to the ridge of mountains dividing the two oceans up to the old Spanish lines, and thence northwestwardly, passing eastward of Tayagalpa and Matagalpa, and thence north to Cape Honduras, containing about seven thousand one hundred square miles. From the earliest authentic period subsequent to the discovery of America, it was inhabited by different tribes of Indians, the most warlike and numerous of which were the Mosquito and Valientes. They neglected the tillage of the soil, had made little or no progress in the arts of civilized life, and had no fixed habitations, but were a wandering race without a home, subject to the promptings of fancy or necessity.

The followers of Cortés, or Pizarro, who had over-run Mexico and Peru, from the jeweled palaces of the Incas or Aztecs did not seek these barren heaths or rocky recesses; and thus with nought to attract the avaricious Spaniard, it is averred the Mosquitos maintained their primal independence. Upon the King of Spain, by virtue of a bull issued by the Pope, the right to this territory, as well as to the major portion of the American Continent, was conferred, as also to his descendants, but as to its occupation, according to the principles of the Law of Nations, there was nothing recognizable. Per virtue of the bull referred to, Spain claimed this territory, and said title was recognized by Great Britain in the Treaty of Paris negotiated in 1783; and yet Great Britain practically repudiated this claim both before and since. For nearly two hundred years, even to the present hour, she has maintained the right of the

Mosquito king to this domain ; and in 1848, when Nicaragua invaded his rights, Great Britain sent a force to expel the latter from the country.

But the question of the entire freedom of this coast should be calmly inquired into ; for under subsequent acts of King Robert, American interests became involved here. By a decree issued in July, 1824, this country was also claimed by the Colombian Government, and all foreigners were forbidden to colonize without the permission of this Republic. By a convention made between Great Britain and Spain in 1786, 'tis true, His Britannic Majesty agreed to evacuate all this coast; but as the Indians showed the same inveterate dislike to the Spaniards as formerly, they, (the natives), were permitted to consider themselves under the protection of Great Britain. Here, then, is a power delegated by Spain to Great Britain, for the guardianship of this people and their homes by the party who claimed this territory, at that time, to the utter exclusion of all other nations. Subsequently, Spain desired to repudiate this jurisdiction, vested by her in Great Britain, which, however, the latter refused to sanction.

Some of the Mosquito kings were educated in Jamaica. A prior king, on his accession to the throne, January 18th, 1816, desired to be crowned at Belize, Honduras, and orders were received by His Britannic Majesty's superintendent to gratify his wish, and to defray the attendant necessary expenses. It may be interesting to give the particulars of this regal ceremony. Cards of invitation were sent to the different merchants of Belize on the previous evening, requesting their attendance at the Court House early in the morning. The king made his appearance in the uniform of a British major, while his chiefs, in sailor's trowsers, were ranged round the room. The order of the day being given, the assemblage moved toward the church, His Majesty King Robert on horseback, supported on the right and left by two senior English officers in the settlement, the chiefs following after in double file. On the arrival of the cavalcade at the church designated, His Majesty was placed in a chair near the altar, and the English Coronation Service was read by the Chaplain of the Colony, who, on this occasion, performed the part of the Archbishop of Canterbury. When he reached that portion of the service where it is written "And all the people said, Let the king live forever! Long live the king! God save the king!" the vessels in port according to previous signal, fired salutes, and the chiefs rising, cried out, "Long live King Robert!"

After the anointing, His Majesty, admiring his finery, indicated his especial gratification at this portion of the Service, by thrusting his hands through his bushy hair, and applying his fingers in an expressive manner to his nose Prior, however, to the chiefs swearing allegiance to their monarch, it was necessary that they should profess Christianity, and accordingly, they were baptized "in the name of the Father, Son, and Holy Ghost." They displayed the most total ignorance of the meaning and intent of the ceremony; and when asked to give their names, they took titles of celebrated English officers, such as Lord Nelson, Lord Rodney, and others, and seemed much disappointed when told they could only be baptized by simple Christian names.

After this mockery had been concluded, the entire assemblage adjourned to a large school-room to eat the coronation-dinner, where the usual healths were drank; and the poor Indians, king as well as subjects, intoxicated by English rum, soon found one common bed—the floor—truly a fit finale to a farce sufficiently ludicrous, could it have been divested of its blasphemic character. In the month of March, 1824, George Frederick, the father of this king, was strangled by his wife, and his body thrown into the sea.

It may be asked, if the English were so far interested as to instal the king, and in this coronation to deprive the chiefs of their birthright and their own peculiar religious notions, by what title did they so assume a sovereignty over them? and why was it necessary for the poor Indian to renounce his religion and embrace that of a foreign nation, with whose tenets and precepts he was totally unacquainted? Was it necessary or vital to the assuming of the throne? Did England then claim this territory? or was the Mosquito Coast's sovereignty merged in that of Albion's by the espousal of Christianity? Truly these are vexed questions with me; like Truth, they lie at the bottom of so deep a well, that it seems unfathomable, unless the result be unfavorable to Great Britain's interests.

The Mosquito Territory, renounced by Spain, and it is also said subsequently, by Nicaragua, was free, entirely independent. She had her king, and that sovereign occupied its throne; but the needs of the Indians were such, that England, by her advances of money and supplies, acquired a foothold in the province, and a consequent ascendancy in the country. She found San Juan del Norte, favorably situated for commerce, at the mouth of the Rio San Juan. She saw its future prominence, changed its name to Greytown, and upon the same staff on which flew the colors of Mosquito, soon floated far above the Cross of Saint George. Thus England set her foot on the soil, and from a money-lender and provider, became dictator, or, as she meekly terms it, the Protector of the kingdom.

The King Robert Charles Frederick was crowned April 23d, 1825. In 1839, having become indebted largely to Peter and Samuel Shepherd, formerly of Georgia, while under the reign of His Britannic Majesty, conveyed to them a large body of lands, beginning on the south bank of the Rio San Juan, and running south and east along the sea-shore, taking in the Boca del Toro and Chiriqui Lagoon, and running thence up to the rock called King Buppan, adjoining New Granada; from thence southerly to the ridge of the mountains which divides the two oceans up to the Spanish lines; thence, nearly parallel with the sea-coast in a northerly direction, crossing the San Juan, and running thence to where the Bluefields' Main River intersects the Spanish lines; thence, back by the northern banks of Bluefields' River to Great River; thence by the said river to the sea, and thence by the coast southerly to the mouth of San Juan. It included all islands, and especially Little Cow Island and the Island of Escuda de Varagua: containing in all upward of 22,500,000 acres.

This grant, made on the 24th of January, 1839, was solemnly confirmed on the following 28th of November; and as set forth in the deeds of conveyance, was made by the king in the presence of, and by the advice and consent of his chiefs and head men; and not only contained a cession of the lands therein described to the grantees, their heirs and assigns forever, but likewise stipulated for their enjoyment and possession free from taxation. It also conferred upon the grantees the right of colonization, and provided for the exemption of the colonists from the burdens usually incident to citizens or subjects. The grantees were put in possession of these ceded lands, as fully as it was possible for them to be of so vast an extent of territory; nor was their title, until lately, ever questioned by any claimant. The consideration for these lands was part money and part provisions, needed greatly by the natives, their turtle-shell harvest having been but small; consequently, the grantees having paid a large sum of money, and having provided for the nation an immense supply of provisions, the consideration was not a nominal, but a fixed and valuable one. Subsequently, however, the English consular agent deprived the grantees, per force, of some portions of the land.

By the maxims of international law, the lands belonging to such tribes may be appropriated by any coterminous civilized nation that has the power to expel the original occupants, and maintain possession of the territory wrested from them. Yet no possession, it is averred, has ensued by any adverse claimants, and hence the Mosquito flag is held to be the virginal and valid symbol of the country, and still floats from the staffs at Greytown, and Bluefields the summer residence of the sovereign. These lands subsequently were conveyed to eighteen gentlemen of the United States, who organized a company, October 16th, 1855, called "The Central American Company," the stock of which was issued valued at twenty-five dollars per share, each share representing one hundred acres of land. The objects of the Company were the colonization of the land and development of its resources.

CHAPTER XVIII.

BLUEFIELDS—THE MOSQUITO KING—THE SHEPHERD GRANT DENIED UPON VARIOUS GROUNDS—ENGLAND PLAYS HER HAND—COLONEL KINNEY—HIS TRIALS AND HARDSHIPS—DENOUNCED AS A FILLIBUSTER—HIS EXPEDITION—WRECKING OF HIS VESSEL—ARRIVAL AT GREYTOWN—BURNING OF GREYTOWN PRIOR TO HIS ARRIVAL—RESULTS AND ALLEGED CAUSE—PRESIDENT PIERCE'S DECLARATION OF WAR—THE MUSE OF HISTORY—COLONEL KINNEY ELECTED GOVERNOR—PREAMBLE AND RESOLUTIONS OF THE NEW GOVERNMENT—CONSTITUTION—OFFICERS ELECTED—THE CENTRAL AMERICAN COMPANY AT A DISCOUNT—KINNEY'S RESIGNATION—HIS VISIT TO GRANADA AND EXPULSION THENCE—WALKER'S EMPTY BOAST—SALE OF THE GRANT TO THE MORMONS.

BLUEFIELDS, the residence of the present Mosquito king, George William Clarence, is situated on a bluff surrounded by a country rich in vegetation, and remarkable as well for its scenery as for its healthiness, although, at times, his Majesty occupies a house in Greytown. He is young, well-formed, lighter in color than the majority of his tribe, is very agile and muscular, wears the undress cap of an English naval officer, and is seemingly satisfied with his title and total freedom from want—his requirements being attended to by the English government. Some time subsequent to the decease of his father, in 1841, the grant made to the Messrs. Shepherd was denied, in fact, revoked by the present king, acting under the instigation of the English, based upon the following reasoning, viz.: that the consideration was insufficient, that the grant was fraudulently obtained, the Sire being intoxicated, as also his chiefs and head men, and that this intoxication was the result of a conspiracy upon the part of the grantees. The present monarch not having reached his majority, the kingdom convulsed with threatened alarms proceeding from Nicaragua proper, and the treasury exhausted, Great Britain became the guardian of the kingdom, as by this course alone she could ever hope to be returned her pecuniary advances, and it is under the prestige of such protection that she has maintained a certain qualified, but truly inexplicable position in the affairs of the country.

The Company referred to, in our last chapter, was organized by Colonel Henry L. Kinney, a well-known gentleman of Pennsylvania, and based upon said grant, which subsequently was purchased by him and other parties. From this arose an expedition, rarely, in its results, trials, and exposures, equalled in the annals of modern times. The expeditionists were to have left New York in the steamship United States, and although for months the Company were openly advertising their object, and desiring actual settlers, at the very moment of departure, the United States Government interposed, prevented the vessel from leaving the harbor, and denounced Colonel Kinney and party as fillibusters, and as such held them for trial. These suits subsequently ended without credit to the prosecution.

Col. Kinney had apprized the President in person of the objects of his Company, as also of his contemplated day of departure, and the latter having broached the idea of colonization, had also advised the former to lead the Central American enterprise; and yet, after immense sums of money had been lavished in preparing himself and followers for the voyage, the entire expedition was crushed for a time, and Kinney himself denounced and branded as a fillibuster. Subsequently, however, with a few comrades, he left New York in a small brig, and after being shipwrecked near Turk's Island, and suffering many hardships, reached San Juan del Norte, where his arrival was hailed with enthusiasm. Thus the Kinney Union, surmounting every obstacle, reached the point of destination, their avowed objects finding an echo in the hearts of the depressed people of the Mosquito Kingdom.

The Transit Company occupied Punta Arenas, a point of land immediately opposite the bay, from Greytown; prior to Kinney's arrival an emeute arose between it and the inhabitants of the town, which ended in the Government of the United States sending the sloop-of-war, Cyane, commanded by Captain Hollins, to that port. The place was bombarded, frame dwellings and cane huts were destroyed by fire, and helpless women and children were driven from their humble homes, without shelter or food, to brave the inclemency of a sickly climate. Many deaths ensued consequent upon this exposure. The results of the conflagration visited alike, Americans, Spaniards, French, and Germans. A debt owed by the little town, which could not be paid in twenty-four hours, was the principal cause of this overwhelming affliction, and the once flourishing village of San Juan was levelled to the earth.

Now that Col. Kinney had arrived, unwonted alacrity was everywhere visible; houses were erected, stores opened, hotels built, and without exception, the new settlers were busy in regenerating the fallen town, upon which the Government of the United States had thus wreaked its vengeance. This act of the Government found no favor with the country at large. It was considered to be a declaration of war by a President without the consent and advice of the Senate, which alone, it was held, possessed this power. Against whom was this war waged? A weak tribe of Indians—a defenseless town, inhabited not by Mosquitians, but by foreigners, many of whom were Americans. When the Muse of History, in after years, pores over her pages stained with reckless spoliation, she will blush to meet this act recorded on her annals. Would that she could drop a tear thereon, and blot it out forever.

Upon the 6th of September, 1855, Col. Kinney was unanimously chosen Civil and Military Governor of the City and Territory of San Juan del Norte, or Greytown; and on the day following, the Convention reassembled, and the oath of office was duly administered. The Preamble and Resolutions set forth were as follows:

Whereas, We, the people of San Juan del Norte, or Greytown, and the Territory thereunto belonging, in Convention assembled, do recognize it as an inalienable right of all men living together as a community, to secure for themselves protection of life and property, and the suitable maintenance of order and good conduct; and believing and affirming such to be a *fundamental* principle, without the sacred observance of which *no* community can exist and prosper;

And, whereas no recognized authorities, civil or military, for the purposes above-named, do now exist in this place, to the great detriment and drawback of its manifold interests;

And whereas, from the urgency of the case, in view of the numerous recent additions to our population, and the large numbers expected soon to arrive amongst us, it is expedient and indispensable that a Provisional Government should be established without further delay.—Therefore be it Resolved,

1st. That a Civil and Military Governor be chosen by the

people, to whom full powers shall be delegated for the appointment of such subordinate officers, (except the Council hereinafter named), and the establishment of such offices and *wholesome* laws and regulations as shall appear to him best adapted for, and the carrying of such laws and regulations into effect, the same to be done with the advice and consent of the Council.

2d. *Resolved,* That a Council, to be composed of five persons, be chosen by the people, whose duty it shall be to consult with and advise the Governor upon all matters connected with the public interest, and the consent of a majority of whom shall be necessary to the appointment of any officer, and the enactment of any law or regulation.

3d. *Resolved,* That the deliberative meetings of the Governor and Council shall be open to the public, unless in the opinion of the Governor the public good should otherwise demand.

4th. *Resolved,* That the Council be empowered by the people to draft a Constitution, which, after receiving the sanction of the Governor, shall be submitted to them for their adoption by ballot.

5th. *Resolved,* That the Provisional Government now established shall continue in power until such time as it may seem fit and expedient to the people to meet, and elect a permanent one under the new Constitution.

6th. *Resolved,* That no Taxes shall be levied on the citizens of San Juan or Greytown and its Territory, without the consent of a majority of the citizens, being owners of Real Estate or personal property to the amount of two hundred and fifty dollars, excepting such inhabitants as have been residents six months and upward.

7th. *Resolved,* That all foreign vessels (excepting Mail Steamers), entering the harbor, shall pay the same port charges as formerly levied in this port, from and after the first day of October next.

8th. *Resolved,* That the former printed Constitution of Greytown, or San Juan del Norte, shall be adopted as a basis to govern the action of the Government.

9th. *Resolved,* That nothing in the foregoing articles shall be construed as depriving the people of their rights to assemble together and discuss matters relative to the public good, and to instruct the Governor and Council upon any subject affecting the same.

We observe a freedom to be admired in the spirit of these Resolutions; the Provisional Government subscribed to the former Constitution, which was modeled after that of the United States, with few exceptions of trifling character. The Inaugural Proclamation of Governor Kinney is high-toned, succinct, and views the bombardment, the poverty following said piratical action, and difficulties with the Transit Company, properly and ably. Schools and churches were erected and opened. Physicians, attorneys, merchants, land agents, and others flocked to support the new administration, and Governor Kinney's assumption of power was brilliant, though unfortunately brief. A printing-press was properly located, and a paper called "The Central American" was published, the first number of which was issued September 15th, 1855. Editors, W. H. Young and F. Lewellyn. The officers of the Government were—

Henry L. Kinney, Civil and Military Governor; W. S. Thayer, Secretary of the Government; J. R. Swift, Captain of the Port and Collector; S. T. Haly, Chief Judicial Magistrate; W. H. Young, Attorney-General; F. Salter, Post Master and Recorder of Deeds; S. H. Shock, Provost-Marshal; Thomas S. Codd, Deputy Provost-Marshal; John Jackson, Surveyor; B. Wark, Constable; Thomas Cody, A. M. C. Wood, Benjamin Mooney, Walter Sutherland, and Samuel Shepherd, Jr., Members of the Council, of which the first-named was President.

The English Government refused to acknowledge the new party in power, but consented, provided a re-election be had, which should give no offense. Gov. Kinney resigned, and other matters pressing upon the tapis, obscured the position of affairs upon this coast for the subsequent period. Illy provided with the means of sustenance, betrayed by the Association with whom he had covenanted, Col. Kinney in vain looked for the reinforcements and provisions which were to have been forwarded by the organization in New York and Philadelphia.

Sick, poor, a stranger in a strange land, having spent his means in the establishment of his Colony, one by one hopes fled, and his men went to the interior to join another cause, whose course was marked by blood-stained battle-fields, and the silent hearths of deserted and spoliated homes.

Had Col. Kinney desired to lead any revolutionary organization, his opportunities for so doing have certainly not been isolated. Overtures were made him by the Nicaraguans through their then Provisional Chief, Don Patricia Rivas, by whom he was urged to visit the City of Granada. Had he desired to grasp the reins of Government, ere Gen. Walker had been tempted to do so, Kinney would have occupied the position of Commander-in-chief, by the unanimous consent of the nation. Costa Rica also sent deputies to confer with him, entreating him and his followers to settle in its province, but he was wedded to his tract on the Mosquito coast. He had sought it for a particular and distinct purpose, and the improvements everywhere visible were endorsements of his high integrity.

His subsequent visit to Granada, and his expulsion thence at Gen. Walker's instance, reflects but little credit upon the latter, whose boast to hang Col. Kinney proved an empty one. Col. Kinney, after enduring many hardships, it is rumored, has sold his Grant to the Mormons for two million dollars, receiving an instalment of one tenth of the purchase-money.

CHAPTER XIX.

INHABITANTS OF THE MOSQUITO COAST—THEIR WEALTH—CLIMATE—INTRODUCTION OF RELIGION—THEIR OWN BELIEF—BURIAL OF THEIR DEAD—PRODUCTS OF THE COAST—TURTLE—BIRDS—FISH—ANIMALS—VINES—TREES AND WOODS—RIVERS—EXPLORATION OF INDIAN RIVER BY THE GOLDEN CLUB—A BEAUTIFUL COUNTRY—MAGNIFICENT FORESTS—BLACK RIVER—GOLD—INDIAN RIVER AGAIN—SHEPHERD'S RANCHE—GRAND FALLS—PROSPECTING FOR GOLD—SUCCESS—DROVES OF WILD HOGS—NO COUNTRY FOR SNAKES—CAPTAIN WILKINSON'S PARTY—PROSPECTING AGAIN—RICH RESULTS.

THE natives of the Mosquito shore, like savages of other countries, are distinguished for their apathy; fruits furnish them with sustenance, chief among which, are the banana and plantain, and these are extremely nourishing. The wild boar, deer, birds, and the fish, all of which are abundant, supply their few necessities. Their wealth consists in a canoe and its accessories; and protected by mountains and morasses, with no accumulated wealth to tempt the pirate or the adventurer, they are exposed to no incursions from without. A healthy climate removes the necessity of clothing, while their huts are easily constructed; thus they have remained in a dormant state, gradually decreasing.

The Dominican monks of Guatemala failed in the introduction of their creed; the Baptist Missionary Society of England sent one of their body there, who died, however, on his arrival at Belize, Honduras. The king has heretofore expressed his willingness to receive and protect any teachers who might be sent. Of their religious belief, scarcely aught is known, save that they acknowledge a Good and Bad Spirit. The latter is worshipped more particularly from dread of his anger, and as they consider the former too merciful to injure them, they plead this as sufficient palliation for their neglecting to adore him. They bury their dead with the paddle and harpoon the owner used when alive, supposing that the deceased will need them in the other world to provide for his sustenance.

The many valuable products of this coast render its exploration and development necessary. The Indians collect immense quantities of turtle-shell, up the Coast, the Hawksbill species being the most valuable, and from whence, if properly and attentively pursued, this article alone would prove highly remunerative as an export. Turtles are abundant, and the expense is merely nominal for the obtaining of the shell. To those who may not be informed on the subject, we may add, that the female turtle lays her eggs on the sea-shore, which she scoops out with her fin-like feet. She then scrapes back the sand over the eggs, and the surface is made smooth as before. They are soon hatched by the genial warmth of the sun, and the little turtles crawling forth from the sand, find their way to the moaning sea with wonderful rapidity. They are of two species—one, called by Linnæus, *Testudo coriacea*, is an inhabitant of the sea; the other, *Testudo lutaria*, is found in fresh water, particularly in the lakes and rivers.

Then we find the Thula, a species of heron, the *Ardea thula*, a name derived from the Chilian—it is entirely white, and its head is adorned with a crest of the same color. Then, too, the gray and red partridge, very large, though about marshy places is found a smaller species. The chicken is said to be domestic; it is smaller than in North America; this may be true, since the hog and dog seem to be animals met with everywhere, especially in the Islands of the Pacific. Then, too, the wild duck, of two or three classes, as also a species of water-hen, with armed wings, similar to the Brazilian hen, called Jacana. The wing is armed at the joint by a spur. It feeds upon the plains, keeps in pairs, builds its nest in the grass, and is jealous of its little home, which if intruded upon, it will defend bravely. This bird never makes any noise during the day, but at night, when it hears some one passing, it will cry. It is good game, equal to the woodcock. Then they have the vampire, an account of which we have given elsewhere, together with bats, ducks, and a variety of birds too numerous to be recorded in the present volume.

Sea-cows, monkeys, and alligators are found in the various rivers, as also the shark, the sword and black-fish, and an endless variety of the finny species. The sea-cow, or sea-wolf, or whatever may be its proper name, is similar to the sea-hog, yet distinguished from it by very striking characteristics. In Indian River the sea-hog is abundant. It resembles the urigne in shape, hair, and manner of living, but its mouth is longer, like the snout of a pig. Its ears are more raised, and the fore-feet divided into five distinct toes covered with a membrane. This *Phoca* is from three to four feet in length. There, too, the porcupine is found. It does not differ from the *Histrix prensile.* The cattle are not very large, but the meat is firm and juicy; the milk is rich, and a large quantity of mild cheese is annually manufactured.

Of the climbing plants, an abundance are found. Among others is one similar to the copiù; its flowers are composed of six petals three inches in length, of the most beautiful crimson, spotted within with white. This plant creeps up the tallest trees; its leaves are disposed by threes, are of a beautiful green color, and oval in shape. The fruit is about an inch in diameter, cylindrical, of a dull yellow color, and contains a white, tender pulp, pleasant to the taste. The passion flower, the sensitive plant, which is very large, the caracol, the sarsaparilla, and many species of the French lianes are discovered. A vine found everywhere as you ascend the Rio San Juan, noticed in our first chapter as falling from tree-tops to the earth, and then creeping up again, weaving a mesh of imperviable network, resembles in its flowers the copiù. It climbs without attaching itself. It produces a leguminous purple flower. It can be used for making hedges, baskets, or for cable for bungos, much more efficient than hemp, for it is capable of resisting moisture for a longer time.

The grasses are numerous, and the rushes grow to the height of four feet; from a certain species I made a basket which held water. Tobacco is of two kinds, the cultivated and wild. It is strong, highly-flavored, but is badly cured. The medicinal plants are very numerous, as also the herbs used in dying, and the alimentary plants or herbs are as abundant as the most ardent student could desire. I have met also with the rosebush, which, however, I cannot believe to be domestic, but, as it was introduced into Peru from Spain, its presence, here, no doubt, is sufficient evidence of its Hispanian origin. The domestic animals live in the fields all the year round, and from feeding on aromatic plants their flesh acquires a peculiar and pleasant flavor. The plains, valleys, and mountains are covered with elegant trees, each season producing new herbage in great perfection; and from the uniformly genial climate of this section, there is no doubt that all the plants of our latitude could be cultivated there without difficulty.

Prior to entering into a view of the minerals, it were well for us to turn to Indian River, which has been partially explored, and as the account has not been publicly given, it may interest the reader. The Rio Escondido and Great River are both considerable streams, and flow through a country of surpassing fertility. These lands so rich have the advantage of an outlet to the sea, through which their products may be carried to market, even prior to the opening of roads. There are several rivers in the southern portion of the territory, and they all abound with many varieties of fine fish. Pearl River, Aula Tara, Rio Grande, Prizapalka, Boshwash, Rain River, Rama, Corn River, Spanish, Indian, Escondido, Tauro, San Juan, Rio Colorado, Juanilla, Serapaqui, Estero Real, Tipitapa, Ochomogo, Gonzales, Sapoa, Nino, Zapatero, Rio Frio, Poco Sol, Melchora, Salvatos, Sarmosa, Machuca, Chorrsa, Francisco, Cruz, San Carlos, Las Miras, Guaspore, Tepanaguasapa, San Rafiel, Burro Negro, Mayales, Tecolostote, Malaxoge, Metape, Papaturo, and Coco: these are the streams found on the face of Nicaragua, embracing the Mosquito Coast.

Little or nothing, or literally nothing reliable, can be col lected relative to the expeditions formed prior to 1855, for the exploration of Indian River, although in this same year several companies ascended probably twenty or twenty-five miles, meeting only with hardships, being illy equipped, and provided scantily with provisions. The report of the miners bearing the name of "The Golden Club," we shall insert. This Company was composed of six gentlemen, commanded by Captain S. H. Shock, of Philadelphia. "The first day's journey from Greytown was not characterized by any event differing from a plain travel over a known region of fertile land and rank vegetation. Twelve miles from the mouth of Indian River, however, the aspect of this country changes entirely, becoming extremely beautiful, which for variety of landscape equals any known portion of the Isthmus. Numerous plantations, old and new, are seen on and near the banks of the river; some of which," says the historian of the Company, for I have his report before me, "seemed as if the owner cared little in reaping to reimburse his labor, so heavily were the trees laden with fruit, showing the more to advantage in the want of the undergrowth, so ruinous where there is no attention given. Some localities, selected by members of our own band, may be seen as the path gradually winds into the forest, lined with lofty cedars, oaks, mahogany, and all other descriptions of timber to be found in tropical regions.

"Upon proceeding about thirty miles up the stream, we found our instructions required us to change our course to the left, up Black River, leading us further into the interior, where, to all appearance, mortal foot had never before trodden, but to our surprise, the country was still the same in variety of landscape and apparent fertility of soil. The river is narrow, and its banks high and sloping, across which, in many places, heavy pieces of timber had fallen, obstructing our progress much. We concluded, after a halt, that the party should here separate, a part to proceed as far up as practicable, the others to remain. Those who ascended the river forced their way, twelve miles, through dense foliage and over high, rugged banks, making a distance of fifty-seven miles from the mouth of the river. Here they found high falls, and after a short prospecting, obtained some gold. This was in the midst of the rainy season, and they were unable to perfect their examination, as well on account of the high stage of water, as their short stock of provisions and insufficient implements of labor. We joined the waiting party, and began to descend to Indian River, following its course, whence we turned to the left, which was the proper route, and the one pursued by Captain Wilkinson's party, which had preceded us a few days.

"On entering the right trail, we found at our several camping places, for some distance, a scarcity of game, and at intervals deserted Indian ranchos. Shepherd's ranche, on the river, was the best camping spot we had, and near this we discovered several deserted plantations. The scenery became broader and more beautiful, as we proceeded, the timber finer and more lofty, and we observed a total absence of undergrowth, enabling us to view to greater advantage the mountain scenery, valleys, and glens, so sweet to all lovers of Nature. On leaving this ranche, the journey becomes picturesque in the extreme, there being a continuation of rapids until our arrival at the Grand Falls. Here pilots became essential. This is one of the most particular points to be observed by parties who may feel inclined to visit the mines in this district, the difficulty of the passage over the rapids rendering great care necessary, as the least want of skill on the part of the pilot might endanger life. The canoes should be unloaded at the foot of the Falls.

"Moving onward, the scenery becomes grander, and from day to day the cataracts and falls, with the picturesque landscape around, present to the eye something to be admired beyond description. The total absence of musquitoes, the freshness of the water, which in coolness almost equals ice, suggests healthiness and comfort; our journey, although slow and difficult, has been a pleasant one. We observed the camp of Captain Wilkinson's party ahead, and soon shook hands with undisguised pleasure with our friends. The further ascent of the river being considered very questionable, we selected three of the combined party to prosecute it, having provided them with rations for ten days. In the interim, the remainder of the party prospected on a gravelly beach, between two large falls or cataracts, in the neighborhood of our encampment. We commenced operations, but found the water too high for effecting a fair test of its yielding capacities, although we shovelled up five pans, all of which were proved, and gold was obtained.

"The river subsided slightly, and we again tried the gravel bar. We dug a hole four feet wide, twelve long, and six deep; this brought us to the rock, where we found each pan to yield ten cents value in gold. That found on the sands was simply drift. The river commencing again to rise prevented us from reaching a spot where not a doubt could exist of our being amply repaid for our exertions.

"We expected to receive from the party who had left us, very favorable reports, which would induce us to abandon the idea of digging; until they arrived, the water being now too high for prospecting, we turned our attention to exploring the valleys, hills, nooks, and dells in our neighborhood, in all of which we found cedar timber in abundance, the trees ranging from fifty to seventy feet in height, without a single knot or limb intervening, plenty of dye-woods, and beautiful table-land, though the continuance of heavy rain prevented our making as full an inspection as we could have wished. We did not find, in any case, gold in any of these Valles. We met with an Indian trail of recent date. Indian River affords a plentiful supply of fish of the finest quality. The stone-bass in this vicinity has the preference. I may mention the almost entire absence of snakes in this region also, which may be attributed to the large herds of wild hogs roaming about—as many as three hundred being frequently found in a drove—the Mountain Cow, Curacoas and Deer, are also to be found in great quantities.

"Upon our return to camp, we were surprised to find our friends already there. They reported, that after five days travel through forests of cedar, they arrived near the bed rock of the river. Here they found formations of slate and granite, and on scooping up a handful of sand from this, it yielded twenty cents of gold to the pan. From their inability to take with them a supply of shovels, long-toms, or other utensils, with the danger of too frequent exposure at this season, they were compelled to relinquish further developments, and rest satisfied with the result already attained. We had journeyed one hundred and twenty-five miles to where our prospects were fully realized, and deciding to return in December, during the more propitious season, we promised ourselves, with all confidence, a full field for our labor."

CHAPTER XX.

WAR IN THE INTERIOR—UNITED STATES MARSHAL IN A FIX—ARRIVAL OF GEN. WALKER—BATTLE OF VIRGIN BAY—DEFEAT OF GUARDIOLA—SUBSEQUENT BATTLES—WALKER'S TRIUMPHANT ENTRY INTO GRANADA—TREASON AND ITS PUNISHMENT—SCHLESSINGER SURPRISED AT GUANACASTE—CHARGED WITH TREACHERY—HIS TRIAL, CONDEMNATION, FLIGHT, AND SENTENCE OF DEATH—BATTLE OF RIVAS—WALKER AGAIN VICTORIOUS—INAUGURATION OF CHAMORRO—A NINE MONTHS' SIEGE—HIS DEATH—ESTRADA HIS SUCCESSOR—PADRE VIGIL'S LETTER TO MR. MARCY—MY OPINION—HENNINGSEN'S GLORIOUS DEFENSE OF GRANADA—ATTACK ON SAN JORGE—GALLANT CONDUCT OF CAPT. HIGBY—SAN JORGE AGAIN—THE CANNONADE—SHARP OPERATION OF THE COSTA RICANS—CAPTURE OF CASTILLO—ENGLISH AND AMERICAN OFFICERS—WHAT WALKER HAD TO CONTEND WITH—EVACUATION OF THE COUNTRY—OFFICIAL REPORT OF WALKER'S FORCE—THE RESULTS OF THE INVASION.

We must now turn to the interior, for since Col. Kinney and his lands have been receiving our attention, the revolution in Nicaragua proper has grown desperate and stirring. The Liberals invited foreigners to aid them in destroying the power of the Servile faction, and on the 4th of May, 1855, Gen.

Walker, with fifty-eight men, arrived at San Juan del Sur. The United States Marshal had interposed to prevent his vessel from sailing, when Walker finding that further delay would only be adding fuel to the flame, invited him into the cabin, feted him with wines, and during the tête-à-tête, the anchor was weighed, and the government officer awoke to the consciousness of being on his way to an unknown port. However, with a delicacy peculiar to the moment, the General advised the officer of his position, and after a few friendly exchanges, sent him back to San Francisco, while the vessel sought the coyal palm-groves of Nicaragua.

The Serviles learning of his arrival, immediately marched from Rivas, and attacked him with four hundred men. In vain the advancing columns of the enemy strove to break the serried and firm front of this invading, friendly force; in vain, Guardiola cheered his men to the attack; in vain, the loud shriek of the swarthy islander or the deep cry of the mountaineer; the deadly rifle, handled by willing hands and able men, swept death and devastation through the enemy. Walker's loss was one white man and four natives, while Guardiola lost fifty of rank and file. The enemy charged again, but Walker, at the head of his small battalion of reserve, rushed to the rescue, and swept the blue and white flag of Nicaragua from the field. The foe were routed, and the moon rose upon a battle-field far bloodier than those fought between the Serviles and Liberals heretofore, while she lighted to the distant shelter a broken and dispirited band of harassed and wounded soldiers. Thus was fought the first regular battle, and from that field the banner of Liberty arose rebaptized and regenerated.

Shortly after the battle of Virgin Bay, Gen. Walker returned to San Juan del Sur. The Government, of which Don Jose Maria Estrada was the President, demanded the arms and ammunition in the possession of the Transit Company. These consisted of four cannon, forty-eight muskets, and a large supply of cartridges shipped from New York by this Company, and landed at the Castillo Rapids, for the use of the forty-eight soldiers, or, as they were termed, "Invincibles," who had been sent out to counteract an influence which was preponderating against them. The arms and ammunition were on board the steamer Virgin, at that time lying off Granada.

Battle succeeded battle—step by step the strangers advanced into the country. From a small detachment of eighty, the ranks were soon swollen to hundreds. The Liberals flocked round their new chief, upon whose banner victory sat—the influence of Walker was at once felt. He summarily punished defections in his ranks, whether among the American or native troops, till every man felt there was nothing left but to obey and execute. The city of Granada, which had so long withstood the Liberal party, yielded to the new-comers, and the entrance of Walker, October 13th, 1855, was hailed with enthusiasm. The church bells welcomed him, and everywhere banners and handkerchiefs waved in his honor. The Serviles, now grown desperate, called upon the adjoining States for assistance, but the knell of Monarchism had been sounded, and the former friends of this once powerful party heeded not the invitation.

A truce ensued, however, between the rival forces. Gen. Corral, the most prominent officer of the so-styled legitimate Government, and chief of the hostile forces, had, prior to this, ratified Walker's triumph in the church, and had sworn friendship to the new Government, of which Don Patricio Rivas was, by virtue of said treaty chosen President, or Provisional Chief. He now dispatched a letter to General Guardiola, who had flown from Granada, representing that affairs under the management of Gen. Walker were not being properly conducted. He also appointed a certain time for Guardiola to invest the city with his entire force, when Walker, unprepared, might be taken by surprise, and his men put to the sword. This letter having been intercepted, and delivered to Gen. Walker, a civil and military tribunal was formed, and Gen. Corral was brought to trial on a charge of treason against the then existing Government.

It has been stated, that after his trial he confessed having written the letter. He was found guilty and condemned to death. He was brave and intelligent, a man of warm attachments and generous disposition. The Minister from Nicaragua, Padre Vigil, besought his pardon with all that eloquence which distinguishes that truly good and merciful-hearted man, but his doom was sealed. He was shot on the plaza, and died universally regretted, leaving three sisters, whom he had revered and loved, in indigent circumstances to mourn his untimely loss. The entire country was shocked upon learning of his condemnation and death, and even the friends and supporters of the Cause felt that the stroke had been too hasty and severe, and for a time it is said even Walker himself shared the same opinions. But to succeed, treachery must be summarily punished. This decisive blow was succeeded by battles, and the incoming of recruits soon erased the gloom of the late execution.

Costa Rica, in the interim, declared war against Nicaragua, and ere the news had fairly been flung to the breeze, Walker had a detachment on the march to the former State to meet the foe on their own soil. Col. Schlessinger commanded this arm of the force, and after marching to Guanacaste, allowed himself to be surprised while in fortification, and many of his men were butchered. Three thousand Costa Ricans, fresh in the field, swept after the broken ranks of the invaders, and straggling over hills and mountains, through morasses and swamps, the shattered remnant of Schlessinger's command, in a state of utter exhaustion, finally reached their Commander-in-Chief in Granada, to accuse Schlessinger of treachery, negligence, and general imbecility.

Subsequently, the leader of this unfortunate expedition found his way to headquarters, but his soldiers had already been heard, and charges were preferred. A tribunal was summoned, and Schlessinger, who had the patrol on honor of the city, escaped while his trial was pending. Sentence of death was pronounced upon the traitor if found on the territory of Nicaragua, and his infamy was published to the world.

The army of Walker heard of the advance of the enemy with impatience, and at the head of about eight hundred men, well armed, but illy ammunitioned, the Commander-in-Chief marched upon the city of Rivas, where the Costa Ricans, three thousand strong, were posted. The latter, commanded by foreign officers, well-armed with Minnie rifles, and flushed with their late victory, expected an easy prey. Street by street was fought through, barricades were overthrown, houses fired and sacked, carnage reigned supreme, and the best and bravest of Walker's army fell dead on that eventful day. Still, the threat of Costa Rica to shoot every man found with arms upon his person nerved even the most timid. To retreat was certain death, to be conquered instant execution ; and between the two there seemed nothing left but to battle on against tremendous odds.

The foreign officers of the Costa Ricans displayed much military skill, and the troops under them executed their commands efficiently; but the cool, undaunted American, who advanced to the thundering cannon, while yet the smoke kissed its warm lip, this to the foe was beyond all conception. The enemy retreated, pierced with the bullets of the sharpshooters, till the evening drawing on, and the ammunition of the Nicaraguans getting low, the army amassed, and after beating the enemy from every tenable position, coolly retreated with colors waving and drums beating. Walker's loss in the engagement was about eighty-five, while that of the enemy was from six to eight hundred.

Walker marched to Granada, leaving the Costa Ricans to nurse their wounded, bury their dead, and to manage a retreat attended with unexpected and unlooked-for disasters. Instead of interring their comrades, they threw their bodies into the various wells of the city, and from the decaying corses emanated sickness and cholera, which thinned, with fearful rapidity, their broken ranks. They reached San Juan del Sur, and hastily embarked, leaving behind many of their sick and wounded, with a total loss of at least one-third their original number.

We shall now refer to the inauguration of Don Fruto Chamorro as Director of Nicaragua. It has been stated in political circles at Washington, by those high in authority, as also, I believe, by Don Augustin Vigil, then Minister from Nicaragua, "that this step was the commencement of the storm; that Chamorro began to show his tendency to despotism, and usurping the sacred rights of the people who had elected him, commenced to forge the chain of their misfortunes. Fearing, however, a number of the citizens who were adverse to him, he commenced criminal proceedings against them. The greater part of these citizens were Liberal Members of the Constituent Assembly, which had convened for April, 1854, and who possessed too much integrity to vote away the liberty of the Republic. Among them were Don Francisco Castillon and General Jerez. These, with others, were imprisoned, and banished subsequently to Honduras.

"General Jerez, at the head of a few men, returned, however, and at Chinandega organized a Provisional Government. They then marched to Leon, where Chamorro had his camp, and as soon as the forces met, the army of the latter went over to Jerez. Chamorro fled to Granada, and by sacrificing the wealthy portion of the citizens, he assembled a force of one thousand men, and stood a nine months' siege on the plaza, during which time the most beautiful portions of the city were destroyed. The Provisional Government was compelled to raise the siege, and invited American citizens to aid them. Ninety of them responded to the invitation, and became naturalized citizens of Nicaragua.

"Chamorro died, and Don Jose Maria Estrada was appointed his successor; thus, (says the Padre in his letter to Mr. Marcy of May 14th, 1856), did the Constituent Assembly trample on the very constitution and charter they had made but a few days before, arrogating to themselves the ordinary legislative power. This," further adds the Padre, "is the style of government which has been styled legitimate, and which was not and could not be so accorded to the Constitution of that State, because Chamorro's term of office having expired, only the people of Nicaragua, represented by the Justas of the Departments, and *never* the Assembly, ought to have appointed the successor."

After entering the city of Granada, as before stated, the Government of Estrada being overthrown, the Padre says: "The new Government invited General Corral, the chief of the hostile forces, to a conference; this officer being fully authorized by the late Government, they agreed to appoint a Provisional chief, for which Don Patricio Rivas was selected, and General Walker, General-in-Chief of the whole military force of the Republic."

The worthy Padre has offered, I fear, but sorry reasoning for the subsequent acts of his Government. He educes an argument against Estrada, because the Justas of the Department only had the power to elect a successor, and yet he tells us, General Corral, a rebel chief, conferred with the enemy, and selected Rivas the successor of Chamorro and Estrada. Is it to be supposed that any such power was vested in Corral by his partizans, as to yield the supreme Directorship of the country, and would he willingly resign his position as Commander-in-Chief, had not force been employed? Are we to believe that this assumption of power on the part of the Rivas party was valid?

Facts are stubborn, and they justify the *selection* of Rivas; but there is no shadow of any legal *election* by the Justas, but by the prescribed Assembly, composed, subsequently, at the moment of the making of this compromise, of friends to the new Government! Was this agreement between Corral and the enemy valid? Was Rivas elected by the Justas? Was any election held at all? Certainly not! The enemy had evacuated Granada, and consequently they had no voice in it. Would they empower their chief, Corral, to treat in this crisis with the enemy?

Is it not absurd to justify the position of the Rivas-Walker Government by such arguments? Was it not certain, that Corral's vote, upon any question, would be over-ruled, and that any advantage he might wish to claim would be denied? And yet a treaty was made, and Corral, instead of returning to his friends, was detained in Granada, and subsequently tried, convicted, condemned upon a charge of treason, and shot. How was this charge sustained? Not by influential parties; they condemned the accusation and the verdict, and the subsequent Minister of Nicaragua, appointed by the Rivas-Walker Government, strenuously besought his pardon, believing him to be innocent.

There was no election, but an unanimous selection of Don Patricio Rivas, a worthy, quiet man, formerly Custom Officer at San Carlos, for the post; a tool, 'tis said, in the hands of General Walker, and against whose interests, it will be remembered, even his son fought, fully feeling that his father was a titled prisoner, a second Montezuma, in the hands of his victor.

By whom was the city shorn of her beauty? By the enemy, not by the Chamorro party, whose interests would have suffered, and that Chamorro defended the plaza for nine months against the enemy, is sufficient endorsement of his valor, for had he been obnoxious to the citizens, he would soon have felt their vengeance. A rebellion had occurred—one party was beaten —the victors claimed the spoils; and they selected their officers, as was usual, and held from that time the country *vi et armis.*

The headquarters of General Walker were at Granada, and the gallant and determined defense of the plaza, by Henningsen, will be remembered as one of the most glorious achievements of modern fillibusterism. With his retreat entirely cut off, supplies diminishing, an hospital immense in proportion to his fighting men, yet there was no show of the white flag; determined to fall or conquer, he braved his foes; and when relief came, small though it proved, responding to the hearty shouts of his fellow soldiers, he leaped from his island barricade to punish the too sanguine enemy.

Reduced to the narrow and circumscribed limits of Rivas and environs, with a clear outlet, however, to San Juan, Walker refused to retreat, and vainly essayed to bring the enemy into a general battle. San Jorge was barricaded, but he resolved to attempt its capture. On the 3d of February, 1857, he returned from San Juan del Sur with forty-three recruits, reaching Rivas at half-past one P. M. That night, with these, he forced an attack on San Jorge,—his men were worn out, had been illy provisioned, and his total force only numbered two hundred. Walker led in person. It was defended with cannon, and proved a very strong post; within the church and plaza was the whole Costa Rican force; Walker had no artillery, for he intended to surprise the village. He would have succeeded, had his men supported him, for when they entered the streets, not a sound was heard, not a picket challenged—the whole place was wrapped in dangerous, almost fatal sleep. The courage of his worn-out men deserted them, and when ordered to the attack, they faltered—they refused. He called for forty volunteers to storm the village—only fifteen advanced. With these he approached the barricade. The whole camp slept within—not a sentry on the alert. They fired into the plaza, which aroused the camp, and met a response of musketry. The volunteers fell back—the whole body began to scatter, when Captain Higby of Mobile sprang forward into the midst of his Company, and taunting them, finally compelled them to amass, and marched them up to the plaza. In the interim the Costa Ricans had entered the square from the surrounding houses, and were firing from thence upon them.

Higby led his men in single file, crouching low along the walls, so as to escape the muzzles of the enemy's guns, and as the Costa Ricans discharged their vollies, up rose the Walker-ites, and through the same port or loopholes returned the courtesy. This manœuvre, however, could not stay the battle long, although it told disastrously upon the foe. Higby being unsupported, and exposed to a galling fire from all points of the plaza, while General Walker's party being the focus of a hot serenade from the cannon, compelled the latter to evacuate the village, after losing Col. O'Neil, Capt. Blackburn, and a considerable number of the rank and file, composed of the First and Second Rifles and the Rangers. He retired to Rivas.

On the 7th, in the morning, at 3 A. M., he marched again to San Jorge, with three field-pieces and at 7 A. M., at a distance of six hundred yards, commenced a cannonade which lasted for several hours, but he was disappointed in drawing the enemy from their retreat. General Cañas, the Costa Rican commander, having an opportunity to communicate with Gen eral Walker some days subsequent, addressed him a note, in which he stated that the cannonade had killed three beeves, thereby saving the butcher some trouble, and that his men had picked up fifty round-shot, which he should with pleasure return to him some time soon—*poco tiempo*.

Upon the Rio San Juan, Walker's officers had taken Serapaqui, the Castillo, and other points, and held Punta Arenas also, but were unsupported, and finally outwitted by the Costa Ricans who succumbed at Castillo. The latter desired twenty-four hours to evacuate, but in the meantime sent messengers for aid to San Carlos, who returned with reserves sufficient to compel Cols. Titus and Lockridge to abandon all hopes of its capture. Had Walker's officers refused time, and forced them at once to surrender, the whole country would have been in his hands. Was this the result of an over-supply of confidence, or "manifest destiny"?

Col. Anderson had succeeded in taking Serapaqui, and was left with a garrison to defend it until the return of Col. Lockridge. Lockridge landed a detachment of one hundred and fifty men under Col. Titus, one mile below Castillo, with orders to march through the woods, and enter the town on the rear; whilst he, in person, proceeded up the river to cannonade it. When he (Lockridge) came in sight of the fort, he found the houses in flames below, and also two of the river-steamers.

Without delay, and under a shower of balls from the fort, he boarded the J. N. Scott, put out the fire, cut her adrift, and floated her out of range of the guns. The other boat, The Machuca, was entirely consumed. The Scott was riddled with balls, and otherwise injured. Lockridge's loss, exposed thus, was five privates and one officer. Titus found the ruins when he reached the Rapids, sent in a flag, and demanded instant surrender, having ascertained previously that the force amounted to only twenty-five men.

The rest I have told. On the 2d of March, Titus descended the river in the Rescue, with Col. Lockridge, having the J. N. Scott in tow. The English officers boarded the steamers *ad libitum*, offering protection to all who desired to leave Walker's service. General Walker's camp at Rivas was also visited by American and English naval officers, but the latter generally felt they had rated the General far too feebly.

Rivas was well fortified. It was defended by stone barricades, and eleven pieces of ordnance—three six-pounders, two mines, two howitzers, and four mortars, the latter very small. The Costa Rican forces were about ten times the number of Walker's. Reduced to a circumscribed space, the latter felt his necessity for action. Not a boat on the lake, no communication with Lockridge on the Atlantic, one hundred men sick and wounded, two hundred more, limping, terribly crippled, and unfit for marching, four hundred only were left together with two hundred natives to battle against this overwhelming odds.

Of how many well-fought fields have these rude untutored troops been the victors! In a strange clime, unaccustomed to its water, or its changing temperature, war from the moment they placed their feet upon its soil, till they sought the "sick-bey," foes around them, about them, starvation at their elbows, and no reserves on the march, what prevented Despair from gathering his share of the laurels? Pride! Pride! On their Leader's brow they saw a dogged resolve, a fixed determination to outfast, outsit, or outfight the enemy. All that perseverance could have accomplished, was certainly his. He penetrated to the Capital—he had it in his power. He governed the State, but his forces were insufficient. Had Lockridge been able to join him, and hence given him possession of the lake and river steamers, the flag of the vanquished would undoubtedly now float from the mast-heads at Realejo, and the flag-staff of Greytown!

From the official report of Ph. R. Thompson, Adjutant-General of the Nicaraguan army, dated Rivas, Feb. 24, 1857, we find that the original number of men enlisted were 2,288, of which 61 were officers. The total of deaths were 685, of which 109 were officers; 37 resigned, 206 were discharged including one officer, 9 were dropped or stricken from the roll, 293 deserted, of which 9 were officers, leaving a total of 733 officers and men, with 141 unaccounted for.

To the number joined, as herein stated, are to be added about 100, who joined singly, re-enlisted, and others employed in the different departments of the army. Of the 141 unaccounted for, about 70 should be added to the killed.

The evacuation of the country by General Walker and compatriots from the port of San Juan del Sur, on the Pacific, and the interference of Captain Davis, of the Ship-of-war St. Mary, is patent. His general successes and discomfitures have been dwelt upon succinctly, but briefly, and we refrain from dilating upon the motives which induced either the first or second visit of the leader to Nicaragua, lest we may do injustice, but we shall publish an official document relating to his capitulation according to the Convention of Rivas. Suffice it for us to ask, what of good hath eventuated from all the turmoil? Many wrongs had been committed by the Government upon Americans, resident and transient. The Transit route has been brought into notice, and many who have visited the country from other motives than commerce, can fully endorse my opinion of it, when I add, that it possesses a regular and good climate—fertile soil—the finest fruits in the world—immense mineral wealth, and a population, with whom, after our Cass and Yrisarri Treaty is fully confirmed, we can affiliate, and enter into commerce, with many chances of success.

CHAPTER XXI.

WALKER'S CONTEMPLATED SECOND INVASION OF NICARAGUA—SENORS YRISARRI AND MOLINA—THEIR LETTER TO SECRETARY CASS—WHAT THEY THINK WALKER WILL DO—WHAT THEY HOPE THE UNITED STATES WILL DO—CIRCULAR OF SECRETARY CASS—CALLS ON THE OFFICIALS—EXPECTS THEM TO DO THEIR DUTY—WALKER SPEAKS—APOLOGISES FOR DOING SO—CLAIMS TO BE THE LAWFUL EXECUTIVE OF NICARAGUA—DOES NOT WANT ANY INTERFERENCE FROM COSTA RICA AND GUATEMALA—DENIES VIOLATING ANY ACT OF CONGRESS—SENOR YRISARRI AGAIN—WANTS THE AMERICAN GOVERNMENT TO DO THE RIGHT THING—TALKS HARD ABOUT WALKER—SAYS THE FILLIBUSTERS ARE NOTHING BUT PIRATES—CANNOT DECEIVE THE CENTRAL AMERICANS, AND WONDERS AT THE IMPUDENCE OF THE MAN OF DESTINY.

In relation to General Walker's second invasion of Nicaragua, we insert the following official documents, which prove the desire of the United States to maintain her position for probity with the world at large. The letter from Señors Yrisarri and Molina to Secretary Cass, dated New York, September 14, 1857, apprises our Government of an intended invasion, and is as follows:

"The undersigned, Minister Plenipotentiary of the Republics of Guatemala and of Salvador, and the Chargé d'Affaires of the Republic of Costa Rica, have the honor of bringing to the knowledge of his Excellency the Secretary of State, that there is no doubt as to the fact that there is now in course of preparation, in the southern section of the United States, an Expedition under the orders of Walker, the adventurer; which Expedition, according to the notices published in the public journals, will sail about the middle of this month, or the beginning of the next, bound for Boca del Toro, where it will take the armament, which, now ready in the port of New York, is to be transferred to that point. It is probable that the collecting of the members of the Expedition and of the armament, at that point, have for their object the entrance of these new invaders into Nicaragua through the port of San Jnan del Norte, since they can have no other point from which they could effect such entrance.

"The undersigned hope that the Government of the United States, though they may not be able to prevent the embarkation of this expedition, like former ones, so publicly and shamelessly proclaimed, will direct that a vessel of war of the United States shall prevent the debarkation of these aggressors in Boca del Toro, and give formal orders to the United States vessel that may be stationed at San Juan del Sur to repel, also, the landing of the expedition along that coast, and to turn them back to the United States as violators of their laws, and as disturbers of the peace and security of friendly nations.

"With the highest consideration, the undersigned have the honor of subscribing themselves the respectful and obedient servants of the Honorable the Secretary of State of the United States."—(*No.* 1, *Ex. Doc. No.* 24, 35*th Cong.*, 1*st Sess.*)

Upon the receipt of which, Mr. Cass issued the following circular, directed to the various Attorneys, Marshals, and Collectors of the United States. It is dated from the Department of State, Washington, September 18, 1857.

"From information received at this Department, there is reason to believe that lawless persons are now engaged within the limits of the United States in setting on foot and preparing the means for military expeditions to be carried on against the territories of Mexico, Nicaragua, and Costa Rica, Republics with whom the United States are at peace, in direct violation of the sixth section of the Act of Congress approved 20th of April, 1818. And under the eighth section of said Act it is made lawful for the President, or such person as he shall empower, to employ the land and naval forces of the United States, and the militia thereof, 'for the purpose of preventing the carrying on of any such expedition or enterprise from the territories or jurisdiction of the United States.' I am therefore directed by the President to call your attention to the subject, and to urge you to use all due diligence, and to avail yourself of all legitimate means at your command, to enforce these and all other provisions of the said Act of 20th April, 1818, against those who may be found to be engaged in setting on foot or preparing military expeditions against the territories of Mexico, Costa Rica, and Nicaragua, so manifestly prejudicial to the national character, and so injurious to the national interest. And you are also hereby instructed promptly to communicate to this Department the earliest information you may receive relative to such expeditions."—(*No.* 2, *Ex. Doc. No.* 24, 35*th Cong.* 1*st Sess.*)

The instant reply of Walker to Mr. Cass is worthy of insertion, and is dated September 29, 1857.

"It is correctly reported that the ministers of Costa Rica and Guatemala have asked for the active interposition of the United States for the purpose of preventing me and my companions from returning to Nicaragua. This request, it is further said, is based on the assumption that I have violated, or intend to violate, the neutrality laws of the United States.

"The want of all official intercourse between the Government of the United States and that of Nicaragua will, I hope, be a sufficient excuse for my addressing you on the faith of a public report. But the rumor comes in such a form that I am satisfied the ministers of Costa Rica and Guatemala have attempted to dishonor the Republic of Nicaragua in the eyes of the United States; and I am further convinced of this fact by a decree of

President Mora, dated at San José, on the 7th of August last, and ordered to be communicated to the diplomatic corps generally.

"The ministers of Costa Rica and Guatemala attempt to humiliate Nicaragua by presenting themselves to the United States as her protectors and guardians. In behalf of the Republic in which I claim to be rightful and lawful chief executive, I protest most earnestly against this assumption on the part of Costa Rica and Guatemala, and ask that the Government of the United States will not permit itself to be influenced by such pretensions on the part of these two Central American powers. On the contrary, it is to be hoped that the United States will, by its conduct, assert and vindicate the independence of its sister Republic, the sovereign State of Nicaragua.

"It is my duty further to say, that the people of Nicaragua have not consented to the military authority at present exercised over them by the agents of Costa Rica and Guatemala, and that they, therefore, cannot be held responsible for any interference of these latter States in the administration of the municipal laws of your Government. Conceiving that the ministers of Costa Rica and Guatemala cannot justify any suggestions they make to the United States concerning the execution of its own Acts of Congress, I desire to relieve Nicaragua from any responsibility for such intermeddling suggestions.

"So far as any violation on my part of the Acts of Congress is concerned, I deny the charge with scorn and indignation. Having been received in the United States when forced for a time to leave Nicaragua, I have in all respects been obedient to its laws. And permit me to assure you that I shall not so far forget my duty as an officer of Nicaragua as to violate the laws of the United States while enjoying the rights of hospitality within its limits."

The letter of Señor Yrisarri, asking for the intervention of the United States, dates October 8, 1857, a portion of which we here insert.

"Nicaragua, unhappily, has been the scene of frequent and sudden revolutions. Her internal dissensions and strifes have produced her national weakness and invited the attacks of the corrupt and the wicked. From such an attack upon her sovereignty and national rights she has just been freed. But scarcely had the last one of these miserable fillibusters been expelled from her territory, when we find the same contemptible leader—who only has ability enough to perpetrate crime—ready again to invade our shores and repeat the same outrages so lately enacted by him. Can the United States Government prevent this new invasion? It can. But not by means of the neutrality laws, for these are too weak, as experience has repeatedly proved, to restrain any body, much less to restrain the defiant and mad enterprises of fillibusterism, that scandal of the age. But this Government has the power sufficient to prevent the projected invasion by the performance of an act of simple justice and comity toward a weak but friendly and confiding people."

The notice of General Walker's letter to Secretary Cass by Señor Yrisarri, dated November 10, 1857, embraces the position of Nicaragua relative to Walker's claim to its Executive, and as we have given one party full latitude, equity demands that the other should be heard. Señor Yrisarri says—

"The undersigned, Minister Plenipotentiary of the Republics of Guatemala and of Salvador, has the honor of imparting to the Hon. Secretary of State of the United States that he has seen, in the public papers printed in these States, a letter addressed to His Excellency, and said to be written by the Sonora and Nicaraguan adventurer, William Walker, who has unduly arrogated the name of President of Nicaragua, by which he has never been recognized in the States of Central America, in any of the Spanish American Republics, in this Government of the United States, or in any other Government of the world, and who never could have been President of that Republic, because the Nicaraguan Constitution excludes any one not a native of Central America from the exercise of the executive power of that State.

"Under the assumption that the letter alluded to has actually been addressed by said Walker to the Honorable Secretary of

State of the United States, it is the duty of the undersigned to contradict the assertions by which the writer has endeavored to mislead this Government and to continue deceiving the people of the United States.

"Truly astonishing is the impudence with which this adventurer, expelled from Nicaragua by her forces and those of all the Central Americans, attempts to constitute himself the Champion of Nicaragua. The man, whose course in that country was an exclusive one of assassination of the defenders of that country—the burner of whole villages, the spoiler of national property, the trampler on all rights, the plunderer of churches, the leader of the foreign stipendiaries which he gathered under his own banner—alone could have alleged his right of citizenship in Nicaragua, and thereby held as dunces all men else on earth.

"This same man, without bitter insult on the common sense of mankind, could not have contrived a more absurd pretext under which to carry into effect the expedition which he has levied to recover a treacherously-usurped authority, than this claim that his expedition is not one hostile to the country, but a peaceful colonizing enterprise! He himself has, time and again, and with characteristic impudence, published that his projected expedition looks to a recuperation of power in that country; whilst in the very letter attributed to him, and addressed to the Honorable Secretary of the United States, he claims for himself the title of 'Lawful Executive Power of Nicaragua.'

"This is ample to prove that the expedition, composed of spurious colonists, is, in reality, one of soldiers, moving with the design of supporting this dream-begotten legitimate executive power of the country. But whatever may be the character of this colonizer, and of those colonists under a new patent, they cannot set foot on the territory which they are about to invade, nor be there received, save as real pirates; because, in Nicaragua and in Costa Rica, as well as in the other Republics of Spanish America, Walker is held in no other light than that of a traitor to the party which he went to serve in Nicaragua, of an usurper of the sovereignty of that country, of a blood-shedder, whose object was to destroy the defenders of their country; whilst his satellites were nothing else than accomplices of his crimes. In proof of this, I transmit to the Secretary of State the decree of the 31st of August last, officially communicated to me by the Minister of Foreign Relations of Nicaragua, by which it will be clearly seen that the expedition which Walker intends to lead into that country, under the appellation of colonists, will be received as an expedition of pirates; in view of which, communication through the Isthmus has been ordered to be foreclosed.

"Neither in Nicaragua, nor in any Republic of Central America, is any colony desired, formed by Walker, or by any other adventurer, who, like him, has dreamed of mastery over its lands, to divide them among his foreign followers. Experience amply teaches there, as well as here, that the thousands of individuals shipped as colonists for Nicaragua, from New York and New Orleans during the course of the last two years, went there with the exclusive aim of waging war against the natives of the land, under the command of an intrusive usurper. And if, with miserable cunning, they can baffle the laws of the United States, which forbid the citizens of those States to disturb the peace of friendly nations, they will certainly not deceive now, as they never have been able to deceive, the Central Americans; and they must not complain of the fate that may befall them, however hard it may appear to them. Natural law imposes on the Central Americans the duty of making an example of the incorrigible violaters of the laws of all the nations.

"Walker never was, nor can he ever be, President of Nicaragua, or a citizen of that Republic from the time that he was declared to be a traitor to it; nor can any men that may be led by him, or any one else in his name, fail to be received and treated in any other manner than that due to bandits and pirates, by whatever name they may be known, or from whatever quarter they may come. This is a fact which grows out of authentic documents from the true executive power, national, and not foreign, of Nicaragua; and to this should the citizens of the United States rivet their attention, so that they may not venture to follow the private banner of the adventurer of Sonora and of Nicaragua.

"It is of world-wide notoriety that Walker was not elected President of Nicaragua, save by a foreign soldiery, which backed him in the usurpation of the supreme power which could not be vested; and wonderful, I repeat it, is the impudence of the man who pretends to vindicate, as a right, that which bears no other character than that of the worst imaginable outrage.

"The undersigned, as Minister Plenipotentiary of Guatemala and of Salvador, and in his appointed capacity by the Government of Nicaragua to represent her in the United States, cannot but protest against the contemplated expedition of colonization and peace to Nicaragua under the leadership of Walker; declaring that, as it cannot be received in that Republic save as a hostile expedition, it shall be treated by the three States, Guatemala, Salvador, and Nicaragua, as one of real pirates. This the undersigned has deemed it his duty to bring to the knowledge of the Government of the United States."

CHAPTER XXII.

A PROMISE FULFILLED—GENERAL HENNINGSEN'S LETTER TO SECRETARY CASS —HIS COMMISSION FROM PRESIDENT WALKER—WHAT HE SAYS ABOUT WALKER'S ELECTION—HIS PERMANENCY AS A RULER—HIS SOLICITUDE FOR THE SOLDIERY—AN APPEAL TO THE PRESIDENT OF THE UNITED STATES—THINKS CAPTAIN DAVIS DID NOT DO THE RIGHT THING—WHAT PRESIDENT MORA DID—WHAT GENERAL WALKER DID—HOW LONG THE INVADERS WERE KEPT FROM INVESTING RIVAS—HOW THEY ATTEMPTED AT VARIOUS TIMES TO STORM THE PLACE—HOW ANXIOUS THEY EVENTUALLY BECAME TO KEEP OUT—POSITION OF BESIEGERS AND BESIEGED ON THE FIRST OF MAY—WHAT WALKER EXPECTED TO DO, AND HOW HE WAS GOING TO DO IT—WHAT CAPTAIN DAVIS DID, AND THE WAY HE DID IT—HOW IT AFFECTED WALKER'S PLANS—THE SCHOONER GRANADA SEIZED AND HANDED OVER TO THE COSTA RICANS—THE GUATEMALA NAVY PUTS TO SEA AND MURDERS CAPTAIN LILLY.

WE promised, in Chapter Twentieth, to give the documents relative to the evacuation of Nicaragua. We now discharge that promise, by inserting extracts embracing the points at issue, from a letter of General Henningsen's to Mr. Cass, dated, Washington, November 12, 1857.

"On the first of May last, in Nicaragua, I was charged by President Walker with negotiating, drafting, and subsequently carrying into execution the Convention of Rivas. That negotiation was entered into, and the capitulation was made solely with a United States officer, Captain Davis, of the United States ship-of-war St. Mary, under the guaranty of the United States flag that certain terms would be observed by the besiegers.

"General Walker was regarded as the legitimate President of Nicaragua, and without any possibility of influencing the ballot, was elected by a larger majority than any President ever received before, or probably will ever receive again in Nicaragua, because the only classes who labor or produce had witnessed under his auspices the abolition of forced military service, and saw in his election, for the first time in their generation, the prospect of not being coerced by ambitious factionists to fight through interminable revolutions for a cause in which they took no interest. When the pressure of internal treachery, foreign invasion, and extraneous influence, prevented him from protecting them from conscription, they came to regard this as an illusion, and resigned themselves, as they had done from time immemorial, to be dragged from their peaceful avocations, and driven to slaughter by leaders whom it was never my fortune to see or hear of in the front of battle. It is difficult for any one acquainted with facts, not to have regarded

General Walker as the legitimate President of Nicaragua, since no valid election can take place as long as the Costa Rican foreign force occupies any part of the territory of that Republic. It is worth observing that, besides being still *de jure* President, General Walker was *de facto* President of Nicaragua far beyond the average term. In the fifteen changes of Government that have taken place in this respect within six years, there is only Chamorro, whose term of power exceeded by one month, and President Pineda, by four months, General Walker's actual exercise of that office.

"Now, sir," he continues, "so great was the solicitude of President Walker with regard to our Nicaraguan fellow soldiers in Rivas, and so strong was generally the feeling of their American companions in arms, that I am only expressing the common sentiment when I emphatically declare, that if ever circumstances could have driven us to capitulate with the Central American invaders or insurgents, I would have run all risks of dying, sword in hand, sooner than have surrendered these good and true men on any guaranty less strong than the obligation of our opponents toward a powerful nation.

"They naturally looked to the Americans in Rivas efficiently to guaranty their safety. President Walker, who entrusted me with the details of that negotiation, and my companions in arms who know that I was therewith entrusted, look to me, and I, sir, have the flag of the American Union to look to. My duty toward the sufferers, and my honor as a soldier oblige me, therefore, respectfully to appeal for redress of this great wrong to the Chief Magistrate of this Republic, whom I believe it is proper that I should address through you."

Again: "An attempt has been made to create the impression that the Nicaraguan army at Rivas was in an utterly desperate position, from which it was relieved by the intervention of Captain Davis, whose interference is pretended to have been only officious, dictated solely by motives of humanity and undertaken on his own responsibility.

"Now, sir, though I do not wish to impugn the motives of Captain Davis, and though we have never done the Cabinet at Washington the injustice to believe that he acted either upon its instructions or in conformity with its intentions, I must remark firstly, that Captain Davis, as commanding the only United States forces there, represented for us the United States; secondly, that in as far as our position was desperate, it was rendered so by his own act; and thirdly, that after the commission of that act, our situation was not desperate enough for us to have trusted our wounded, or our native companions in arms to the mercy of our opponents without a better guaranty than the word they had so often violated.

"We could not have done so, remembering that in the Spring of 1856, President Mora had preached a crusade of which the avowed object was the extermination of all North

Americans who took any part in the affairs of a (to him) foreign country; that in March of that year he shot all the stragglers and wounded who fell into his hands after the disaster of Santa Rosa; that in the following April he put to death peaceable American citizens in Virgin Bay; and that, being attacked in Rivas, Nicaragua, which he was invading, by President Walker, he (President Mora) fled back to Costa Rica with his brother, General Mora, leaving General Cañas to bring back his shattered forces; that General Cañas was obliged to abandon his sick and wounded Costa Ricans to General Walker's mercy, who had them tended with the same care as his own. We could not have done so, remembering that after this, in the following October, peaceful citizens were massacred at Granada, amongst others a minister of the Gospel, the Rev. Mr. Wheeler, and Mr. Lawless, a merchant long resident in the country, the neutrality of both of whom was beyond cavil or dispute.

"As to the condition of the Nicaraguan army under President Walker, in Rivas, the attempt to besiege that city began on the 27th of January, 1857, he being at that time cut off from all communication with the Atlantic States by the unlawful seizure of the transit steamers. By repeated and vigorous attacks—once at Obraje, four times at San Jorge, on the 29th of January, 3d and 11th of February, and the 16th of March, by sweeping the transit road, and by various skirmishes, the invaders and insurgents were for seven weeks prevented from investing Rivas.

"For the remaining six weeks, up to the 1st of May, Rivas was more or less closely invested by means of four strongly entrenched camps with connecting lines. During the whole of this siege, and indeed for nearly five months preceding the 1st of May, 1857, we had received only one hundred and thirty-five men reinforcement. The besiegers, who reached Obraje, according to their own report, with two thousand one hundred and sixty men, had been during this time reinforced by five thousand men, making the total force brought against us over seven thousand men. After the investment two attempts were made to carry the place by surprise and storm, viz.: on the the 23d of March and 11th of April. On the 23d the besiegers took possession of all the houses outside of our works, but by two o'clock P. M. were driven out of them back to their lines with great loss, leaving in our hands one cannon and thirty prisoners, including a Colonel of Artillery.

"On the 11th of April, 1857, led in by a deserter, they succeeded in capturing one side of the lower plaza, and attempted to storm on other sides. In two hours they were again driven back with great slaughter, leaving in our hands nearly one hundred prisoners, all those who got within our works being killed or compelled to surrender. Their loss on that occasion has been since ascertained to have exceeded eight hundred.

"From that time to the 1st of May they made no further attack and received no reinforcement of any consequence. They had none whatever to expect, except one corps of Salvadorians, whose advent and fidelity was doubtful and unimportant, and whose leader shortly after attempted a revolution. Up to the 11th of April the besiegers had been under the impression that they could capture Rivas if they could enter it. They were then eager to get in. The result of the 11th destroyed this illusion, and they were equally anxious to keep out.

"On the morning of the 1st of May the position of the besiegers and of the besieged was as follows: Of the seven thousand men brought by the allied foreign invaders and insurgents against Rivas (two-thirds of which force had consisted of foreign invaders) there remained six hundred allies, and from one thousand to one thousand two hundred Nicaraguan insurgents. Their entrenched camps had been much strengthened, but they could no longer with this reduced force, man effectively the connecting lines, which were over two miles in extent, and the besieged sent scouts and messengers through them, who almost always returned in safety. The besiegers were, besides, short of powder, and threatened with cholera and the rainy season, both of which had set in a fortnight earlier the year preceding.

The besieged, on the other hand, were straitened for provisions and encumbered with wounded. For a month they had been living on horse and mule meat, sugar and chocolate. They had been much weakened by desertion, but desertion had nearly done its worst. Their force consisted of two hundred and sixty Americans and forty natives capable of bearing arms. They had still left on the 1st of May two or three days' provisions, viz. : two oxen, two mules, three horses, and one thousand pounds of sugar. They were well supplied with ammunition, half their store being in Rivas. In the harbor of San Juan del Sur they had the war schooner Granada, which contained the other half of their ammunition, besides several hundred stand of small arms.

"President Walker had remained thus long in Rivas, apprehending that Colonel Lockridge might march round by Chontales, and because there was every reason to believe that shortly after the action of the 11th April, the enemy would be obliged to raise the siege. It was his intention, after ordering the schooner Granada to sail for Realejo or some point northward, to evacuate Rivas when he came to his last day's provision. He had no doubt, by a night attack, of being able to force his way through their now weakened lines; no thought of the besiegers attempting to pursue him till after daybreak, nor fear of being easily able to route their vanguard with his rear if they did. There was then nothing to impede his march to Realejo, or other points where the schooner Granada with the ammunition and spare arms would have met him. In the adjoining districts, where, but for the necessity of protecting the transit, he long since would have carried on the war, his native friends were anxiously awaiting either till the besiegers exhausted their strength on Rivas, or till we appeared amongst them. It is true that the besieged would have had to destroy the ammunition and heavier pieces at Rivas, and would have been compelled to leave their wounded behind them, but they would have carried with them the substantial guaranty of one hundred prisoners as hostages.

"If it be doubted whether the besieged were strong enough to break through the lines of the besiegers, I have only to refer to many examples in the war, where, with a smaller force, greater obstacles were overcome. I will cite only three: On the 11th of November, 1856, with two hundred and sixty-five men, and one gun, President Walker carried the entrenched camp and all the barricades on the transit route, held by General Cañas, with eight hundred Costa Ricans, and at least four times stronger than the lines of investment at Rivas. On the 17th of the same month, with two hundred and sixty men, and three guns, he forced his way into Masaya, defended by two thousand men, captured half the city, held it for three days, and was hourly gaining ground, though ninety of his small force were killed and wounded. On the night of the 11th of November, one hundred and sixty men, landed by him three miles from Granada, carried successively four lines of barricades, and reported to me at daybreak on the 12th, at the Guadaloupe church.

"To the schooner Granada, in the harbor of San Juan, there was no difficulty in communicating orders. Its immense importance at this juncture to the besieged is apparent, both as a magazine and as a means of conveying material of war, which they had no other means of transporting.

"Now, sir, just at this critical juncture, and before the question of capitulation had been discussed, Captain Davis formally declared to me, on the night of the 30th of April, that he had embargoed the schooner by leaving orders with the United States force, which he commanded, to prevent her from leaving the harbor of San Juan, and he expressed his unalterable determination to take possession of her before he left the harbor. It was this act of intervention on the part of a United States officer which alone caused President Walker to entertain the proposed terms of capitulation. For the act, that is to say, the order to prevent the Nicaraguan schooner-of-war from leaving the harbor had already been given before he declared his intention of seizing her.

"The schooner Granada, (whose commander, Fayssoux, had fought her through as gallant an action as any living officer in any navy in the world has fought,) had been lying for many weeks next to the St. Mary, their officers interchanging courtesies. There could be no reason or pretext for preventing her leaving the port or taking possession of her on the 1st of May, which had not existed for many weeks previously. There could be no motive for so doing, except that the besieged in Rivas had never before been reduced to depend on her possession, a motive so base that if Captain Davis endeavored thereby to justify the change in his conduct from professed friendship to active hostility, which I cannot believe, I am sure that neither the American people nor its Executive would hold this a justification.

"The only explanation of Captain Davis' conduct is in the supposition that he had already pledged himself to give up the Granada to the besiegers, and, in fact, we afterward learned that when he first announced his action and future determination with regard to the schooner Granada, and proposed the outline of a capitulation to the besieged, he had for many days been negotiating it with the enemy, a fact of which the besieged were utterly ignorant, and which explained the unaccountable perseverance of the besiegers in continuing their siege, or their ability to keep their forces together through the end of April, they naturally concluding that these propositions were made with our knowledge and concurrence. By embargoing the Granada he constrained President Walker into the acceptance of terms which otherwise he would never have thought of. But even after Captain Davis had thereby rendered our position so precarious, President Walker would sooner have run the last hazard of war than have trusted his men, his wounded, or his native fellow-citizens to the faith of the invading or insurgent leaders without some such solid guaranty as either hostages or the flag of some powerful and civilized nation. Under circumstances more desperate than Captain Davis had rendered ours in Rivas, we persistently refused to do so.

"On the retreat from Granada, there were in Granada, or between Granada and the Lake, four hundred and nineteen souls. Of these seventy-three were wounded men, seventy women and children. Of the two hundred and seventy-six men capable of bearing arms, forty-seven were cut off within ten minutes of the first attack. Of the remaining two hundred and twenty-nine, seventy-five were subsequently killed or wounded, besides those who died of cholera and typhus, (amounting to one hundred and twenty of all sexes and ages). They were exposed for seventeen days to rain and sunshine, without shelter, night or day, living on horse and mule meat, short of ammunition, incessantly fighting, and surrounded by a force larger than remained to beleaguer us in Rivas on the first of May—yet surrender or capitulation was never contemplated. At Rivas, the responsibility of the United States flag was held to be sufficient security for the safety of those whom we were bound to protect at every sacrifice.

"Captain Davis put into execution his threat of seizing the schooner Granada, after we had carried out, on our part, the terms of the capitulation, in which that vessel was not mentioned He caused her to be seized by his first lieutenant, who sprung upon her the broadside of the St. Mary, and started a hundred men in boats to board her. Captain Fayssoux, with his crew, (then of seventeen men,) prepared for action, and only surrendered her on the written order of President Walker, who ordered him to yield to this demonstration of overwhelming force.

"After taking possession of her, Captain Davis handed over this Nicaraguan schooner, not to the Nicaraguan insurgents, but to the Costa Ricans, who had no claim to her, and who could never have taken her, for the simple reason that they had already lost in the attempt their only man-of-war, the brig Onse de Abril, which, of the burden of two hundred and twenty-five tons, with four nine-pounders, and a crew of one hundred and eighteen men, was destroyed after a desperate action by the little schooner Granada, of seventy-five tons, with two sixes, and twenty-eight men crew. Her gallant captain had the mortification of seing her given up by Captain Davis to a Costa Rican Captain, a Jamaica negro, who had formerly been servant to an American officer. After this step, the two vessels which constituted the Guatemala navy, and to which the Granada had vainly offered battle, put to sea, and thereby obtained the opportunity of recently murdering, for the sake of his cargo, Christopher Lilly, an American neutral, trading on the coast." (*Ex. Doc. No.* 24, 35*th Cong.*, 1*st Sess., p.* 22.)

CHAPTER XXIII.

NICARAGUA THREATENS TO SUSPEND THE TRANSIT—HER PREAMBLE AND DECREES—LIEUT. ALMY APPLIES FOR INSTRUCTIONS—SUPPOSES A CASE IN WHICH FILLIBUSTERS FIGURE LARGELY—DELICATE POINTS GROWING OUT OF IT—DOES NOT WISH TO COMPROMISE OUR GOVERNMENT—SECRETARY TOUCEY POSTS HIM UP—SAYS HE MUST PREVENT FILLIBUSTERS FROM LANDING—COMMODORE PAULDING HEARD FROM—SAYS HARD THINGS ABOUT WALKER AND HIS MEN—CONSIDERS HIS REASONS QUITE SUFFICIENT FOR SENDING THE FILLIBUSTERS HOME—REFUSES ANY CO-OPERATION FROM OTHER POWERS—WALKER GIVES HIS PAROLE OF HONOR—GOES HOME AT HIS OWN EXPENSE—GIVES HIMSELF UP TO MARSHAL RYNDERS—SENOR YRISARRI WRITES TO MR. CASS—SAYS NICARAGUA CONFIRMS THE CONTRACT WITH THE TRANSIT COMPANY—THANKS THE UNITED STATES FOR TAKING WALKER AWAY—THINKS SHE DID THE HANDSOME THING—WANTS HIS LETTER PUBLISHED.

THE decree of Nicaragua to suspend the Transit, in the event of the appearance of freebooters in Central America is dated Managua, August 31, 1857, and is as follows:

"Administrative Department of the Supreme Government of the Republic of Nicaragua—God! Union! Liberty!—The

Supreme Executive Power has been pleased to issue the following decree:

Whereas, the Atlantic and Pacific Maritime Canal Company are about to commence the re-establishing of the line of Transit from one sea to the other, from San Juan del Norte, to San Juan del Sur, and *vice versa*, as it is stipulated in the agreement of the 22d of September, 1849, the supplementary one of the 11th of April, 1850, and in the last of the 19th of June of the present year, which resolves the conditions of Article 30 of the original contract; and—

"Whereas, said establishment is of the highest interest to the United States of North America, and for the nations of the world in general, which advantages the Government of Nicaragua protects, so long as the freebooters shall not make attempts against the Independence of this Republic, and that of the other States of Central America: Decrees,

"*Article* 1. The Republic of Nicaragua protests against all and whatever attempts which freebooters and pirates, of any denomination or from any quarter, may make against her independence, or against that of any other of the States.

"*Article* 2. From the moment that such freebooters may make their appearance, and that it shall be known that they are preparing a new invasion, or that in effect they intend such against the Republic or against the other States of Central America, the Transit shall be suspended, as all the effects of the agreement entered into with the Maritime Canal Company on the 19th of June.

"*Article* 3. Should such an attempt or invasion take place after the re-establishment of the Transit by said Company, and the latter have complied strictly with the conditions of the contract relative to assistance to Nicaragua in defending her independence, her sovereignty over the Isthmus, and the neutrality of the same; or should said Company, before the restoration of the Transit, lend efficient aid and co-operation in said defense, it will, in the former case, continue in operation, and in the latter, the Transit shall not be closed, nor will any change be allowed in the exercise of the rights stipulated for the Company in said contract.

"*Article* 4. Let this be communicated to the Minister Plenipotentiary in Washington, to the President of the Company, and to the Ministers on the Diplomatic list."

The following letter from Lieut. Almy, dated Oct. 7, 1847, to the Secretary of the Navy, asking for instructions relative to the course to be adopted by him in the event of seizing a "suspicious vessel," bears upon the question of the Right of Search, and is highly interesting, as is also the Secretary's reply thereto, dated Oct. 12, 1857.

"In regard to the instructions received by me from the Navy Department, dated the 3d instant, I am there referred for my guidance to the law enacted by Congress, approved

April 20, 1818, entitled 'An Act for the punishment of certain crimes against the United States,' and am also referred to a Circular issued by the State Department, dated September 18, 1857, addressed to various civil officers of the United States.

"These directions to preserve the neutrality of the country are very plain for the government of officers where they are required to act in the ports of, or in the jurisdiction of, the United States; but I must confess that I might find myself embarrassed when required to act in a foreign and neutral port. Therefore, I must be pardoned for soliciting from the Honorable Secretary of the Navy answers to certain questions, and more specific instructions in the premises.

"Suppose, for instance, that, while lying in a port of Central America, an American steamer should enter having on board a large number of men whom I suspect of being 'fillibusters'—people intending to land for the purpose of obtaining possession of the country, and of forming a Government there. Must I seize this vessel and bring her into a port of the United States, or merely use the force placed at my command to prevent their landing?

"It is generally conceded that American citizens have a right to travel and go where they please. Suppose that this suspicious body of men inform me that they are going to travel—that their intention is to cross the Isthmus, or intend to settle peaceably in the country for the purpose of developing its agricultural resources; indeed, that they have been invited to come and settle there?

"These and other delicate points and kindred questions which may suggest themselves to the Honorable Secretary of the Navy, I deem it necessary to be enlightened upon in order that I may not compromise the Government, and at the same time be enabled to assert and exercise the power entrusted to my hands with due spirit, dignity, and justice."

The Secretary writes as follows:

"In reply to your letter of the 7th instant, it is true that American citizens have a right to travel and to go where they please, when engaged in lawful pursuit, but not to violate the laws of their own or of any other country. They have a right to expatriate and to become citizens of any country which is willing to receive them, but not to make that right a mere cloak and cover for a warlike expedition against it or its Government. Your instructions do not authorize you to act arbitrarily, or upon mere suspicion. You will not seize an American vessel, or bring her into port, or use the force under your command to prevent her landing her passengers upon mere suspicion. You will be careful not to interfere with lawful commerce. But where you find that an American vessel is manifestly engaged in carrying on an expedition or enterprise from the territories or jurisdiction of the United States against the territories of Mexico, Nicaragua, or Costa Rica, contrary to the 6th section of the Act of Congress of April 20, 1818, already referred to, you will use the force under your command to prevent it, and will not permit the men or arms engaged in it, or designed for it, to be landed in any part of Mexico or Central America."

The following letter from Commodore Paulding, dated December 15, 1857, Flag-Ship Wabash, off Aspinwall, to the Secretary of the Navy, is *apropos*—

"My letter of the 12th instant informed the Department that I had broken up the camp of General Walker, at Punta Arenas, disarmed his lawless followers, and sent them to Norfolk in the Saratoga. The General came here with me, and will take passage in one of the steamers for New York, where he will present himself to the Marshal of the District.

"The Department being in possession of all the facts in relation to Walker's escape with his followers from the United States, as well as the letters of Captain Chatard and Walker to me after he landed at Point Arenas, the merits of the whole question will, I presume, be fully comprehended.

"I could not regard Walker and his followers in any other light than as outlaws who had escaped from the vigilance of the officers of the Government, and left our shores for the purpose of rapine and murder, and I saw no other way to vindicate the law and redeem the honor of our country than by disarming and sending them home. In doing so, I am sensible of the responsibility that I have incurred, and confidently look to the Government for my justification. Regarded in its true light, the case appears to me a clear one; the points few and strong. Walker came to Point Arenas from the United States, having, in violation of law, set on foot a military organization to make war on a people with whom we are at peace. He landed there with armed men and munitions of war, in defiance of the guns of a ship-of-war placed there to prevent his landing. With nothing to show that he acted by authority, he formed a camp, hoisted the Nicaraguan flag, called it the 'head-quarters of the Army of Nicaragua,' and signed himself the Commander-in-chief.

"With this pretension he claimed the right of a lawful general over all persons and things within sight of his flag. Without right or authority he landed fifty men at the mouth of the river Colorado, seized the fort of Castillo, on the San Juan, captured steamers and the goods of merchants in transit to the interior, killed men, and made prisoners of the peaceful inhabitants, sending to the harbor of San Juan del Norte some thirty or forty men, women, and children in the steamer Morgan.

"In doing these things without the show of authority, they were guilty of rapine and murder, and must be regarded as outlaws and pirates. They can have no claim to be regarded in any other light. Humanity, as well as law and justice, and national honor, demanded the dispersion of these lawless men. The remnant of these miserable beings who surrendered at Rivas were conveyed in this ship last summer to New York, and their sufferings are yet fresh in the memory of all on board.

"Besides the sufferings that would necessarily be inflicted upon an innocent and unoffending people, these lawless followers of General Walker, misguided and deceived into a career of crime, would doubtless have perished in Central America, or their mutilated and festering bodies have been brought back to their friends at the expense of their country.

"For the above reasons, which appear to my mind quite sufficient, I have disarmed and sent to the United States General William Walker and his outlawed and piratical followers for trial, or for whatever action the Government in its wisdom may think proper to pursue.

"Captain Ommanny, of H. B. M. ship Brunswick, offered to co-operate with me in removing the party from Point Arenas, but as they were my countrymen, I deemed it proper to decline the participation of a foreign flag."

General Walker accordingly took passage in a mail steamer from Aspinwall for New York, preferring this to a Government vessel, as will be seen by the following. It is dated United States Steam Frigate Wabash, off San Juan del Norte, December 11, 1857, and signed "WILLIAM WALKER."

"The option being given me to go to the United States in the Saratoga, or take passage at my own expense from Aspinwall to New York, I have preferred to return by way of Aspinwall, and will deliver this communication, in person, to the Marshal for the Southern District of New York."

The communication referred to was addressed by Commodore Paulding to Isaiah Rynders, Marshal for the Southern District of New York. It is of the same date as the above, was duly delivered, and is as follows:

"This will be handed to you by General William Walker, who has given me his parole of honor that he will present it to you in person. With the naval force of this squadron I arrested General Walker on Punta Arenas, on the 8th instant, for a violation of the neutrality laws of the United States, he having set on foot in the United States an unlawful military organization to make war upon a people with whom we are at peace, and was, at the time of his arrest, at the head of said organization, in the act of making war, as above stated.

"As Marshal for the Southern District of New York, I consign him to your custody."

The following, from Señor Yrisarri to Mr. Cass, contains the confirmation of the contract made with the Atlantic and Pacific Ship Canal Company, and other matters of interest. It is dated December 30th, 1857.

"The undersigned, Minister Plenipotentiary of the Republic

of Nicaragua, has the honor of communicating to his Excellency the Secretary of State of the United States, that on the 15th of last month the authority of the Republic of Nicaragua was assumed by General Martinez, elected to the presidency by an immense majority of votes, and that one of the first acts of the new head of that Republic was to confirm the appointment made in the person of the undersigned by former national governments as Envoy Extraordinary and Minister Plenipotentiary to the Government of the United States.

"The undersigned deems it also to be his duty to inform his Excellency the Secretary of State, that the Constituent Assembly of Nicaragua has approved and confirmed the contract made by the undersigned with the American Atlantic and Pacific Ship Canal Company, the only one vested with the privilege of carrying across the Isthmus—as the only one, also, which, for the present and so long as the Government will not have otherwise disposed—has the right to carry emigrants to that country, under such conditions as have been imposed on said Company. All other emigrants or colonizers, whatsoever, that may be conveyed to that country will be refused admission, and compelled to depart from the territory of the Republic; or they will be dealt with as enemies of the Republic should they appear there in the character borne by those lately introduced by the incorrigible adventurer William Walker.

"The undersigned, in the name of the three governments which he represents, returns thanks to the Government of the United States for having taken away the adventurer William Walker and his invading band from the point of which they had taken possession on the coast of Nicaragua; thus freeing those friendly countries from the evils with which they would have been visited had these disturbers of the peace of nations been allowed the possibility of increasing their forces by new recruits. Those who, in the service which the Government of the United States has rendered to its friend, the Republic of Nicaragua, would seek for a warrant to say that the Nicaraguan territory has been violated, will hardly find it, from the moment that the world will have learned that the Government of Nicaragua, far from complaining of a violation of her territory, looks upon that act as an assistance, directed in behalf of its inviolability, which was wounded, in effect, by certain adventurers from the United States; and that it considers such assistance extended by this Government, as a consequence of the measures which, by his note of the 14th of September last, the undersigned had asked this Government to adopt, giving orders to the navy of the United States to capture the violators of the laws of neutrality.

"The point from which Commodore Paulding forced away those bandits, the violators of the laws of all nations, and, as such, justly assimilated, by the law of nations, to pirates and foes of mankind, is an almost desert one, on which there exists no Nicaraguan authorities that could have managed the apprehension of those felons. Nicaragua, therefore, considers that the proceedings of Commodore Paulding against Walker and his horde were entirely justifiable; for, as a man-of-war of any nation may take up pirates from a desert island, or one so thinly peopled that they can assert their dominion over it, although that island might belong to another sovereign nation, just so can bandits be apprehended, as enemies of the human race, by the armed vessels of a friendly nation, on a point of a foreign coast, which may be placed under circumstances like to those of the island mentioned by way of illustration.

"Considering it highly important that the tenor of this note—especially the portion touching emigration to Nicaragua—should be made public, the undersigned would enter tain the hope that the Secretary of State will find no objection to have its contents published.

"The undersigned, with highest consideration, has the honor of tendering to the Secretary of State the renewed assurance that he is his respectful servant."

CHAPTER XXIV.

LANDING OF COLUMBUS ON THE MOSQUITO SHORE—ARE THE MOSQUITOES AN INDEPENDENT NATION?—WHAT VISCOUNT PALMERSTON SAYS ABOUT IT—THE CLAYTON AND BULWER TREATY—CONFLICTING VIEWS AS TO ITS CONSTRUCTION—THE ENGLISH CHARGE D'AFFAIRES TO THE GOVERNMENT OF NICARAGUA—A RUNNING FIRE OF GASCONADE—THE SAME OFFICIAL ON BOUNDARY LINES—WHAT BONNYCASTLE SAYS—TREATIES OF PEACE, BOUNDARIES AND COMMERCE BETWEEN GREAT BRITAIN AND SPAIN—WHAT AN OLD ENGLISH AUTHOR SAYS—MOTION TO CENSURE IN THE HOUSE OF LORDS—REFUSAL—THE SAMBOES—PROBABLE ORIGIN OF THE MOSQUITO NAME—THE MOSQUITO SHORE COMPLETELY EVACUATED—THE SAMBOES IN A REAL ESTATE OPERATION—THE DOG IN THE MANGER—REVOLTED NEGROES FROM ST. DOMINGO—THE PRODUCTIONS OF THE MOSQUITOES—BELIZE—ITS ARMORIAL BEARINGS—SURPLICE FEES.

COLUMBUS landed upon the Mosquito Coast, on Sunday, August the fourteenth, A. D. 1502, and is said to have taken formal possession of the country. A gun bearing his name, has been found imbedded in the sand, about twelve miles north of Greytown. This territory, held by the Republic of Nicaragua, to be but the Atlantic margin of her domain, and as strongly controverted by Great Britain, has a present historic importance, as to whether the Moscos or Mosquitoes, in fact, be an independent, sovereign nation. Whether they ever have been, is a mooted question, and hence we approach the subject, aware of the importance of our position, nor shall we exceed the bounds of evidence in endeavoring to illustrate our pages.

A previous chapter on this subject, was general in its tone. We shall particularize now, and uphold the views of the United States. When the question was broached, the subjoined was presented to Mr. Lawrence, in which, as to whether the Protectorate is of modern data or not, as claimed by Great Britain, is set forth. It is dated, Foreign Office, Jan. 5, 1850, and is as follows:

"Viscount Palmerston presents his compliments to Mr. Lawrence, and begs to communicate to him, for his perusal, a translation in Spanish of a letter from Mr. Chatfield, her Majesty's Chargé d'Affaires in Guatemala, addressed to the Government of Nicaragua, on the 5th of September last, containing a statement of facts, showing the nature of the connection which has existed since the middle of the Seventeenth century, between Great Britain and the Mosquito nation."—(*Senate, Doc.* 27, *p.* 50.)

We must not overlook the fact, that the "Clayton and Bulwer Treaty" was concluded between the United States and

Great Britain, April 19, 1850, and proclaimed in July of the same year. John M. Clayton, in his letter dated, Department of State, Washington, May 7, 1850, informs the Country, that he has "negotiated a Treaty with Sir Henry Bulwer;" and in conclusion, he adds, "Her (Great Britain's) protectorate will be reduced to a shadow—*stat nominis umbra*, for she can neither occupy, fortify, or colonize, or exercise dominion or control in any part of the Mosquito Coast or Central America. To attempt to do either of these things, after the exchange of ratifications, would inevitably produce a rupture with the United States. By the terms, neither party can occupy to protect, nor protect to occupy." Sir Henry Bulwer denied this construction in his letters to Mr. Webster, in which he holds, "that the Convention was not designed to affect the position of Her Majesty in respect to the Mosquito Shore."

On the 15th of August, 1850, the English Representative in Central America, addressed the Government of Nicaragua as follows: "Instead of insisting on its supposed rights to the Mosquito Shore, Nicaragua would best consult her interests by at once making good terms with England; for resistance in this matter will be of no avail. It is impossible that Nicaragua should be ignorant of her Britannic Majesty's relation to the Mosquito question, as she has before her the letter of Viscount Palmerston, of the date of April 15th last, (written, as will be seen, after the note to Mr. Lawrence,) which was sent to Nicaragua at a later period, in which he declares in the most clear and direct terms, the utter impossibility of acceding to the pretensions of Nicaragua. On the other hand, the Treaty of Messrs. Clayton and Bulwer, about which you have so much to say, and in which you express so much confidence, expressly recognizes the Mosquito Kingdom, and sets aside the rights which you pretend Nicaragua has on that coast. The true policy for Nicaragua, is to undeceive herself in this respect, and to put no further confidence in the protestations or assurances of pretended friends, (viz. Americans). It will be far better for her to come to an understanding without delay, with Great Britain; on which nation, depends not only the welfare and commerce of the State, but also the probability of accomplishing any thing positive concerning inter-oceanic communication through her territories; because it is only in London that the necessary capital for such an enterprise can be found."

This certainly is gasconading to some purpose, though the Government of Nicaragua still believed there was almost as much capital to be had, for a remunerative enterprise, in the United States as in London. Again, on December 5th, following, the same official informed, in writing, the Government of Nicaragua, of the boundaries "which Her Majesty's Government proposes to assert for the Mosquito King"—Thus:—

"The undersigned, her Britannic Majesty's Chargé d'Affaires

in Central America, with this view, has the honor to declare to the Minister of Foreign Relations of the Supreme Government of Nicaragua, that the general boundary line of the Mosquito Territory, begins at *the Northern extremity of the boundary line between the district of Tegucigalpa, in Honduras, and the jurisdiction of New Segovia ; and after following the Northern frontiers of New Segovia, it runs along the South-eastern limit of the District of Matagalpa and Chontales, and thence in an Eastern course, until it reaches the Machuca Rapids, on the River San Juan.*"

"The Mosquito Shore, (says Bonnycastle), was held by Great Britain for eighty years," which agrees with the date 1783, when a Treaty of peace, boundaries, and commerce, was declared between it and Spain. Article 6th of said Treaty stipulates, that "English subjects shall have the right of cutting, loading, and carrying away logwood in the District lying between the River Wallis, or Belize, and Rio Hondo." *Remember that this is distant hundreds of miles from the Mosquito Coast.* "Therefore, (we continue), all the English who may be dispersed in any other parts, whether on the Spanish Continent, (main land,) or in any of the Islands whatsoever, dependent on the aforesaid Spanish Continent, and for whatever reason it might be, without exception, shall return within the District which has been above described, in the space of eighteen months, and for this purpose orders shall be issued on the part of His Britannic Majesty."—(*Sen. Doc* 75, *Vol. X.*, *page* 16.)

Was this then not an actual abandonment of any heretofore, or then pretended claims upon the part of Great Britain to the Mosquito Territory ? By their covenanting to the foregoing, did they not solemnly waive all claim to space, outside of the therein-prescribed bounds and metes ?

In 1786, July 14, in a further Treaty between the same parties, by Article 1st, it was stipulated, "His Britannic Majesty's subjects and the other colonists who have hitherto enjoyed the protection of England, shall evacuate the country of the Mosquitoes, as well as the Continent in general, and the Islands adjacent, without exception, situated beyond the line hereinafter described as what ought to be the position of the extent of territory granted by His Catholic Majesty to the English, for the uses specified in the third Article of the present Convention ; and in addition to the country already granted to them in virtue of the stipulations agreed upon by the Commissioners of the two Crowns in 1783. The lines specified in the other articles of the Treaty, as the boundaries of the special possession of the English, were the Rio Hondo on the North, and the River Sibun on the South, together with the small Island of Casino, St. George's Key or Cayo Casino, and the cluster of small islands which are situate opposite that part of the coast occupied by the cutters, at the distance of eight leagues from the River Sibun, a place which has always been found well adapted for that purpose."

In Article 7th, all the foregone conclusions of the Treaty of 1783 are confirmed, with added stringent restrictions, liberty being granted on the part of Spain, for the English to cut mahogany, &c. Upon the part of Great Britain, in Article 2d thereof, His Britannic Majesty agreed, that "should there still remain any persons so daring as to presume, by retiring into the interior country, to endeavor to obstruct the entire evacuation already agreed upon, His Britannic Majesty, so far from affording them the least succor, or even protection, will disown them in the most solemn manner, as he will equally do those who may hereafter attempt to settle upon the territory belonging to the Spanish domain."—(*Sen. Doc.* 75, *Vol. X. p.* 23.)

Article 14th stipulates, to wit: "His Catholic Majesty prompted solely by motives of humanity, promises to the King of England, that he will not again exercise any act of severity against the Mosquitoes inhabiting in part the countries which are to be evacuated by virtue of the present Convention, on account of the connections which may have subsisted between the said Indians and the English; and His Britannic Majesty, on his part, will strictly prohibit all his subjects from furnishing arms or warlike stores to the Indians in general, situated upon the frontier of the Spanish possessions."—(*Sen. Doc.* 75, *Vol. X. p.* 13.)

In this connection we furnish, as worthy of attention, the following from Vol. 2, p. 423, of "A Journey through Spain," by Townsend, published in London, 1792. "Ever since the war, the exertions of Spain have been incessant to render her marine respectable; but more especially when I was there, all was in motion, and the Minister of the Marine was making the most strenuous efforts to equip a formidable fleet. This was done to vindicate their claims upon the Mosquito Shore, although that territory was never subject to the Crown of Spain, and the independent Princes who have dominion there had been for ages in alliance with the English Nation. When I returned to England, I examined the nature and extent of the settlement which caused so much uneasiness to Spain. It consisted of no more than five hundred and sixty-nine freemen, including the women and their children, with one thousand seven hundred and sixty-three black slaves, and two hundred and four head of cattle.

"The uneasiness arose, therefore, not from the number of the settlers, but from their contraband trade; from their communication with the Mosquitoes, who, in time of war, had been used to molest the Spaniards; and from the apprehension that, by their means, the English, in some future war, might establish themselves in force on the Lake of Nicaragua. This settlement was certainly valuable to England as the connecting medium between Jamaica and the Spanish Main for the exchange of our manufactures with Guatemala against indigo, cochineal, silver, and nard dollars. Indeed, the indigo, growing wild on all that coast, yields the best commodity, and no country produces finer sugar-canes.

"The infant colony made about a hundred and fifty hogsheads in one year; but being obliged to pay the foreign duty in England, the mills were suffered to decay. Mahogany was a principal article of their commerce; and of this the annual export was about three million feet. Besides these articles, they sent to England four tons of turtle-shells, paying a duty of one shilling a pound, with a hundred and twenty thousand pounds weight of sarsaparilla, the duty of which, at seven pence a pound, was three thousand five hundred pounds; a sum more than sufficient to discharge all the expenses of this new settlement.

"Such was the value of our possessions on the Mosquito Shore, that neither the Minister who signed the preliminaries of peace at the close of a disastrous war, nor his immediate successor in office, who ratified that peace, would agree to their relinquishment; yet, in the year 1787, the settlement was evacuated, and our most faithful allies were abandoned to the mercy of their inveterate enemies."

March 26th, 1787, Lord Rowdon brought a motion in the House of Lords to censure the king's ministers for having given up the Mosquito Shore to Spain. (Contents, 17; Noncontents 53.) The ministry defended the treaty, holding "that the British settlement on the Mosquito Shore was not a regular and lawful settlement, and that the Mosquito nation were not allies, and therefore Great Britain was not bound to protect them." The vote of censure was refused by a large majority of the peers. We have here, then, a *total* abandonment by Great Britain of all claim, affiliation, or even *interest* in the regal brother whom they lately embraced so warmly.

We have given the account of the coronation of a Mosquito king at Belize, in a former chapter. When the Duke of Albermarle was Governor of Jamaica, the Indians put themselves under his protection, and their king had a commission granted him from Great Britain. Since that time, it is asserted, the new monarch always goes to Jamaica to receive this document, the Indians refusing to acknowledge his authority until he does so. They are confidently asserted by many authors to be descendants of slaves from Guinea, who were wrecked on this coast. They are called Samboe Mosquitoes. (Very significant of the Red-man's origin.) The crown is succeeded to hereditarily, and the king (as he is called) is a despotic monarch. The musquitoes annoy them excessively, and probably hence they may have received their title.

July 4th, 1787, Colonel Grimarest, as Commissioner from the King of Spain, and His Majesty's Superintendent, Despard, went up the rivers to mark the limits, and to endeavor to discover the sources of the Belize and the Sibun. The said Commissioner published, on his return to Belize, permission to the English settlers to enter upon the new district, agreeable to the late treaty with Spain, viz.: 1786. July 7, 1787, Colonel Lawrie, late Superintendent on the Mosquito Shore, arrived at Belize in His Majesty's ship Camilla, Captain Hull, and the Mosquito shore was completely evacuated, conformably to treaty.

July 10th, 1787, David Lamb, Surveyor, was employed by the Superintendent to lay out lots fifty feet by one hundred, to be ballotted for, on the south point of Belize River mouth. August 2d, 1787, the ballot took place, and the Superintendent in person delivered possession to those who drew them; chiefly amongst the settlers from the Mosquito Shore. November 19th, 1791, two hundred and seventeen revolted negroes from St. Domingo were disembarked on English Key, distant seven leagues only from Belize, by the French ship, L'Emanuel, Captain Colmin, he having been prohibited from selling them by the magistrates.

The legal territory for Great Britain, hence, was Belize and its dependencies, as described. It was to this point, then, that this power induced the Mosquitoes to flock, where they employed themselves in fishing among the Keys, particularly for the hawksbill, a species of turtle, which are plentiful, and from which is obtained the tortoise-shell. For this they received from six to seven dollars per pound, and at times more. Here, then, they centred, and here their kings were crowned, that the tribe, *in toto*, might be concentrated about or near the merchants. But while England forbade the sale of the revolted slaves from St. Domingo, we find she dealt in the article, probably *sub rosa* in a manner, yet *de facto*.

The town of Belize is at the mouth of the river of the same name, and was so called from its discoverer, Wallice, a noted Buccaneer, who made it his place of retreat. The Spaniards write it Waliz, and subsequently it became corrupted into Balleze, or as it is now called Belize. Its armorial bearings may be read thus: Chief Dexter—Argent—the Union Jack, proper; Chief Sinister on the Proper—the Chiefs di vided from the Body of the Shield by a chevron-shaped Partition from the Fess of the Dexter and Sinister base—Points—the intermediate space, azure—a Ship with set sails on the Sea, passant proper—Crest, Mahogany tree; Motto, "*Sub umbra floreo*"—Supporters, NEGROES; that to the left, with a paddle—to the right, with an axe over his shoulder. The motto is appropriate. The poor fellows flourish everywhere in the shade—and—clover.

But Great Britain disavows slavery; her aim ever has been to its extinction; and yet before me lies a document, official, confirmed by the magistrates of the settlement, dated September 19, 1817, wherein is embraced the Table of Fees payable to the Clerk of St. John's Church. Items three and four, under head of Baptisms. Slaves, if ten in number, or under, at one time, each three shillings and four pence; above ten, at one time, and if owned by one person, each two shillings and six pence. Under the head of Marriages, we find—Of slaves, gratis!—Burials.—Of slaves above ten years old, five shillings; under ten, three shillings and four pence. The above are classed in Table of Surplice Fees. Confirmed June 27, 1817. "The Law requires that these Fees be paid at the time of service, and in default of which, they are recoverable by Warrants of Distress. Slave Fees are invariably defrayed by the owners."

CHAPTER XXV.

THE MOSQUITO COAST AGAIN—USURPATIONS OF ENGLAND—CLAIMS OF SPAIN—INDEPENDENCE OF GUATEMALA—ENGLAND'S ACKNOWLEDGMENTS—THE COLONY OF BAY ISLANDS—CONFLICTING CLAIMS—AN ACT OF THE ENGLISH PARLIAMENT—THE TREATY OF 1850—THE PROTECTORATE FICTION AND LORD JOHN RUSSEL—THE UNITED STATES AND GREAT BRITAIN—LORD CLARENDON'S ARGUMENT—MR. CLAYTON AS RENDERED BY MR. LAWRENCE—LORD CLARENDON AGAIN—MR. WEBSTER MISCONSTRUED—LORD JOHN RUSSEL TO THE POINT.

WE shall pursue the history of the Colonization of Great Britain on this coast, and shall prove her desire to act in bad-faith with Spain prior to meeting her demands upon the United States, and upholding the position the latter assumed, predicated upon the Clayton and Bulwer Treaty.

The frequent and continued breaches of the Treaty of 1786, and consequent usurpations upon the part of England, were sustained by Lord Clarendon, who alleged "that the Treaty of 1786 was abrogated in 1814 by the war between the contracting parties, at which time the Belize Settlement extended to the Sarstoun River, which is far South of the Sibun the prescribed boundary. In 1812 Spain adopted a new and written Constitution, in defiance of the despotic powers of Europe; said Constitution contained this Article: "Guatemala, with the internal Provinces of the East and West, and the adjacent Ialands in both Seas form part of the Spanish dominion." Under this Constitution, Spain was recognized by England, who guarantied her sovereignty.

Guatemala in 1823 discarded the Spanish yoke, and became a Confederated Republic, and its Constitution thus described the domain claimed: "The Territory of the Republic is the same which formerly comprised the ancient Kingdom of Guatemala, with the exception for the present of Chiapas." This territory included the whole of the Mosquito Coast. The British settlement between the Silver and the Rio Hondo, called Belize, belonging within the Spanish Province of Yucatan, by the revolution came under the sway of Mexico. England acknowledged the latter's independence, stipulating that British subjects, dwelling in its territories, "should enjoy the rights which had been granted to them by Spain in the Treaty of 1786."

Did not England herein reaffirm her own exclusion from Central America? Where then was in fact, any Mosquito Kingdom, as a distinct and independent territory? If such had existence, they were heathens, having neither king, churches, ministry, parliament, schools, or council; no army, navy; no treasury, customs, taxes, revenue, police, industry, trade, and no intercourse diplomatic with any other people. True, the English authorities were present; and from Great Britain did they derive their powers and salaries.

On the 17th of July, fourteen days subsequent to the negotiation of the "Clayton and Bulwer Treaty," a proclamation was issued by the Government of Great Britain, constituting the Islands of Ruatan, in the Caribbean Sea—in Central America, and not in British Honduras, four hundred miles distant from Belize—Bonacca, Utilla, Barbaret, Helene, and Mocrat, a colony under the Colony of the Bay Islands. Ruatan and Bonacca are said to be, on account of their fine harbors, good soils, fine air, abundant animals, and their commanding sites, "the Gardens of the West Indies, the Key to Spanish America, and a new Gibraltar."

The United States insist upon England's discontinuing this new Colony. The latter refuses, alleging that the Colony is within the Belize Settlements, or British Honduras, and being so, is excepted from the Treaty. The Islands excepted are only small ones in the neighborhood of and assigned to the Belize in the Treaty of 1786, while the Bay Islands are neither small, nor in the vicinity of the Belize; they are certainly of vast importance as to location and wealth.

The Treaty of 1786 assigned them to the "Spanish Continent," and expressly excludes Great Britain from them. Spain held them until the Revolution in Central America. In 1829 the State of Honduras assumed possession, and their ensign was planted on Ruatan. In 1839, England supplanted it with her own, yet this was soon lowered, and that of Honduras was restored.

In 1817 the English Parliament passed a law, entitled "An Act for the more effectual punishment of murders and manslaughters committed in places not within His Majesty's dominions." The preamble runs thus: "Whereas grievous murders and manslaughters have been committed at the settlement in the Bay of Honduras, in South America, the same Bay or settlement being for certain purposes in the possession of and within the protection of His Majesty, by persons residing within that settlement, &c." Parliament amended this statute, in 1819, and reaffirmed that "Belize was not within the territories and dominions of Great Britain."

I have now proven that England never occupied the Belize, save in subordination to the Spanish title. That in 1826, Great Britain, in recognizing the Independence of Mexico, expressly stipulated "for her settlement at the Belize, the privileges granted by the Treaty with Spain of 1786." And again, I have shown that England, although in 1819 reaffirming that this settlement "was not within her territories and dominions, yet alleges that by the war in 1812, the Treaty was abrogated in 1814, although she did not even then challenge Spain's title, or allege a change in the nature or extent of her possessions. To conciliate and to calm this vexed question forever, the Treaty of 1850 was entered into, in which Great Britain solemnly and forever relinquished and abandoned whatever pretensions she may have ever before made to the Bay Islands."

The imposture of the Mosquito King failed, and the protectorate fiction dissolved upon the publicity of Lord John Russel's statements, of January 19th, 1853. "It is evident (we quote him) that since Great Britain first assumed the protection and defense of the Mosquito Indians, the positions of all parties have changed. First, Spain, instead of exercising absolute sovereignty over Central America, and prohibiting all commerce on the coast under her sway, has entirely lost her domain over the Continent from Cape Horn to Florida; secondly, the Mosquito Indians, instead of governing their own tribe, according to their own customs, furnish a name and title to Europeans and Americans, who carry on trade at Greytown, and along the Coast of Mosquito, according to the usages of civilized nations; thirdly, Great Britain, instead of having an interest in the defense of the Mosquito Indians, for the sake of rescuing part of the territory of Central America from Spanish control, and obtaining an outlet for her, has no other interest in Mosquito than that which is derived from an honorable regard for her old connection with the Indian nation at Mosquito."

The United States from the foregoing, and especially insisting upon the stipulations of the Treaty of 1850, hold, that Great Britain is bound to withdraw from the Mosquito Coast. This is in turn denied by England, who asserts that the stipulations are only prospective, and do not seize upon, or terminate occupancy in a colony of hers which was existing at the time of the concluding of the Treaty. She argues, such effect is only inferential; for, should it have been intended, it would have been embodied, as an express renunciation. Great Britain stipulates therein, that she will not, that is to say, after this time henceforward, enter into, maintain any colony or occupancy, or exercise any dominion over the Mosquito Coast. Then why not have retired from, discontinue, give up, relinquish, and abandon whatever colony, occupancy, or domain, of whatever nature, she subsequently has maintained therein or thereon? This entire concession she repeats; "she will not, from this time henceforward make use of any protection which she now affords to any state or people, for the purpose of maintaining any colony or occupation, or exercising any dominion whatever on the Mosquito Coast."

The United States have no colony, occupancy, or dominion of any nature on the Coast, or in any portion of Central America, and they stipulate, that "they never will obtain or assume any such." Great Britain further agrees, not only that she will not obtain or assume any new colony, occupation, or dominion there, but will not hereafter maintain or exercise any such that is now existing."

Lord Clarendon argues, that the English construction is based after the principle of "neutrality." He writes,—"Great Britain has colonies, occupations, and dominions in Central America; the United States have none; if England abandons hers, she receives no equivalent for her surrendered advantages." But the United States deny *in toto* her title to these colonies, occupations, and dominions, and say that of Nicaragua, was held to be the more valid. Here they conflict, and hence the mutual agreement to abandon Central America to the States "existing there, to whom it belongs."

Abashed, yet not entirely mortified, England resumes the contest of words, and Lord Clarendon shelters his argument under the conduct of Spain and the United States previous to the Treaty; true, Spain did not remonstrate against the protectorate during her last hours in America, for she was elsewhere completely occupied and harassed with her insurgent provinces; but prior to 1849, Central America, and the States of Honduras, Guatemala, and Nicaragua, invited the United States to challenge the loyalty of the said protectorate. Then we had no interest there, but subsequently we did acquire a title and interest, and our Government promptly announced its opposition to the continuance of the protectorate.

The language of Mr. Clayton, as rendered by Mr. Lawrence, is certainly very explicit: "Is Great Britain eager, or willing that the question of her alleged protectorate should be tried at the bar of the public opinion of the world? Does she believe that she can obtain credit for having undertaken it from a conviction that the Mosquitoes were competent to discharge the duties of sovereignty? Or is she disposed to hazard the notoriety of the fact, that the visor of royalty which she would fain place upon the pseudo-monarch of that region, is too transparent to conceal the features of a real sovereign? Can Great Britain imagine that the commercial nations of the world will tacitly allow her, by means so invidious, to obtain substantial and exclusive control over the right of way to the Pacific, by the Port of San Juan, and the river of that name, or to wrest the sovereignty over that region from the rightful proprietor? In such pretensions, we trust that the United States, at least, will never acquiesce."—(*Sen. Doc.* 27, *page* 19, *Vol. III., Sess.* 2, 32*d Cong.*)

The resort of Lord Clarendon next is to the stipulation by which the parties agree to invite all powers friendly to enter into stipulations similar to those contained in the Treaty, arguing that this agreement would include the Central American States, while if they should accept the invitation, and sign the Treaty, they would thereby, according to the construc tion of the United States, renounce the territories in which they exist. A glance at the context shows that two classes of States are here contemplated: one, not existing in Central America; the other, those which are already established there. The first, only, are invited to imitate the example of the contracting parties, and enter into their present stipulations with the second class, to wit, the Central American States.

Lord Clarendon in his statement of September 11th, 1855, resumes the argument thus: "If the Treaty had been intended to act upon and terminate the protectorate, it would have contained in specific terms a renunciation on the part of Great Britain of the possessions and rights which, up to the conclusion of the convention, she had claimed to maintain. The treaty," he adds, "would then have imposed upon Great Britain the obligation to renounce possessions and rights without any equivalent renunciation on the part of the United States. And still," he proceeds, "if the convention was intended to impose upon Great Britain an obligation to withdraw from portions of territories occupied by it, then the Government of the Central American States would, by the mere act of accession, sign away their rights to the territories in which they were situated." And upon the same hypothesis, he writes: "The British Government neither have the wish to extend the limits of their possessions or the sphere of their influence in that quarter, nor would any British interest be promoted by doing so. But the British Government are not prepared to contract either the one or the other."

And in contrast here, let me insert his statement, dated May 3d, 1854. "It is proper that Her Majesty's Government should at once state that Her Majesty has never held any possessions whatever in the Mosquito country. But although Great Britain held no possessions in the Mosquito country, she undoubtedly exercised a great and extensive influence over it as the protecting ally of the Mosquito king." Here are exhibited variations we little expected; but his lordship proved his expertness upon the diplomatic-chromatic scale in an eminent degree. His continuation will enlighten us probably. "Mr. Buchanan confounds the conditions of a sovereignty and a protectorate, and, under this error, treats the agreement 'not to colonize, or occupy, or fortify, nor assume, nor exercise dominion over,' as an agreement not to protect. With respect to sovereignty, Great Britain never claimed, and does not now claim or hold any sovereignty over the Mosquito."

By custom of both European and American states, savage tribes, though suffered to exercise some municipal powers, have no actual sovereignty, for this is vested in the State or nation which directly exercises or derives to itself the title acquired by discovery. Did not Great Britain acquire and maintain until the Treaty of Versailles, in 1783, sovereignty within the domain of the original United States? Did not France also acquire and maintain the same in Canada and the West India Islands until the fall of Quebec in 1764, when she transferred to Great Britain? Did not Spain acquire title to the Floridas and the vast territory in Louisiana as also in Mexico, Central and South America? How, otherwise, did Denmark acquire her hold in the West Indies? Portugal her possessions in Brazil, the Empire of which now rests on the same title?

By referring to the conversation had between Mr. Rives and Lord Palmerston, will be perceived the apposite confession of Great Britain to the present occasion. Lord Palmerston admitted the general doctrine for which we contended "was the principle on which they conducted (*i. e.* the English) all their relations with the Indian tribes in Canada; but that the case of the Mosquitoes was "*sui generis*," and stood upon its own peculiar circumstances." Admitting the universal law, if there are to be cases "*sui generis*," the totality ceases, and the universal fractured, becomes the customary, usual law.

Lord Clarendon contends that the English construction of the Treaty of 1850 was sanctioned by Mr. Webster, then Secretary of State. It is said that Mr. Webster advised Mr. Marcoleta, the Nicaraguan Minister, to accept a Treaty proposed to his State and Costa Rica by England, upon "the basis of that construction;" but no doubt it was intended solely as a compromise. It failed, however, and the United States never endorsed the opinion of the Secretary, maintaining their own construction rigidly and inviolate.

Lord John Russel's letter, already in part inserted, speaks pointedly and frankly and the conclusion of it is so direct and positive, that we quit the discussion, assured of the validity of the position assumed thereon by the United States. His lordship writes: "The peculiarity of this case is, that certain neighboring States deny altogether the independence of Mosquito; and the Mosquito nation are liable any day to new incursions upon their territory. We can make no new provision against this danger. Our policy is to do all that honor and humanity require in behalf of the Mosquito nation; but we intend to adhere steadily to the Treaty of Washington of the 19th of April, 1850, and not to assume any sovereignty direct in Central America."

CHAPTER XXVI.

THE INTER-OCEANIC CANAL—CHARTER FOR THE TRANSIT ROUTE—SYNOPSIS OF ITS PROVISIONS—ITS IMPORTANCE TO THE UNITED STATES—POSTULATE OF PRESIDENT MONROE—BRITISH INTERFERENCE—NICARAGUA PROTESTS—THE CLAYTON AND BULWER TREATY MOOTED—MR. RIVES TO LORD PALMERSTON—REPLY OF THE LATTER—CARDINAL POINTS OF THE TREATY—TREATY OF COMMERCE AND FRIENDSHIP WITH NICARAGUA—THE CANAL COMPANY'S CHARTER AMENDED—LEONEZE PROTEST—SAVE ME FROM MY FRIENDS!—VIVE LA CHAMPAGNE!—THE CANAL IN NUBIBUS—THE TRANSIT TANGIBLE.

THE Transit, or in other words, the route per the Rio San Juan, from Greytown on the Atlantic side to Lake Nicaragua, thence across to Virgin Bay, and thence overland twelve miles, to San Juan del Sur on the Pacific, is a highway in which, save as a speculation, Nicaragua itself has but little interest, inasmuch as it develops no internal resources, no agricultural or mineral wealth, conciliates neither the Serviles or the opponents, but is solely a source whence the State receives a profit, an annual subsidy. That the route should be under a protectorate, joint if desired, there cannot be a doubt, since Nicaragua convulsed by revolutions is unable at present to maintain either its tranquillity, or neutrality.

On the 27th of August, 1849, a Grant was obtained, and ratified with an American Company on the 23d of September, from which a Charter was consummated under the assurance that if of a proper character, the American Government was willing to extend to it its guarantees. A synopsis of the provisions therein contained, may prove at present, interesting. It is as follows:

1st. That the American Atlantic and Pacific Ship Canal Company may construct a Ship Canal, at its own expense, from the Port of San Juan, or any more feasible point on the Atlantic, to the Port of Realejo, or any other point within the territories of the Republic, on the Pacific, and make use of all lands, waters, or natural materials of the country for the enterprise.

2d. The dimensions of the Canal shall be sufficiently great to admit vessels of all sizes.

3d. The Grant is for the period of eighty-five years from the completion of the work; the preliminary surveys to be commenced within twelve months; the work to be completed within twelve years, unless unforeseen events, such as earthquakes or wars, shall intervene to prevent it; if not completed within that time, the charter to be forfeit, and whatever work may have been done, to revert to the State; at the end of eighty-five years the work to revert to the State free from all indemnity for the capital invested; the Company, nevertheless, to receive fifteen per cent. annually of the net profits, for ten years thereafter, if the entire cost shall not exceed twenty million dollars; but if it does exceed that sum, then it shall receive the same per centage for twenty years thereafter.

4th. The Company to pay to the State ten thousand dollars upon the ratification of the contract, and ten thousand dollars annually until the completion of the work; also to give to the State two hundred thousand dollars' worth of stock in the Canal, upon the issue of stock; the State to have the privilege of taking five hundred thousand dollars of stock in the enterprise; to receive for the first twenty years, twenty per cent. annually out of the net profits of the Canal, after deducting the interest on the capital actually invested, at the rate of seven per cent.; and also to receive twenty-five per cent. thereafter, until the expiration of the Grant.

5th. The Company to have the exclusive right of navigating the interior waters of the State by steam, and the privilege, within the twelve years allowed for constructing the Canal, of opening any land or other route, or means of transit or conveyance across the State; in consideration of which, the Company shall pay, irrespective of interest, ten per cent. of the net profits of such transit to the State, and transport, both on such route, and on the Canal, when finished, the officers of the

Government and its employees, when required to do so, free of charge.

6th. The Canal to be open to the vessels of all nations, subject only to certain fixed and uniform rates of toll, to be established by the Company, with the sanction of the State, graduated to induce the largest and most extended business by this route; these rates not to be altered without six months previous notice, both in Nicaragua and the United States.

7th. The Contract, and the rights and privileges conceded by it, to be held inalienably by the individuals composing the Company

8th. All disputes to be settled by referees or commissioners to be appointed in a specified manner

9th. All machinery and other articles introduced into the State for the use of the Company, to enter free of duty; and all persons in its employ to enjoy all the privileges of citizens, without being subjected to taxation or military service.

10th. The State concedes to the Company, for purposes of colonization, eight sections of land on the line of the Canal in the valley of the River San Juan, each six miles square, and at least three miles apart; with the right of alienating the same, under certain reservations; all settlers on these lands to be subject to the laws of the country, being, however, exempt for ten years from all taxes, and also from all public service, as soon as each colony shall contain fifty settlers.

11th. It is expressly stipulated, that the citizens, vessels, products, and manufactures of all nations shall be permitted to pass upon the proposed Canal through the territories of Nicaragua subject to no other, nor higher duties, charges, or taxes than shall be imposed upon those of the United States; provided always that such nations shall first enter into the same treaty-stipulations and guarantees, respecting said Canal, as may be entered into between the State of Nicaragua and the United States.

Such are the provisions of the Charter, and as we now tread upon the threshold of new and thickening events, let us cautiously survey them, ere the fogs of bigotry and clouds of dissension have arisen to dim the horizon.

The acquisition of California in 1848 by the United States, the disclosure of its vast mineral wealth, its consequent political organization, and social development, precipitated upon the world the solution of a communication across the Isthmus, and such a passage, however desirable to other nations, became doubly so to the United States, for the purposes of commerce and defense. With our sympathies, we had extended the Spanish American States favorable commercial treaties.

In 1823, was announced the postulate of President Monroe. —" The American Continents, by the free and independent condition which they have assumed and maintained, are henceforth not to be considered subjects for further colonization by any European power." The United States declined to interfere in the political affairs of the Spanish States, though frequently invoked to do so. Dawn was breaking in this benighted region, and new life, with young, and healthy blood was about being infused into the decrepit Asiatic branches, who, though richer, and more imperial, had been outstripped in the race. The Isthmus was about to be opened; the youngest family on this Continent had assumed a position where its voice commanded, and its skill directed the noble enterprise.

Three routes, each rivals for preferment, presented themselves; the Tehuantepec, in Mexico—the subject before us, the Transit in Nicaragua—and the Chagres Route, in New Granada. The United States essayed to open them all. The Charter alluded to in our chapter, proposes, in Section Eleventh thereof, equal terms to all nations who should enter, of course, into the same stipulations and guarantees as should be agreed upon by the United States and Nicaragua. Still did we hesitate, owing probably to the presence and intervention of Great Britain in Central America.

During Spain's dominion on the Continents, she excluded foreign powers from commercial intercourse with her colonies. Between them and those of the British, contraband trade grew up, wars ensued, and when peace was declared, Great Britain possessed two settlements: the Belize or British Honduras, in the department of Yucatan, and the Mosquito Coast in Nicaragua—their title to both, disputed by the Central American States. The Agent of Great Britain announced to Honduras and Nicaragua the determination of England to sustain her protectorate on the Mosquito Coast, (September 10, 1847,) from Cape Honduras to, and including the lower part of the Rio San Juan. (*Vide Ex. Doc.* 75, *p.* 44, *Vol. X.*, 1st *Sess.* 31st *Cong.*)

Subsequently, on the 8th of February, 1848, two English ships of war arrived at San Juan del Norte, or Greytown, expelled the State officers of Nicaragua therefrom, and four days afterward proceeding up the Rio San Juan, took the fort at Serapaqui, after a determined resistance on the part of Nicaragua, the latter having succumbed under protest, on the 17th of March, 1848. In October, 1849, an English man-of-war captured Tigre Island, belonging to Nicaragua, off the Pacific coast, together with the Island of Ruatan or Roatan, belonging to Honduras, commanding an unexcelled position for protecting or molesting every passage between the oceans. Capable of being admirably fortified at a small expense, it invited the rapacity of her English foe. Costa Rica, the late ally of Nicaragua, disputed with the latter the boundary of the Rio San Juan, and claiming the southern portion of Lake Nicaragua, seemed, in this struggle, to favor Great Britain. Honduras and Nicaragua implored the aid of the United States.

Under these circumstances, the Clayton and Bulwer Treaty was mooted between Lord Palmerston, Prime Minister of Great Britain, and Mr. Rives, American Minister to France, in an interview held in London, September 24th, 1850, the latter, being *en route* to the French court; it was ratified July 4th, 1850, but took effect from its date, April 9th, 1850. The interview alluded to we embrace here, as we propose submitting the complete data, which has never been fully understood by the country at large, and no doubt will prove interesting.

Mr. Rives stated to Lord Palmerston that "the British Consul in New York had publicly claimed for the Mosquito Indians sovereignty and ownership of the mouth and lower part of the Rio San Juan; that the United States had now become a party to the question in their own right by virtue of the contract by which Nicaragua had granted to American citizens, the right to construct an inter-oceanic Canal by the way of the River San Juan and Lake Nicaragua; that the United States, on examination, were satisfied, as well on legal as on geographical grounds, that the State of Nicaragua was the Territorial Sovereign of the River and Lake, and that they had already concluded, or were about concluding, a Treaty with that State for securing a passage; that the United States, however, sought no exclusive privilege, and sincerely wished to see the passage dedicated to the use of all nations, on the most liberal terms, and on a footing of perfect equality for all; that even if they could, they would not obtain any exclusive right or privilege, and so, on the other hand, they would not consent to see so important a communication fall under the exclusive control of any other great commercial power; that the Mosquito Coast at the mouth of the San Juan could be considered in no other light than as British Possession; and he proposed that Great Britain and the United States should come to a frank understanding with each other, and unite to carry the undertaking into effect, as one of the highest importance to themselves and the rest of the world."

Lord Palmerston replied, that "from an early period the Mosquito Indians had been treated by the British Government as a separate and independent State; had a king; that Nicaragua having never before been in possession of San Juan, had taken possession of that town, and that England had dispossessed her of it; that the Nicaraguans had, in bad faith, granted to American citizens a right to open the proposed passage through a territory of which she was not in possession; and that the English Government had therefore given notice to those grantees of its (England's) intention to regard the contract as a void one."

Moreover, he added, "a suspicion seemed to be entertained by some persons in the United States that the English Government wished to plant a new colony on the San Juan; that there was not the slightest foundation for that suspicion, as Great Britain had already more colonies than she could manage; that as to any idea of her holding exclusive possession of the mouth of the Rio San Juan as the key of the contemplated inter-oceanic passage, nothing conld be further from her mind; and that, if any plan could be suggested by which Great Britain and the United States could unite in promoting, by their joint influence and mutual co-operation the opening of a great channel by the way of Lake Nicaragua, and declaring it a common highway for the use and benefit of *all* nations, it would receive the most favorable consideration of Her Majesty's Government." (*Sen. Doc.* 27, *p.* 18.)

Mr. Rives reports to Mr. Clayton a conversation between himself and Lord Palmerston thus: "I concluded with saying that it resulted from this long course of universal usage and conventional practice, that actual possession was in no wise necessary to the exercise of a rightful sovereignty on Indian territory; and that, although Indian tribes were possessed of some of the attributes of a separate political existence, such as that of governing their communities by their own internal laws, also of sustaining the relations of peace and war, yet it was impossible to recognize in them a complete national independence, such as that which was claimed for the Mosquitoes, without subverting the whole fabric of public law belonging to our peculiar position, which had grown up with the general concurrence and assent of all the civilized nations of Europe."

To these remarks Lord Palmerston replied by saying that he "fully admitted the general doctrine for which we contended; that it was the principle on which they conducted all their relations with the Indian tribes in Canada; but that the case of the Mosquitoes was *sui generis*, and stood upon its own peculiar circumstances." (*Sen. Doc.* 27, *p.* 22, *Vol. III. 2d Sess. 32d Cong.*)

The Treaty recites the purpose of the parties, namely: the consolidating of amicable relations, but expressing and fixing their views and intents mutually in any inter-oceanic Canal that may be constructed *via* the Rio San Juan and either of Lakes Nicaragua or Managua, or both. The cardinal points of said Treaty I annex.

Article 1. Neither party will ever obtain or maintain for itself any exclusive control over the contemplated Canal.

Neither will ever erect or maintain any fortification commanding the same, or the vicinity thereof.

Neither will occupy, or fortify, or colonize, or assume, or exercise any dominion over Nicaragua, Costa Rica, the Mosquito Coast, or any part of Central America.

Neither will use any protection which either affords, or may afford, to either alliance, which either has, or may have, to or with any State or people, for the purpose of erecting or maintaining any such fortifications, or of occupying or colonizing Nicaragua, Costa Rica, the Mosquito Coast, or any part of Central America, or of assuming or exercising any dominion over the same.

Neither will take advantage of any intimacy, or use any alliance, connection, or influence that either may possess with any State or people, through whose territory the Canal may pass, for the purpose of acquiring or holding, directly or indirectly, for its own citizens or subjects, any unequal rights, or advantages of commerce or navigation. Again, in

Article 4. The parties will use their influence with any State or States, or Governments possessing or claiming jurisdiction or right over the territory through which the Canal shall pass, to induce them to favor its construction, and to use their good offices, whenever or however it may be most expedient, to procure the establishment of two free ports, one at each end of the Canal. In

Article 6. The parties engage to invite every State in friendly intercourse with both or either of them, to enter into stipulations similar to those contained in the Treaty, so that all other States may share in the honor and advantages of having contributed to the construction of the contemplated Canal. And each of the contracting parties shall enter into treaty-stipulations with such of the Central American States as they may deem advisable, for the purpose of carrying out the object of the Treaty—namely, the construction and maintenance of the Canal, as a Ship Canal between the two Oceans, for the benefit of mankind. In

Article 7. The parties determine to give their support and encouragement to the persons or Company who shall first offer to build the Canal with the necessary capital and the consent of the local authorities, and to any such Company, already existing, as may have a contract which is justly unobjectionable to the parties.

Article 8. The parties declare that, besides the particular purpose of the Treaty before stated, they have the further and broader object, to establish a general principle; and so they agree to extend their protection, by treaty-stipulations, to any other practicable communications, whether by canal or railway, across the Isthmus, and especially to those contemplated to be made by the ways of Tehuantepec and Panama.

Such is the "Clayton and Bulwer Treaty," ample in design, simple in construction, and generous in spirit. Yet there was no necessity for it, for already on the 23d of September, 1849, simultaneously with the sealing of the Charter of the Canal Company, was a Treaty of Commerce and Friendship negotiated with the Government of Nicaragua, and ratified unanimously by the Legislative Chambers. It was forwarded to the United States, where it received the commendations of the

President (Gen. Taylor) and Cabinet, but owing to the protracted debate on the Slavery question, it did not receive immediate attention.

I shall here add the second and third stipulations of the Treaty of Commerce, which prove the utter waste of powder in the negotiation of the much-abused "Clayton and Bulwer."

Section 1st is purely commercial in its character.

Section 2. And inasmuch as a Contract was entered into on the 27th day of August, 1849, between the Republic of Nicaragua and a Company of Citizens of the United States, styled "The American Atlantic and Pacific Ship-Canal Company," and in order to secure the construction and permanence of the great work thereby contemplated, both high contracting parties do severally and jointly agree to protect and defend the above-named Company in the full and perfect enjoyment of said work, from its inception to its completion, and after its completion, from any acts of invasion, forfeiture, or violence from whatever quarter the same may proceed; and to give full effect to the stipulations here made, and to secure for the benefit of mankind the uninterrupted advantages of such communication from sea to sea, the United States distinctly recognizes the rights of sovereignty and property which the State of Nicaragua possesses in and over the line of said Canal, and for the same reason guaranties positively and efficaciously the entire neutrality of the same, so long as it shall remain under the control of citizens of the United States, and so long as the United States shall enjoy the privileges secured to them in the preceding section of this Article.

Section 3. But if by any contingency, the above-named "American Atlantic and Pacific Ship-Canal Company" shall fail to comply with the terms of their Contract with the State of Nicaragua, all the rights and privileges which said Contract confers, shall accrue to any Company of Citizêns of the United States which shall, within one year after the official declaration of failure, undertake to comply with its provisions, so far as the same may at that time be applicable, provided the Company thus assuming said Contract shall first present to the President and Secretary of State of the United States satisfactory assurances of their intention and ability to comply with the same; of which satisfactory assurances, the signature of the Secretary of State, and the seal of the Department shall be complete evidence.

Section 4. And it is also agreed, on the part of the Republic of Nicaragua, that none of the rights, privileges, and immunities guarantied, and by the preceding Articles, but especially by the first section of this Article, conceded to the United States and its citizens, shall accrue to any other nation, or to its citizens, except such nation shall first enter into the same treaty-stipulations, for the defense and protection of the proposed great inter-oceanic Canal, which have been enterec into by the United States, in terms the same with those embraced in Section Second of this Article.

It will be seen by a comparison, that the spirit, intent, and conception even of both Treaties are similar. Why, therefore, a new compact? Great Britain, by subscribing to Section Fourth, shared all the advantages to be enjoyed by the United States. There was a non-desire at this early date to forego her colonies, and her cherished hopes of "an hereafter" in our midst, as I shall prove as we proceed.

Subsequent to the consummation of the last-named Treaties, the Canal Company experiencing difficulties in properly arranging the details of their proposed work, procured a separation of the privilege of exclusive steam-navigation in the interior waters (which amounted to Lake Nicaragua solely), from the remainder of the original Charter, and secured and established the monopoly of Transit across from Greytown to San Juan del Sur. This is known as the "Nicaragua Transit."

War having occurred in the interior, and there being two distinct Governments, one at Leon, sustained by the Bishop and General Muñoz, and the other at Granada, supported by Gen. Chamorro, the question, if at all admissible, was not at least debatable, "which of the two to choose?" as both claimed precedence and authority. Joseph L. White, Esq. Agent for the Canal Company, in a mode entirely *sui generis*, succeeded in negotiating the desired separation. The Leonese Government, however, entered its protest as follows:

"The Provisonal Supreme Government will see with satisfaction the interests of the aforesaid Company arrayed in harmony with those of this State when it shall have recovered its internal peace, and when its Government is qualified to enter upon affairs of this kind; but any negotiations concluded in the meantime are not authorized by it, nor will they be recognized as legal and subsisting."

The President of the State, (Pineda) having been shortly after this, gagged and blindfolded in Leon, by some of his ardent admirers (in the very house too, subsequently occupied by our Minister, Mr. Kerr of Maryland), and placed on a mule and trotted off to Chinandega, was subsequently permitted to leave for Granada, *via* Realejo and San Juan del Sur.

The Transit went into active operation, and the frequent charges *from*, and discharges *of* imported Champagne, never suffered either of the Governments to be sufficiently qualified to enter into the equality or inequality of the Contract or Charter, as subsequently amended. One fact, however, is apparent. The Canal is not in existence, and the Transit has been successful.

CHAPTER XXVII.

RIVAS REVOKES THE TRANSIT COMPANY'S CHARTER—WHAT NICARAGUA CLAIMS IN THE MATTER—THE REPLY THERETO—WHAT THE UNITED STATES AND NICARAGUA AGREED TO DO—WHAT RIVAS DID AND THE REMEDIES THEREFOR—THE CASS AND YRISARRI TREATY—WHAT PRESIDENT BUCHANAN SAYS—WANTS AN ARMED FORCE TO PROTECT THE TRANSIT—WHAT THE POSTMASTER-GENERAL SAYS—IMPORTANCE TO FOREIGN RESIDENTS OF KEEPING THE ROUTE OPEN—MONSIEUR BELLY NEGOTIATES FOR A ROUTE—REMARKS OF THE FRENCH PRESS THEREON—CHRISTOPHER COLUMBUS, BARON HUMBOLDT, AND LOUIS NAPOLEON ON INTER-OCEANIC COMMUNICATIONS—OVERLAND ROUTE—GEN. CASS ON THE INTERVENTION OF FOREIGN POWERS—THE POLICY OF THE AMERICAN CONTINENT.

In August, 1852, the Accessory Transit Company made its first inter-oceanic trip over the Nicaraguan route, and continued in successful operation until February 18th, 1856; then it was suddenly closed, and the Grant and Charter of the Company were arbitrarily revoked by the Government of Rivas. It will be remembered that at this period General

Walker was Chief of the forces of the State. Prior to this, in 1854, serious disputes had arisen between Nicaragua and the Company concerning the settlement of accounts, and even at that date the interruption of the Transit was threatened. The United States, desirous of harmonizing all the existing difficulties, interposed in vain.

From the date of the discontinuance of the Transit, the route has been closed, greatly to the prejudice of the United States. Nicaragua contends that the Charter is void, inasmuch as the Company did not complete the necessary surveys in the time specified in the Grant. This is one of the chief allegations. In reply, by referring to Section 3d of said Charter, we find: "The Grant is for the period of eighty-five years from the completion of the work; the preliminary surveys to be commenced within twelve months." Surveys were duly made by the Company. The time for the completion of the work, according to the section already referred to, was "within twelve years, unless unforeseen events, such as earthquakes or wars, shall intervene to prevent it." Hence, upon this allegation, Nicaragua fails to sustain her action.

In the Treaty of Commerce and Friendship, negotiated on the 23d of September, 1849, we shall perceive that Nicaragua and the United States "do severally and jointly agree to protect and defend the Company in the full and perfect enjoyment of said work from its inception to its completion, from any acts of invasion, forfeiture, or violence, from whatever quarter the same may proceed."

If the Rivas Government was an unlawful one, since the Company's Charter was forfeited by it, and the route summarily closed, why has not the subsequent Government reinstated the Company? If damages have been sustained by the latter, by reference to the eighth section of the original Charter, we find: "All disputes to be settled by referees or commissioners, to be appointed in a specified manner." Until Nicaragua shall have adhered to her stipulations, the Company have complaints to urge and justice to demand; and should that State refuse to acknowledge the validity of its claims, the United States, being a party to the Treaty of Commerce and Friendship, should receive the petition of the claimants.

On the 16th day of November, 1857, a treaty was signed by Secretary Cass and Señor Yrisarri, Minister of Nicaragua, under the stipulations of which the use and protection of the Transit Route would have been secured, not only to the United States, but equally to all other nations. But by reference to all the Treaties and Charters herewith connected, the neutrality of the route was stipulated for on terms of equality to all other countries. This latter treaty contained a provision authorizing the United States to employ force to keep the route open, in case Nicaragua should fail to perform her duty in this respect. This was the principal objection, and this clause being insisted upon by the United States, the Treaty has, as yet, failed to receive the ratification of the Nicaraguan Government. President Buchanan, in his Message of December 8th, 1858, in relation to Central America, says:

"The political condition of the narrow Isthmus of Central America, through which transit routes pass between the Atlantic and Pacific Oceans, presents a subject of deep interest to all commercial nations. It is over these Transits that a large proportion of the trade and travel between the European and Asiatic continents is destined to pass. To the United States these routes are of incalculable importance, as a means of communication between their Atlantic and Pacific possessions. The latter now extends throughout seventeen degrees of latitude on the Pacific coast, embracing the important State of California, and the flourishing Territories of Oregon and Washington.

"All commercial nations, therefore, have a deep and direct interest that these communications shall be rendered secure from interruption. If an arm of the sea, connecting the two oceans, penetrated through Nicaragua and Costa Rica, it could not be pretended that these States would have the right to arrest or retard its navigation to the injury of other nations. The Transit by land over this narrow Isthmus occupies nearly the same position. It is a highway in which they themselves have little interest when compared with the vast interests of the rest of the world.

"Whilst their rights of sovereignty ought to be respected, it is the duty of other nations to require that this important passage shall not be interrupted by the civil wars and revolutionary outbreaks which have so frequently occurred in that region. The stake is too important to be left to the mercies of rival Companies, claiming to hold conflicting contracts with Nicaragua. The commerce of other nations is not to stand still and await the adjustment of such petty controversies. The Government of the United States expects no more than this, and it will not be satisfied with less. It would not, if it could, derive any advantage from the Nicaragua transit not common to the rest of the world.

"Its neutrality and protection for the common use of all nations is her only object. She has no objection for Nicaragua to demand and receive a fair compensation from the companies and individuals who may traverse the route; but she insists that it shall never hereafter be closed by an arbitrary decree of that Government. If disputes arise between it and those with whom they may have entered into contracts, these must be adjusted by some fair tribunal provided for the purpose, and the route must not be closed pending the controversy. This is our whole policy, and it cannot fail to be acceptable to other nations.

"All these difficulties might be avoided if, consistently with the good faith of Nicaragua, the use of this Transit could be thrown open to general competition, providing at the same time for the payment of a reasonable rate to the Nicaraguan Government on passengers and freight."

And again: "A Treaty was signed on the 16th day of November, 1857, by the Secretary of State and the Minister of Nicaragua, under the stipulations of which the use and protection of the Transit route would have been secured, not only to the United States, but equally to all other nations. How and on what pretexts this Treaty has failed to receive the ratification of the Nicaraguan Government, will appear by the papers herewith communicated from the State Department. The principal objection seems to have been to the provision authorizing the United States to employ force to keep the route open, in case Nicaragua should fail to perform her duty in this respect.

"From the feebleness of that Republic, its frequent changes of government, and its constant internal dissensions, this had become a most important stipulation and one essentially necessary, not only for the security of the route, but for the safety of American citizens passing and repassing to and from our Pacific possessions. Were such a stipulation embraced in a Treaty between the United States and Nicaragua, the knowledge of this fact would of itself, most probably, prevent hostile parties from committing aggressions on the route, and render our actual interference for its protection unnecessary.

"The Executive Government of this country, in its intercourse with foreign nations, is limited to the employment of diplomacy alone. When this fails, it can proceed no further. It cannot legitimately resort to force without the direct authority of Congress, except in resisting and repelling hostile attacks. It would have no authority to enter the territories of Nicaragua, even to prevent the destruction of the Transit, and protect the lives and property of our own citizens on their passage. It is true, that on a sudden emergency of this character, the President would direct any armed force in the vicinity to march to their relief; but in doing this he would act upon his own responsibility.

"Under these circumstances, I earnestly recommend to Congress the passage of an Act authorizing the President, under such restrictions as they may deem proper, to employ the land and naval forces of the United States in preventing the Transit from being obstructed or closed by lawless violence, and in protecting the lives and property of American citizens traveling thereupon, requiring at the same time that these forces shall be withdrawn the moment the danger shall have passed away. Without such a provision, our citizens will be constantly exposed to interruption in their progress, and to lawless violence."

On the subject of ocean and foreign mail service, the Postmaster-General, among other things, says "By the time the contract for the California line, *via* Panama and Tehuantepec expires, October 1st, 1859, it is probable that the route by Lake Nicaragua will have been reopened and in successful operation. This presents the question whether one, two, or three of these routes shall thereafter be employed for mail purposes. The Tehuantepec route is the shortest and most readily protected against interruptions, but it will be comparatively too new, and the line of stages too long, to furnish with certainty adequate and satisfactory communication between our Atlantic and Pacific possessions.

"While it is destined, no doubt, to become a Transit of the first importance, and will deserve the highest patronage and encouragement, still it cannot supersede the necessity of one or more routes through Central America. It is of the highest importance that the route by Nicaragua should be reopened, and its undisturbed use for the transportation of the mails, passengers, troops and munitions of war secured by the solemn guarantee of a public Treaty. Without this, in view of the unstable condition of the local Governments of Central America, the safety and security of the transportation can hardly be relied on."

We need not expatiate upon the tenets embraced in the President's Message. The importance of the demands therein contained speak for themselves. If, as has been fully tested already, Nicaragua is incapable of protecting the Transit Route, and thereby preventing it from being at any time summarily closed, it is proper that the United States should, in common with all other nations, see that its neutrality be preserved.

At Leon, Granada, Managua, Masaya, and Rivas in the interior of the State, many Americans, as also other foreigners, have located; at Realejo and San Juan del Sur on the Pacific, at Virgin Bay on the Lake, and at San Juan del Norte or Greytown on the Atlantic side, numbers of our citizens have embarked their fortunes in mercantile pursuits. As merchants, trading to and from the United States and Europe, they must be deeply and vitally interested in the opening of the Transit. Why should they be compelled to suffer damage, and even utter bankruptcy, if Nicaragua possesses the power to keep the route open? Claims for losses through the neglect of Nicaragua might be sustained, if the State admits her efficiency, yet fails to interpose her strong ,arm. The truth is, she is weak, her Governments are spasmodic, meteoric, and Mr. Buchanan has but demanded that, which will find an echo in the heart of every American that throbs on Nicaraguan soil.

At a later period, Monsieur Belly, from France, negotiated a Charter for a canal through Nicaragua, which has been the cause of much controversy in this country and Europe. If the Charter granted to the American Atlantic and Pacific Ship Canal Company is in force, then M. Belly and his associates must survey a new route altogether.

The Paris Press publishes the full correspondence which took place between the United States Minister to Nicaragua, and the Foreign Minister of Nicaragua, touching M. Belly's Conventions. The former says that no arrangement with M. Belly shall be recognized or assented to in any thing contrary to the just rights acquired by American citizens, and that a liberal policy, resulting from the Transit Treaty of November last, shall be constantly maintained.

The Nicaraguan Minister replies that his Government wishes only for justice and its rights, and desires to maintain friendly relations with the United States; but declares that the Transit Treaties are of no value, because the route was not opened at the stipulated period. M. Belly had appealed to the Clayton-Bulwer Treaty for protection, and Lord Malmesbury's letter to him says that the stipulations thereof will, in his own opinion, apply to his scheme, if carried out.

The Courier de Paris gives an account of M. Belly's plan for opening a communication between the Atlantic and Pacific Oceans, by means of a canal through the Isthmus of Panama. This project is one which Englishmen often read of in New York papers, where it is seldom mentioned without angry depreciation, although few, perhaps, could state its features off-hand. M. Belly, who some short time back obtained a concession of the ground required for the undertaking, has lately published a pamphlet in which he sets forth the advantages of the enterprise, and shows by maps the line of country through which the proposed canal is to pass. The Courier de Paris, in remarking on the project, adds some explanations which are of interest. It says:

"The first name which we meet with in examining the history of the project is that of Baron de Humboldt, who, after having examined in Central America the positions best adapted for the junction of the two coasts, gave the preference to the basin of Nicaragua. His 'Historical Essay on New Spain,' in which his opinion was expressed, was published in 1804.

"After that of the patriarch of modern science, we find the name of the prince who was destined to be Emperor of the French. Prince Louis Napoleon, during his stay at Ham, occupied himself with the grand idea of cutting through Isthmusses, and more particularly that of Panama. Like M. de Humboldt, he saw that Nature had taken care to indicate to the industry of man the line of communication to be established between the two seas, by the depression of the chain of the Cordilleras, and by the existence of lakes and of the river of San Juan de Nicaragua.

"A small work on the subject, by the Prince, was printed at

London, in 1846, but only a very few copies of it were struck off. It was, however, republished in 1849 by the Révue Britannique. It is reproduced by M. Belly in the volume, 'Percement de l'Isthme de Panama,' which he has just published, and which, in addition to an account of the project, contains all the documents relative to the great question.

"The project of M. Belly only differs from that of the Prince in not making use of the whole of the Nicaragua, and in crossing the Lake in its narrowest part. His plan necessitates a cutting in the ridge which separates the Lake from the sea. But the line would thus be almost straight, and the distance would be considerably shortened, as it would be seventy leagues at the outside, whilst in the plan of the Prince, it is one hundred and twenty. Such is then the result. By a passage of seventy leagues, vessels going from Europe, or from New York, to California, or to the seas of China and Japan, would be saved all the circumnavigation of South America.

"Let us add that the canal, of a depth of eight metres, (twenty-six feet), at a minimum, would admit the largest vessels, and that the total expense is estimated at one hundred and twenty million francs, whilst the annual revenues, according to the estimates of the authors of the preliminary project, would not be less than fifty million francs. And if we consider that the territory passed through is admirably fertile, and that M. Belly, in addition to the privilege of the canal, has obtained a concession of the complete proprietorship of the lands on both banks, to the width of four kilometres, (two-and-a-half miles,) we shall see the full mercantile value of an enterprise which is really of the very greatest value."

It then adverts to the political bearing of the proposed plan, and shows that the intention is to place the canal of Nicaragua under the general protection of the great powers, England and the United States setting the example.

"As to the political basis of the enterprise, they are those which are laid down in the Clayton-Bulwer Treaty. This Treaty, which was signed in 1850, binds England and the United States with regard to the inter-oceanic communication. According to it the two powers mutually undertake to employ all their efforts for the opening of a canal between the Atlantic and Pacific Oceans, by way of the River San Juan and the Lake of Nicaragua, to protect the Company which may be formed for the construction and navigation of the said canal, and to guarantee the neutrality of it.

"They oblige themselves, besides, to form no establishment calculated to menace the independence of the States of Central America, and to oppose any external attempt calculated to encroach on that independence, and they renounce in advance all advantages which may be accorded to their subjects to the prejudice of those of other States. Lastly, the Treaty says that other powers shall be called on to sign it, in order to cover with a common protection an enterorise destined to be for the interest of all.

"Such is the spirit of the treaty which gave rise to the Convention of Rivas. This Convention, which was signed on the 1st of May, 1848, between the Presidents of Costa Rica and Nicaragua and M. Belly, confers on the latter the privilege of constructing and navigating the canal; it consequently only accomplishes what the two Governments which signed the Clayton-Bulwer Treaty wished for.

"In realizing the enterprise dreamed of by Christopher Columbus, indicated by M. de Humboldt, and traced out by Prince Louis Napoleon, the Convention of Rivas completes the system of oceanic circulation, prepares the international fusion of races, and makes the liberty of the seas a reality. The cutting through the Isthmus of Panama, like that of the Isthmus of Suez, is neither French, nor English, nor American, and does not constitute either privilege or preponderance for any nation. France, in both undertakings, desires no other advantage than the honor of being able to say that two of her children have originated these great works."

There is little to be apprehended from this array of new influence on the Isthmus. That a canal is practicable from the mouth of the Rio San Juan to Lake Nicaragua, I do not believe, save at an enormous expense. A railway could be as easily constructed along the banks of the river. Once trade and travel sought the water—canals were dividend-paying enterprises. Now, the route for the traveler and for goods of value is overland. A Canal Company will fail here—they will reap losses, and their employees will die in the morasses after two months' exposure in this wild luxuriance of decaying and decayed vegetation.

The English and French journals frequently enlighten their readers upon the designs of the American Government in respect to Central America. In their view, the Government of the United States is seeking exclusive possession of the routes across the Isthmus, both for commercial and political ends. We are warned against our ambitious projects, and are told that England and France will not allow their commerce to be shut out from a free pass across the American continent.

We hope that the President's explicit declaration in his recent Message, that the United States "would not, if they could, derive any advantage from the Nicaraguan route not common to the rest of the world," will be sufficient to satisfy these European journals of their error. General Cass' letter to Mr. Lamar, upon the same point, says: "The United States do not seek either the control, or the exclusive use of these routes; they desire that the advantages should be equally common to all nations."

It is very plain from these declarations, that the United

States are seeking no exclusive advantages, in the settlement of the Central American question, but that the purpose is to open the routes across the Isthmus to the commerce and travel of all nations. While making these declarations regarding the intentions of the United States, General Cass is equally explicit in respect to the intervention of European powers, in any other way than by joining to secure the freedom of these routes, and to "make them neutral highways of the world, not to be disturbed by the operations of war." Dwelling upon this subject, he says:

"But the establishment of a political protectorate by any one of the powers of Europe, over any of the Independent States of this continent, or, in other words, the introduction of a scheme of policy which would carry with it a right to interfere in their concerns, is a measure to which the United States have long since avowed their opposition, and which, should the attempt be made, they will resist by all the means in their power.

"The reasons for the attitude they have assumed have been promulgated, and are everywhere well known. There is no need, upon this occasion, to recapitulate them. They are founded on the political circumstances of the American continent, which has interests of its own, and ought to have a policy of its own, disconnected from many of the questions which are continually presenting themselves in Europe concerning the balance of power, and other subjects of controversy arising out of the condition of its States, and which often find their solution or their postponement in war.

"It is of paramount importance to the States of this hemisphere, that they should have no entangling union with the powers of the Old World, a connection which would almost necessarily make them parties to wars having no interest for them, and which would often involve them in hostilities with the other American States, contiguous or remote. The years which have passed by since this principle of separation was first announced by the United States, have served still more to satisfy the people of this country of its wisdom, and to fortify their resolution to maintain it, happen what may."

This is language not easily misunderstood, and language that the people of the United States will endorse by their action, if circumstances should require it. They want no exclusive privileges themselves, nor will they permit any other nation to have any. They claim for their citizens no exclusive right to form contracts for opening Transit Routes in Nicaragua. M. Belly or any one else may make such contracts with the Central American Powers. But no contract with him, or any one else, can interfere with previously-existing engagements with American citizens, and the regulations and conditions of the Grant shall be such as to render the routes safe and free to all nations, but controlled by none and upon moderate and reasonable terms.

CHAPTER XXVIII.

A DASH AT POLITICAL HISTORY—EXTENT AND POPULATION OF GUATEMALA—HOW IT WAS GOVERNED UNDER SPAIN—HER LIBERALITY AND ITS ABUSE BY THE MOTHER COUNTRY—DISCONTENT AND INSURRECTIONS—INDEPENDENCE DECLARED—GAINZA CHOSEN PRESIDENT—A GENERAL CONGRESS CALLED—CONSTITUTION—SUBDIVISION INTO STATES—POPULATION AND CAPITALS—BOUNDARIES OF THE UNITED PROVINCES—THE LEGISLATIVE POWER—STATE REGULATIONS—NATIONAL FLAG AND ITS DEVICES—THE DREAM OF THE CASTILIAN.

THE kingdom of Guatemala was governed by a Captain-General, appointed by the mother, Spain, and a Royal Audiencia, with powers to take cognizance over an extent of country estimated at twenty-six thousand one hundred and fifty-two square leagues, and extending from 8° to 17° North latitude, and from 82° to 95° West longitude, with a population of about one million two hundred thousand. It was subdivided into fifteen provinces; five on the margin of the

Atlantic, five on the Pacific, and five in the interior, each governed by inferior officers subject to the Royal Audiencia.

An Archbishop and three suffragans had charge of spiritual affairs. The ecclesiastical division of the kingdom was composed of four bishoprics, comprising two hundred and twenty curacies, seven hundred and fifty-nine parochial churches, and four establishments for the conversion of infidels. Fully impressed with the prowess and greatness of Spain, and believing her to be the mistress of Europe, the military force within her limits was indeed meagre, not more than fifty soldiers being required for the security of her domain.

The present century undeceived them relative to the actual powers of the mother country, and a new era pregnant with important events succeeded the dark years of submission. Remote as Spain was, and tyrannical as was her colonial system, its administration here was comparatively mild, and her stern, harsh edicts were easily evaded. Patents of nobility were purchased by some of the wealthier families, and through flatteries they won upon the Viceroys, whom they in turn ruled *ad libitum.*

About 1803 and '4 the public purse of Spain was so far depleted that a voluntary subscription was required from her colonies. Guatemala generously furnished her quota, and yet, instead of receiving any favor from the mother country, unjust and excessive taxations followed as the recompense for her known liberality. Her literary and scientific societies were incensed and suspended by these glaring and repeated acts of despotism and ingratitude, and during the years of 1812, '13, and '14, feverish symptoms manifested themselves in many of the provinces.

In 1815 an insurrection occurred in Leon (Nicaragua), but it was suppressed, and the leaders of the revolt were sent to Spain. From that time to 1819, discontent displayed itself, secret meetings were held, and the masses seemed swayed by a vast and almost uncontrollable impulse. The spirit of independence which had so long been smouldering, flamed in more than one quarter of the new world, and the fate of Mexico was decided in 1821. News of this reached Guatemala, and only increased the universal fermentation.

At this juncture Gavino Gainza arrived, appointed by the Cortes of Spain, bearing intelligence of the late political changes in the peninsula, and the establishment of the Constitution. Meetings were organized, the leading families, and the influential members of the Church assembled, and on the 15th of September, 1822, the Independence of Guatemala was publicly proclaimed. A proclamation was issued, and it was resolved to call a General Congress for the 1st of March, 1822. In the interim a provisional Government was formed, consisting of a Council composed of individuals selected from the different provinces, of which Gainza was chosen President.

However, the union of this Congress was prevented by subsequent events. Iturbide ascended the Mexican throne shortly after, and strifes occurring between San Salvador and Guatemala, absolute Governments were formed, thus abrogating all ideas of the Union anticipated on Sep. 15, 1821.

A proclamation was issued on the 29th of March, 1823, reconvoking the General Congress, and on the following 24th of June, the Constituent Assembly, as it was termed, met. With the exception of Chiapa, which was firm in its adherence to Mexico—and Nicaragua, which was distracted by internal revolutions, each State sent deputies to this Congress, though San Salvador, having dispatched troops to aid Nicaragua, her deputies were not so soon seated. After the nomination of an executive, one of its first acts was, "the declaring of these provinces independent of Spain, Mexico, and every other power, either of the old or new world." This is dated July 1, 1823.

The basis of its future Constitution, now that the Congress was fully organized, was published Dec. 17th, and Guatemala was declared a Federal Republic, comprising five States confederated, under the title of the "United Provinces of Central America, viz., Guatemala, consisting of thirteen Departments, the Capital of which was Guatemala. These Departments comprised one hundred and fourteen towns and villages, with a population of about seven hundred thousand. San Salvador, embracing four Departments, Capital, San Salvador, and comprising fifty-five towns and villages, and a population of about three hundred and fifty thousand. Honduras, consisting of twelve Departments, Capital, Comayagua, fifty-seven towns and villages, with a population of about two hundred thousand. Nicaragua, consisting of eight Departments, Capital, Leon, comprising fifty-three towns and villages, with a population of about two hundred thousand. Costa Rica, consisting of eight Departments, Capital, San José, comprising twenty-one towns and villages, with a population computed at fifty thousand.

These States contain about twenty-two thousand square leagues, bounded on the north by the Atlantic, south and southwest by the Pacific, southeast by Veraguas, and west and northeast by Mexico, comprising about one million five hundred thousand inhabitants, and were to be governed on the principles of Federal Republicanism. The Legislative power was ordained to reside—first, in a Federal Congress, and second, in a Senate, composed of two Senators popularly elected by each State. The Executive power was vested—first, in a President popularly chosen, second, in a Vice-President, third, in a Supreme Court of Justice. The internal affairs of each State to be regulated independently upon the following basis: first, by an Assembly of Deputies; second, by a Council; third, by a Chief; all to be popularly elected; fourth, by a Vice-Chief; fifth, by a Supreme Court of Judicature.

Wars and revolutions succeeded, and the Constitutions of the different States were decreed as follows: That of Guatemala, October 11th, 1825; San Salvador's, June 12th, 1824; Honduras', December 11th, 1825; Nicaragua's, April 8th, 1826; Costa Rica's, November 22d, 1824. In 1824, the Republic was decreed under the name of "The Republic of Central America," with a national flag, having for its armorial devices five volcanoes, and bearing the motto, "Dios, Union, Libertad,"—God, Union, Liberty.

We close our brief sketch, and as elsewhere we have given the various changes which occurred, we shall now direct attention to the proposed Ship Canal, and present distinctly in outline the progress from the Conquest, with the search after the Secret of the Strait, the grand desideratum of the Castilian, which he supposed would indeed open to the Crown the gates of a Paradise, little less in value than those to be reached by years of contrition, penitence, and prayer.

CHAPTER XXIX.

THE VALE OF ANAHUAC—ORIGIN OF THE MEXICANS—EMIGRATION TO YUCATAN AND GUATEMALA—THE CASAS GRANDES—THE SIX TRIBES AND DESERTION OF THE FIVE—THEIR FORTUNES AND MISFORTUNES—FOUND THE CITY OF MEXICO—SACRIFICE A CHIEF'S DAUGHTER—ELECT A KING—HOME IMPROVEMENTS COMMENCED—MONTEZUMA THE ELDER SUCCESSFULLY WAGES VARIOUS WARS—MONTEZUMA THE YOUNGER—COMING OF THE SPANIARDS—GUATEMOZIN AND HIS FATE—CORTES RETURNS TO SPAIN—DIES OF A BROKEN HEART—WHAT WAS DONE WITH HIS REMAINS—HIS TITLE AND ESTATES—THE BLOOD OF THE MONTEZUMAS IN THE VEINS OF CASTILIAN NOBILITY—ASSASSINATION OF PIZARRO—HIS TITLE, ESTATES, AND DESCENDANTS—WHAT WAS DONE WITH HIS REMAINS—ONE OF HIS FINGERS IN BALTIMORE—THE HOLY CROSS AND ITS IRRESISTIBLE ARGUMENTS—MONTEZUMA TO RETURN AS A DEITY—EL PARAISO DE MAHOMA AND REFLECTIONS.

FROM the Vale of Anahuac, or of Waters, embracing a beautiful district, the whole country, called subsequently by the Spaniards New Spain, received the name of Anahuac. It has since been given to the dominions of Spain in North America, occupying the entire extent of the northern boundaries to the kingdom of Guatemala, and often embracing that territory also.

The origin of the Mexicans, or the nations of Anahuac, is very obscure; but according to Clavigero, the Toltecas, who inhabited the country north of Mexico, left their homes, or were banished, and journeyed south in search of a proper locality whereon to fix their habitation. For the space of one hundred and four years they wandered, till at length reaching the Vale of Anahuac, they erected a city fifty miles east of the city of Mexico. At Tula they founded the capital of a dynasty which lasted three hnndred and eighty-four years. They appear to have been well skilled in arts, industrious, civilized, and living under the government of kings in a peaceable manner.

In the year 1052, a dearth and pestilence nearly desolated the country, and a great number of their people having died of famine, many of those who survived emigrated to Yucatan and Guatemala, leaving but a remnant of this once flourishing empire in Tula and Cholula. For one hundred years the Toltecan country was nearly deserted. After this interval from the North came another race—the Cachemecas—whose manners were less refined. The source whence they emigrated they called Amaquemecan. They settled about six miles from the present city of Mexico, and were governed also by kings, who encouraged them to cultivate the friendship of these poor

Toltecans who survived, and who gratefully taught them in return many of the arts.

This monarchy lasted till 1520, nearly five centuries. Other tribes, of which the Otomies and the Acolhuans were the chief, entered into alliance with the Cachemecas. Eight years afterward came the Tarascas and the Nahuatlacas. The Aztecas, or Mexicans were the last; they came from a country beyond the Gulf of California, in the year 1160, when they moved southward, and traces of the buildings they left are said to exist on the banks of the Rio Colorado, and the Rio Gila. They came from a country called Azatlan. They stopped for a time at some point in New Biscay, about 250 miles North Northwest from Chihuahua, and there built the Casas Grandes, in 29° North latitude.

This large edifice is constructed with three floors, and is crowned by a terrace; the lower floor has no door, and the upper is accessible only by a ladder, which is still the style in which the buildings of New Mexico are constructed. This House or Fort has been surrounded by a wall, Humboldt says, seven feet thick, and in which enormous stones were used; the beams of pine are said still to exist. In the centre is a keep or mound—the whole has a ditch about it, and earthen pots and jars, with mirrors of the Iztli stone have been dug up in the vicinity.

When the Aztecs left their native land, they consisted of six tribes, namely, the Mexicans, Tepauecas, Chalcese, Tlahuicas, Tlascans, and Xochimilcans. They fashioned the image of the Deity Huitzilopochtli, at Culiacan, on a throne, to carry on the shoulders of four priests. The five tribes deserted them on quitting Culiacan, and journeying with the Deity, arrived at Tula, the Capital of which the Toltecans had built, erecting altars at all their resting-places on the road.

Here, and in the neighborhood, they remained for twenty years. In 1216, they came to Zumpanco, a large town in the Vale of Anahuac, where they were kindly received, and the son of the Chief, Ilhuicatl, married one of their women, from which alliance descended the race of Mexican Emperors. They wandered about the Lake of Tezcuco, settling in different places, and at last entered into wars with the Cachemicas and Acolhuans, and were obliged to fly to some islands called Acocolo, in the Southern part of the Mexican lakes. Here they remained for fifty-two years, in great poverty and distress, being enslaved by the chief of a petty state called Coluachan. It is believed by Clavigero and Humboldt, that the Toltecs, Acolhuans, Chichimecas, and Nahuatlacs, spoke the same language, and probably emigrated from the same degree of North latitude.

A few years subsequently, a war ensued between the Xochimilcans and the Cholhuans, in which the Mexicans assisted their masters, and battled so bravely as to win their freedom. The latter, however, treated their captives so brutally, inhumanly cutting off their ears, and offering human sacrifices to their Deity, that the Chief of the Cholhuans commanded them to quit his territory. They moved to a spot near the junction of Lakes Chalco and Tezcuco, which place they named Mexicaltzinco, and thence they went to Iztacolo, nearer the location of the present City of Mexico.

Here they remained some two years, when, wandering about, they discovered on an island in the Lake, an omen foretold by their oracles to be their future home. They built some miserable reed huts, and having taken captive a Cholhuan, sacrificed him to their Deity, erected an altar, and prepared to fix their permanent abode here. To this Island and Town they gave the name of Tenochtillan, and subsequently building their huts round the altar of Mexitli, their God of war, they called the town Mexico, or the City of Mexitli. This took place in 1325.

The omen referred to, was, finding on a rock in the Lake, the "Eagle on the Prickly Pear." Here they dwelt long in a wretched manner; the situation being chosen merely from the omen, was uncomfortable, and also small, and finally they were necessitated to drive stakes, and to make dykes to the adjacent islets, by which means they shut out the water, and connected the islets so as to gain considerable space for building. They then furnished themselves with necessaries, constructed floating gardens on the lake, with mud and branches, and thus struggled on through a press of privations for thirteen years, when an old quarrel having been resumed, they divided into two cliques; one party remained, while the other sought a neighboring island, called by them Tlatelolco, afterward joined to the others by mounds.

The original Mexico was now divided into four quarters, and in the centre was the temple of Mexitli or Huitzilopochtli. They remained in barbarism for some time, and sacrificed a daughter of the Chief of Colhuacan, whom, under a specious pretext, they had invited into their city. The outraged father waged war against them, but they were equally powerful with himself; their Government had been hitherto an aristocracy, the nation obeying a council of their Great Chieftain. They found now, that a Monarchy was best adapted to their views, first, because their neighbors had adopted that form of Government, and second, because their territories consisting only of the City, one person was better able to perform the duties of the kingly office than several. Acamapitzni was therefore selected their King and leader. This Prince married a daughter of Acolmiztli, King of Coatlican.

The Tlatelolcos also chose a king, the son of the King of the Tepanecans, who oppressed them much for fifty years, thirty-seven of which Acamapitzni governed Mexico. He took another wife, and had by her a son, Hiutzilihiutl, and by his concubines several children, of whom Izcoatl was the most renowned. In this reign, buildings of stone were erected, and canals for use, and for the adorning of the city, were commenced. He died in 1389, having swayed his sçeptre with great success. Four months afterward his son Hiutzilihiutl succeeded him by the universal choice of the people. He had two wives, one, the daughter of the King of the Tepanecas, the other also a princess. By them he had two sons, the latter bearing him the famous Montezuma Ilhuicamina. After a reign of twenty years, he died in 1409, and was succeeded by his brother Chimalpopoca, who having been thrown into prison by the king of Acolhuacan, committed suicide.

Itzcoatl was the son of Acamapitzni by a slave. Thence ensued wars between the neighboring rival kings, especially the Tlatelolcans, who were fully equal to the Aztecs. Their first king died in 1339. Itzcoatl, on his accession to the throne, built temples, made many public improvements, subdued neighboring provinces, and concluded an alliance with the exiled prince of Acolhuacan, whose father had been killed, and he the son supplanted by an alien. This Prince declared war against the usurper, and took several cities. Itzcoatl sent Montezuma to congratulate him. He was taken prisoner, but by treachery escaped to Mexico, when Maxtlaton, the usurper of the Acolhuacan throne, declared war against Mexico on account of the Aztecs allying themselves with the exiled Prince Nezahualcajotl. The Aztecs were terrified, and demanded of their king to make peace, but Montezuma urged their commencing hostilities.

War followed: victory sat doubtful on either banner for an entire day: but as night approached, Montezuma, with other chiefs, rushing to the front, captured, with his own hand, the general of the enemy, and completely discomfited them. Next day the battle was renewed, when the Tepanecans were defeated, and their city taken. Subsequently the entire nation was subdued, and became subject to Itzcoatl, who replaced Nerahualcajotl upon the throne. The Tepanecan country he gave to Totoquihuatzin, with the title of King of Tacuba; these kings formed an alliance offensive and defensive. The Xochimilcans, fearing the power of the Aztecs, declared war against them, but their strongholds and cities were taken by Montezuma, and from a petty group of island huts, Mexico, through the address and courage of this Prince became the most powerful of all the adjacent States.

In 1436, at an advanced age, Itzcoatl died, and Montezuma succeeded to the throne. He erected an immense temple, obtaining the victims to be sacrificed at his coronation from a war then waging between the Chalcese and Tezcucans, in which the former were defeated. This coronation was the most magnificent ever witnessed.

Probably next to the Aztecs, the most valiant tribe were the Tezcucans. Although their province was small, it was defended by natural fortifications, high rocky ridges, and deep gorges, upon whose sides bristled loose boulders, and although in a measure subservient to Mexico, the Tezcucans ever evinced their love for their province, and their ability to defend it. Bernal Diaz gives a full and glowing account of the hardy Tezcucan mountaineers, and the old soldier pays them merited tributes.

The King of Tlatelolco having formed a conspiracy against Itzcoatl, and having renewed his designs upon Montezuma, the latter deposed him and placed Moquihuix on the throne. Many provinces were wrested from their chiefs to adorn the coronet of Montezuma. He then engaged in war with the King of the Mixtacas, the Huexotzincas, and the Tlascalans, and suffered a reverse, though he finally defeated them. He conquered also the Cholulans, the Chalcese, and other tribes, until his empire stretched from the Gulf of Mexico nearly to the Pacific. In 1446, Mexico, having suffered from an inundation, he constructed a dyke nine miles long, to prevent any future calamity arising from the same cause.

Montezuma died in 1468, and was succeeded by Axaycatl. It was under the reign of this Prince that the Provinces of the Tlatelolcos were added to those of Mexico, and their king's heart (Moquihuix) was torn out by Axaycatl. He also waged successful wars against the Matlatzincas, and died in 1477. His brother Tizoc ascended the throne. He was succeeded by his son Cacamatzin, who was afterward captured by the Spaniards. Then came Ahuitzotl, his brother, who completed the Great Temple commenced by Tizoc. The human sacrifices he offered at its dedication, it is said, amounted to seventy thousand. This took place in 1486 and 1487, when Mexico was violently shaken by an earthquake. This monarch was a warrior from his birth. His conquests extended to Guatemala, a distance of nine hundred miles from his Capital. The Aztecs, however, were defeated in 1476 by the Atlexcans, under their Chief, Huexotzincas.

Ahuitzotl died in 1502. Then succeeded Montezuma the Second, called Montezuma Xocotzin, or the Younger, who was a Priest, and a Prince of extreme bravery. His coronation was more magnificent than any of his predecessors, while his household retinue was composed solely of people of rank, whom he favored particularly, at the expense of the other classes. His style of living was most sumptuous, and extravagance marked his every measure; he was bigoted—a patron of the arts, generous, and swayed his sceptre with dignity, though his disposition was extremely haughty and tyrannical.

At this period, when Montezuma's kingdom had risen to unusual splendor, the Spaniards having settled in Cuba and Hispaniola, determined to explore the Continent to the West, and Vasco Nuñez de Balboa, having landed on the Coast, descried the Pacific from the summit of the mountains. This was in 1513. The empire of the Aztecs at this time extended five hundred leagues from East to West, and two hundred from North to South. Montezuma died, and was succeeded by his brother Quetlaoaca or Cuitlahuitzin, in 1520, who gave evidence of proving a good king. He prepared to receive the Spaniards in his Capital, but in the same year, during the preparations for the continuance of the war which had been so vigorously carried on by his brother, he died of the small-pox, and his nephew Guatimozin occupied the throne.

The characters of Montezuma and Guatimozin are so well known, that it would be idle and useless to dwell upon them here. The courage and constancy of the latter during his defense of Mexico have been favorite themes of former writers, and it is well known that he was captured in a canoe by Sandoval, one of the officers of Cortés. His address to the latter when he appeared a prisoner before him will never be forgotten. "I have done my duty as a king—sheathe your dagger in my body—my life is now useless to myself and my subjects."

Although a captive, and allowed to remain in the Capital upon certain pretexts, Cortés took him with him in an expedition to Honduras. During the march thither, one of the Indian converts in his train, informed Cortés that a conspiracy had been set on foot by his captive-king with the Cacique of Tacuba and other nobles, to seize a favorable moment when the army should be entangled in the defile or morass, and rise upon the

Spaniards. After the destruction of the latter, the Indians were to march on to Honduras, and cut off the Spanish settlers there, then to return to Mexico, effect a general rising of the tribes, seize the vessels, and thus exterminate the invaders.

Cortés immediately arrested Guatimozin and the Aztec lords in his train. From the latter he learned the truth of the Indian's story, they alleging that the plot had been planned by the Prince, but denying their own participation in it. The Prince neither denied nor acknowledged the accusation, but maintained a dogged and stubborn silence. It was evident, however, that a rising of the Aztecs had been discussed, if not planned. Cortés ordered them to instant execution, and the prince with other nobles was hung from the branches of a ceiba tree by the roadside. Thus closed the line of the Imperial Aztecs in 1525, although the Imperial career was finished on the 13th of August, 1521, the day on which the Capital was taken. Here ended the race of Mexican Emperors, after a period of one hundred and ninety-seven years, and three hundred years from the emigration of the tribe to Mexico.

Cortés pushed on, but subsequently alarmed by tidings of discontent brewing in his Capital, he returned to Mexico. The Conquest of Nicaragua, Costa Rica, Darien, and the Gulf of Panama, would scarce have been too remote for the brilliant schemes of this daring adventurer, had not Fate willed otherwise. Basely treated by the country for which he had gathered immense revenues, he returned to Spain to urge his claims, and to avow his innocence of all preferred charges. After a series of misfortunes, he finally withdrew to the village of Castilleja de la Cuesta, attended by his son, where, on the 2d of December, 1547, in the sixty-third year of his age, he died of a broken heart.

His remains were transported to the Chapel of the Monastery of San Isidro in the City of Seville, where they were placed in the family vault of the Duke of Medina Sidona. In 1562, they were removed by his son Don Martin, to New Spain, and laid in the monastery of St. Francis in Tezcuco, by the side of his wife, Doña Catalina Pizarro, and a daughter. In 1629 they were again removed, and on the death of Don Pedro they were taken to the Church of St. Francis in the City of Mexico. Notwithstanding this removal, they were not permitted to rest by the authorities of Mexico, but in 1794 were taken to the Hospital of Jesus of Nazareth. In 1823 a mob, in commemoration of the era of their National Independence and their detestation of the early Spaniards, prepared to break open the tomb holding the ashes of the Conqueror and scatter them to the winds; the authorities even did not interfere, but the family, or their friends, entered the vault by night, and secretly removed the relics.

Cortes, by his first marriage, had no children. By his

second he left four: a son, Don Martin, and three daughters, who formed splendid alliances. "He also left," says Prescott, "several natural children, whom he particularly mentions in his testament, and honorably provides for. Two of these, Don Martin, the son of Marina, and Don Luis Cortés, attained considerable distinction, and were created Comendadores of the Order of St. Jago. The male line of the Marquesses of the Valley, became extinct in the fourth generation. The title and estates descended to a female, and by her marriage were united with those of the house of Terranova, descendants of the 'Great Captain' Gonsalvo de Cordova. By a subsequent marriage, they were carried into the family of the Duke of Monteleone, a Neapolitan noble."

Montezuma, dying, commended three favorite daughters to the protection of Cortés. After the death of the emperor, they were baptized, and subsequently married to Spaniards of honorable descent and family, and from them descended several noble houses of Spain. To Doña Isabel, Cortés granted the city of Tacuba, and several other places as a dowry. The house at Castilleja de la Cuesta, near Seville, Spain, formerly occupied by Cortés, has been recently purchased by the Duke de Montpensier, with a view to its being repaired and preserved as a national monument. The Spaniards do not often trouble themselves about their antiquities.

And here having traced the career of Hernando Cortés to

its close, we may, without violence to our narrative, advert to another Spanish adventurer, Pizarro, the Conqueror of Peru, who after planting the Cross of the Crusade upon the desolated altar of the Incas, was assassinated in his palace on Sunday the 26th of June, 1541. Pizarro, unprepared as he was, baffled for a long time the combined efforts of sixteen assailants to dispatch him, but finally overpowered, he sank, his body pierced with the swords of several of the conspirators. The dying conqueror traced a cross with his finger on the bloody floor, bent down his head to kiss it, murmuring "Jesu! Jesu!" when a stroke ended his struggling existence.

The friends of Pizarro prevailed on his enemies to suffer them privately to inter his remains. The body was wrapped in a cotton cloth, and removed to the Cathedral; a grave was dug in an obscure corner, the services hurriedly completed, and thus, in secrecy, was the Corse of the Conqueror consigned to kindred dust. In the language of Gomara, "There was none even to say, 'God forgive him!'"

Subsequently, upon the restoration of tranquillity, the remains were placed in a coffin, and deposited under a monument in a conspicuous part of the Cathedral. In 1607, his bones were removed to the New Cathedral, where they reposed by those of Mendoza, Viceroy of Peru. Pizarro was never married, but by an Indian Princess of the Inca blood, he had a son and daughter. Both survived him, but the son died ere reaching manhood. The mother wedded Ampuero, a Spanish cavalier, and removed with him to Spain. Her daughter Francisca accompanied her, and subsequently married her uncle, Hernando Pizarro. The title and estates of Francisco did not descend to his illegitimate offspring; but in the third generation the title was revived in favor of Don Juan Hernando Pizarro, who was created Marquis de la Conquesta, with a liberal pension. His descendants, bearing this title, are still to be found, says Prescott, at Truxillo, in the ancient province of Estramadura, the birth-place of the Pizarros.

In a "Ramble from Sydney to Southampton," published in 1851, the following interesting article appears: "In the crypt, under the high altar, are deposited the remains of the celebrated Pizarro, who was assassinated hard by. A small piece of silver, which I dropped into the hand of the attending sacristan, procured me admission into the crypt. Descending a few steps, I entered a small place, some twenty feet long, quite light, and whitewashed, and which smelt and looked so much like a comfortable wine-cellar, that I caught myself more than once looking round for the bins and bottles. The first object I saw was a large square tomb, surmounted by the erect figure of an Abbot, and, close by, in a narrow opening in the wall, I noticed, what first appeared to me to be a collection of dusty rags, but a closer inspection proved that this was all that remained of the renowned Conqueror of Peru."

He had still on him the clothes and shoes which he wore at the time of his assassination. Of course his body is nothing but a skeleton, covered with dried flesh and skin, so that no features are discernible. The body is covered with what was white linen swathed around him, but the dust of centuries had collected on it, and turned it into a light-brown color, and it almost pulverizes when touched. The body is placed on a narrow piece of plank, in a sloping position, and was put in this hole merely to get it out of the way. The folks in Lima do not think any thing of the remains of poor Pizarro, and I dare say that a little money, judiciously invested, would procure for any curiosity-hunter the whole of his remains." Dr. Cohen of Baltimore has one of the fingers of Pizarro.

Thus closed the lives of the most illustrious leaders of the Conquest known in Spanish history. The followers of Pizarro and Cortés were far from being the chivalry of Old Spain; they were adventurers, whose minds, excited and elated by the returns of gold and precious stones from Mexico and Peru, only saw in those new regions a prodigality of wealth, to be won by the swords of the daring, and who, probably, bankrupt in fortune, dreamed of an El Dorado, where, in a single campaign, they might regain fabulous riches, and riot in Indian pleasures.

The Cross reared upon despoiled shrines, whether of the Aztecas or the Incas, only added a cloak, a solemnity, an earnestness to their purpose; but the cruelties attendant upon the introduction of the Holy Catholic Faith were strange arguments wherewith to justify the Confessor's lessons of Justice, Humility, Good-will, and Love! From the throne to the hut, the population received the new Faith, baptized with the blood of their fellow-beings, and the bigotry and recklessness of the Fathers of the Conquest but illy paralleled the acts of Him, who on Golgotha offered himself for the Redemption of mankind! It is to these scenes of plunder, pillage, and violence, the memory of the exiled Indian reverts, as he gazes upon the Holy Cross—he feels an awe creeping over his soul, as he marks the Fathers, as of yore, chanting the Mass, and he innately shudders as he notes the dominion of the Church extending over his native haunts.

It has been said by some writer, "that from the outermost margin of this Continent to the shores of the Atlantic, the name and fame of Montezuma is cherished by the various tribes." Many of the Indians of Nicaragua, with still unextinguished, though secret veneration for their hidden Idols, nourish the hope, and sacredly cling to the belief, that this most unfortunate of the Aztec Emperors, will yet return and re-establish his Empire, and, hoping for the Paraiso of yore, where, ere the mailed steeds of Castile brought dismay and carnage, Montezuma, to his people, was the reflection of their Deity—the impersonation of Infinity.

We have thus given an extended sketch of the origin of Mexican civilization, because Guatemala at the time referred to comprised Nicaragua, and was peopled by the same tribes or their descendants. The flow of Empire has been westward; the gems of Honduras, the fertile valleys of Costa Rica, with her pearl fisheries, the minerals of Nicaragua, with its salubrious climate—these attracted the avaricious Conquerors, and ere long they broke in upon the peacefully-governed plains whither the shattered remnants of the vanquished had fled, and found a temporary retreat.

Nicaragua was justly termed El Paraiso de Mahoma. The early tribes who had journeyed from the far distant North, where wars were waging, found, as they progressed in their exile, pleasant hills and valleys, luxuriantly covered with shady groves and pleasant fruits, where nature offered them a generous support and exacted but little, if any labor in return. The spirit of the warlike grew more social as he came in contact with his fellow-man, and the magical power of agriculture revealed to him something beyond a subsistence to be gained by weapons imbued in his brother's blood.

The warrior, in his sterner Northern clime, had imbibed a spirit, a love for war, but in the soft luxuriancy of the South, new scenes suggested new ideas, and prompted the erection of protections against the Sun. The love for war was succeeded by enthusiasm, a wish to venerate something. There was a Giver—a God—a Deity—a Parent of all this teeming grandeur and goodness—and in the deep leafy arcades, on the mountain crests, in the dim niches of the echoing valleys, pyramids arose, fashioned by the once bloody hands, and dedicated to a Deity. Although adored by human sacrifices, this was a step toward civilization, inasmuch as the idea born might and would in time tend to the cultivation of ennobling thoughts and humanizing practices. The Deity they worshiped had protected them through their weary pilgrimage, and the Vale of Anahuac, once the scene of sacrifices, soon received the genial influences of the Christian religion, and the sacrificial stone and bloody knives were succeeded by the Baptismal Font and the Rosary.

The remains of ancient cities attract the tourist in Guatemala. Ruins of much interest have been found in Nicaragua, and we may truly hope that the records of the past may not be entirely destroyed, but may yet serve to throw much light on the early history of this interesting country. Nations have fallen, and been succeeded by others on our Continent. We vainly strive to gather data from the archives of oblivion ; the tide of Time remorselessly sweeps important documents beyond our reach, and we must soon rely on the History of the Indian —Tradition !

CHAPTER XXX.

EL SECRETO DEL ESTRECHO—THE SECRET OF THE STRAIT.

CORTES IN SEARCH OF THE STRAIT—WHAT PRESCOTT SAYS ABOUT IT—WHAT OVIEDO THOUGHT OF CORTES' OPINION—ALVARADO IN SEARCH OF IT—CHRISTOVAL DE OLID TRIES HIS HAND—THE SECRET TO MAKE CHARLES THE FIFTH LORD OF THE WORLD—ALL THE MARITIME NATIONS OF EUROPE TRYING TO PENETRATE IT—SPAIN EAGER ON THE SUBJECT—BALBOA CLAIMS THE ENTIRE PACIFIC OCEAN—REVELS IN GOLD AND GEMS—FINALLY SUFFERS AS A TRAITOR—PEDRO ARIAS AND HIS TREACHERY—THE CONQUERORS OF MEXICO AND PERU MEET IN HONDURAS—MUTUAL ASTONISHMENT OF THE WARRIORS—SPECULATION STILL RIFE AS TO THE STRAIT—THE SECRET YET IN EMBRYO—FIVE POINTS OF TRANSIT—THE RIO SAN JUAN AND THE RAPIDS—OBJECTIONS TO A SHIP CANAL—ADVANTAGES OF A RAILWAY—ESTIMATES AND REMARKS.

Cortes in 1524 fitted out an Expedition, the principal object of which was to discover a Strait which should connect the Pacific and Atlantic Oceans. He also had another squadron of five vessels for the same purpose in the Gulf of Mexico, to take the direction of Florida. This discovery was then, as others have been in our times, "the great ignis fatuus of navigators." Prescott very justly remarks: "By some it was supposed that the Rio San Juan had been at one time navigable for frigates, and the Lakes Nicaragua and Managua, as well as the Rio Tipitapa, were also considered to be one vast sheet, and thence, there seemed to the early Spaniards, to be a certain exit to the Pacific."

Oviedo, although he considered Cortés "the greatest captain and most practiced in military affairs of any we have known," thought his opinion relative to the Strait "proved him to be no great cosmographer." The conversations and correspondences of men of science touch frequently upon this subject. Columbus wrote to the Emperor: "Your Majesty may be assured that, as I know how much you have at heart the discovery of this Great Secret of a Strait, I shall postpone all interests and projects of my own for the fulfillment of this grand object." (*Martyr*, *Opus*, *Epist. Ep.* 811.) Alvarado was deputed, with a large force of Spaniards and Indians, to descend the southern plateau of the Cordilleras, and penetrate the countries beyond Oaxaca. This Expedition terminated in the Conquest of Guatemala.

An armament was equipped and placed under the command of Christoval de Olid, who was to steer for Honduras, and plant a colony on its northern coast. A detachment of this squadron was subsequently to cruise along its southern shore toward Darien in search "of the mysterious Strait" The country was reported to be so full of gold, that "the fishermen used gold weights for their nets." (*Rel. Quarta, Ap. Lorenzana, page* 385.)

In 1523, the Emperor Charles V. enjoins Cortés to search carefully for it, and the latter in reply, adds: "It would render the King of Spain master of so many kingdoms that he might consider himself Lord of the World." Cortés, however, was compelled to return to Spain, and the search was abandoned.

The Romans knew little of a world beyond the Western waves; their acquaintance with Southern and Middle Europe, and a portion of Africa and Asia being imperfect and limited, for they were not a maritime nation, and water is the element of the discoverer. Subsequently Europe, being divided into independent nations, the Republics on the Baltic and Mediterranean launched their vessels upon the waves, seeking commercial advantages, while Spain and Portugal competed with the Eastern Caravans in their search for another avenue leading to the Indian Spice Islands.

"The discovery of a strait into the Indian Ocean," says Prescott, "was the burden of every order from the Government. The discovery of an Indian passage is the true key to the maritime movements of the fifteenth, and the first half of the sixteenth centuries." And again: "The eagerness to explore the wonderful secrets of the New Hemisphere became so active, that the principal cities of Spain were, in a manner, depopulated, as emigrants thronged one after another to take their chances upon the deep."

The Venitian Ambassador, Andrea Navagiero, who traveled through Spain in 1525, notices the general fever of emigration. Seville, in particular, he says, was so stripped of its inhabitants, that the city was left almost to the women. "The El Dorado," where the sands sparkled with gems, and golden pebbles as large as birds'-eggs were said to be dragged out of the streams in nets, the emerald mines of Peru, where the gems were found upon the surface, the turquoises and amethysts of infinite varieties, and the massive chains of gold, composed of large lumps of the precious metal, of exquisite quality, wooed the adventurous to this Land of Light, called by the Spaniards, Castillo del Oro—Golden Castile.

What were naked Indians, armed with spears, clubs and primitive weapons, to the shield, helm, and coats of mail of the Castillian Knights? What were hunger, thirst, fevers, death even, to those who, from continuous poverty, heard tales of enchantment, and tottered from their couches, to enrol themselves under the banners of the Conquerors? What to them was the Holy Cause—the Faith? Not what buoyed the Templars and Hospitallers on the arid sands of the East—a watchword of belief—and who dying in defense of the Red Cross, were assured of an eternity in Paradise! No! The incentive was gold, and while the Aztecs mourned their national degradation, new altars were builded, and a new God adored. Even then, the golden shores of the Pacific were yet unexplored—unknown.

How magnificently resounded through Castile the report of Vasco Nuñez de Balboa, the discoverer of the Southern Sea, who while weighing some gold collected from the natives, was accosted by a young chieftain, who had been attentively marking the satisfaction expressed upon the features of the strangers.

"What! is it this you desire?" said the Barbarian.

"Yes!" replied the Chivalry of the Conquest. "Gold! Gold!"

The chief struck the scales with his hand, and scattering the treasure far and wide, contemptuously exclaimed, "If this is what you so much prize that you are willing to abandon your distant homes, and risk even life itself for it, I can tell you of a land where they eat and drink out of golden vessels, and gold is cheap as iron is with you. To the North! To the North!" and Balboa, armed to the teeth, rushed frantically to the Pacific, where he exclaimed, "I claim this unknown sea with all that it contains for the King of Castile, and I will make good the claim against all, Christian or Infidel, who dare gainsay it."—(*Herrera—Dec.* 1, *Lib.* 10, *Cap.* 2.)

Darien was occupied, but Balboa in 1519 transferred his Capital to the ancient site of Panama, which although unhealthy, was favorably located for maritime enterprise. Years elapsed, and the country South of this was unsought, the detection of a Strait which was supposed must intersect some portion of the extended Isthmus, being enforced strictly by the Government. Balboa next landed on the shores of a territory, the name of whose Prince, was Coura. Thence he navigated various streams and bays, and steered toward the dominions of a Cacique named Tumaco.

This Chief opposed the landing of the strangers, but peace ensuing, the Spaniards received many valuable presents in token of entire pacification. Some of the servants of the chief brought gifts of gold to the value of six hundred and fourteen pieces-of-eight, and two hundred and forty-five large pearls, with many others, which, though small, were bright. These gems were not so white as usual, owing tò the Indians having used fire in opening the oysters. The Spaniards evincing such great joy upon receiving the pearls, the Cacique sent some of his Indians to fish, who within four days, returned with as many as weighed no less than ninety-six ounces. The Cacique assured Nuñez that there was a country about five leagues from thence, where there was an abundance of large oysters, which contained pearls as large as beans.

Subsequently, Nuñez was created Lord Lieutenant of the Countries on the South Seas by the Crown, Pedro Arias d'Avilla having been chosen Governor of Castillo del Oro. This officer is commonly called Pedrarias by the Spanish writers. Nuñez in 1517, in the 42d year of his age, suffered as a traitor, for having served his Prince with too much zeal and fidelity. A course of cruelty finally compelled Pedro Arias to think of removing from his palace at Panama, to some remote spot, where his enemies would forget, if they would not forgive him.

About the beginning of 1526, the Court of Spain, wearied with continual complaints against him, determined to send a successor; Pedro hearing of this, determined to retire to Nicaragua, whose conquest, already attempted by Francisco Hernandez, he resolved to secure to himself. Francisco advanced cordially to meet him, but Pedro pretending to have received information that the latter intended to revolt, treacherously seized, and had him beheaded. Hated and despised, yet he was confirmed in his government of Nicaragua, a fitting tool for the Inquisitorial rack and cord.

Veragua and Costa Rica were subsequently occupied by other leaders, and the mailed knights, forcing their way through morasses, over mountains, and through dense jungles, started aghast, when in Honduras, they heard the trumpets of Christian comrades pealing defiance, and rushed astonished into mutual view. Then, and not till then, had the survey of this wild Realm been completed, and the warriors met, only to exchange tales of wonder, feats of daring or legends of pleasure, one exhibiting gold and gems, another magnificently painting the beauties of the soft-eyed Amazons, or the dusky daughters of down-trodden Azatlan.

Since that time speculation has been rife, relative to the Strait, and five points of Transit have been indicated, which we give, although Mr. Squier has already written very ably upon the subject.

First. The Isthmus of Tehuantepec, between the sources of the River Chimalpa and the Haasacualco, falling into the Atlantic.

Second. The Isthmus of Nicaragua, by the River San Juan, Lake Nicaragua to the Gulf of Fonseca, the Gulf of Papagaya, or the Port of Realejo.

Third. The Isthmus of Panama.

Fourth. The Isthmus of Darien.

Fifth. The Isthmus between the Rio Atrato, falling into the Atlantic, and the Rio Choco, falling into the Pacific.

From the Lake Nicaragua, however, several routes have been suggested. One by the River Sapoa to the Bay of Salinas. One by the Rio Lajas near Rivas, (however, utterly impracticable), to San Juan del Sur, the present Transit. Another, by the Rio Tipitapa to the Port of Tamarinda, on the Pacific, or to Realejo, or by the Estero Real to the Bay of Fonseca.

In the first place, the Rio San Juan has many streams issuing from it, which bleed it so profusely, that at times even the boats drawing eighteen inches run aground; the Tauro, Colorado, Serapaqui, and the San Carlos, must first be dammed up, ere a sufficient volume of water could be had upon which reliance might be based. I have weighed maturely the various suggestions of those interested in this Canal, and if I mistake not, Mr. Squier expresses doubts as to the navigability of the San Juan for vessels of large size. He also deems the Castillo Rapids a formidable objection.

I do not believe these Rapids to be the result of any upheaving from natural causes, but are chiefly artificial, and I further believe, that were these mouths, the Colorado, Tauro, and the San Juan dammed, the immense body of water flowing from the Lake, would cut and keep open a very considerable channel, which would greatly improve navigation. The Colorado being the heaviest drain, I paid minute attention to this bleeder, and do not doubt that a comparatively small sum paid to an enterprising Yankee, would sufficiently choke it off.

The Rapids of Machuca, Mico, Los Valos, and the Toro, are inconsiderable, though of course each of these obstructions would receive their quota of a capital raised for their removal. The difficulty of Ship Transit never occurred to me to arise from any of these, but solely from the nature of the base of the River, and in a measure from the nature of its banks, they being so yielding as to add greatly to the alluvial deposits, during the rainy season. The bottom of the river is flinty rock, and an incalculable amount of labor and money would be required for the construction and completion of the Great Ship Canal.

But why should the world at large harp forever on this mode of Transit? Why not attempt a railway from Greytown, on the right bank of the Rio San Juan, to San Carlos? The idea is as valuable as his who suggested the Canal! For all purposes, supposing steamships to augment, trade would be as greatly facilitated, if not in a greater degree, than by a Canal. Supposing the latter to be completed, would not a longer time be required for the passage of ships from the Atlantic to the Pacific than would be necessary for the unloading at Greytown and the reloading at San Carlos together with the overland railroad conveyance? Steamers upon the Lake would be necessary of course, and yet trade would be facilitated immensely, for in the event of such an arrangement, Americans would form a nucleus around each depot, and there need be no necessity for depending upon the Nicaraguans.

A fine trade would ensue from the interior alone—Nicaragua would be benefitted by it, as also Costa Rica, and in a much less time could a railroad be constructed. I believe it to be as practicable as the Canal. But the latter has occupied the general attention, and although the Government of Nicaragua has entered repeatedly into negotiations for such a desirable national improvement, the ignis fatuus survives the attempt. A pamphlet was written upon this subject by the present Emperor of France, Louis Napoleon, when at Ham, but it is devoid, I believe, of the merit claimed for it by its author, and his estimates are certainly incorrect.

Baily estimates the Rio San Juan, including its windings, to be eighty-eight miles in length, and therefore it has a fall of about sixteen inches to the mile. The result of three hundred and fifty-one levels taken by him in 1838 between San Juan del Sur and the mouth of the Rio Lajas, shows that the level of the Lake is one hundred and twenty-eight feet three inches above that of the Pacific. Mr. Lloyd estimates the Pacific at low water in the Bay of Panama, to be six feet six inches lower than the Caribbean Sea at Chagres. Assuming this, we have Lake Nicaragua one hundred and twenty-one feet nine inches above the Atlantic. The variation of the level with the season is about six feet six inches.

Relative to the cost of making such an immense Canal, which would most probably be the largest in the world, and fit to be stamped Napoleon de Nicaragua, could it be constructed for two hundred millions of dollars, would the trade guaranty its outlay? Eight out of every ten laborers sent there would die—provisions could be obtained only at exorbitant prices, while the comforts of a home could not be had on any terms. In many localities on this river it rains every day in the year while heavy fogs lie above the tree tops, producing a close, damp, choking atmosphere, markedly oppressive.

The change is very remarkable as you touch the Lake. There the air is fresher and purer, but as you descend the river you feel at once that you have reached a different climate. And again, fuel along this Transit is fast becoming scarce. The wood being porous and wet, generates but little steam, and the stations are illy supplied. Coal could be transported on the railway from the Atlantic Terminus to the Pacific, but this can be done to little extent now, upon the stern-wheel boats. At times during the rainy season, they can barely carry their load of passengers, and I have known the river-boats to run aground on sand-bars formed within twenty-four hours, and forced to remain there frequently all night, exposing their living freight to the most insinuating rain. There they would anchor till daybreak, when, to lighten the craft, the passengers would have to leap overboard, and give a "helping hand."

To those who dream of a Ship Canal, I only add, be no longer befogged—and to those Capitalists whose expectancies are merged in vessels and foreign trade, I would suggest the Railway as equally feasible. Beds of coal have been discovered in Costa Rica and on the Mosquito Coast, and consequently this article could be had at less expense than the poor wood of the neighboring country.

For purposes beyond a traveling Transit, the Rio San Juan will not be used for many years to come; and should a Railway be constructed through the Chiriqui District, where advantages are greater for a similar mode of transportation, travel would decrease on the Nicaragua Transit, inasmuch as there is wanting capital and energy with the inhabitants, and the state of the country will be no doubt for years as it has been, unsettled, and foreign Capitalists will not venture where there are so many chances for outlay, and so few for revenue, without the Cass and Yrisarri Treaty be fully and fairly entered into.

Should the Government of Nicaragua be once firmly based, and not made the butt for contending factions, as heretofore it has been, this State may occupy the most important position on the Map of New Spain; and should her mines be explored, her revenues would guaranty extensive public improvements worthy of a nation, which in many respects is far superior to the different races which surround her—remnants of the exiles from dismantled Azatlan.

CHAPTER XXXI.

CARDINAL SOURCES OF A NATION'S GREATNESS—THE FUTURE OF NICARAGUA—CONTAINS ALL THE ELEMENTS OF WEALTH—MUST AWAKE OR SLEEP FOREVER—A VIGOROUS REPUBLIC ON THE WING—THE GREAT NATIONS OF THE EAST FEELING HER INFLUENCE—HER SHADOW ALREADY ON THE HALLS OF THE MONTEZUMAS—BLIGHTING INFLUENCE OF THE MOTHER COUNTRY—THE REPUBLICS OF THE GREAT SOUTHERN CONTINENT—CALIFORNIA A VAST NATIONAL MART—SAN FRANCISCO THE CONSTANTINOPLE OF THE AMERICAS—OUR GOLD HUNTERS AND THOSE OF THE CONQUEST—MOUNTAINS NEVER KEEP ACCOUNTS—THE GREAT PACIFIC RAILWAY—THE PRESENT MAIL ROUTE—AN AVENUE NEEDED FOR THE TRADE OF ASIA—OUR CONTINENT A WORLD IN ITSELF—ADVANTAGES OF THE PROPOSED SHIP CANAL—GREAT BRITAIN VERSUS THE UNITED STATES.

THE cardinal sources of a nation's greatness are, no doubt, Agriculture, Commerce, and Manufactures. Nicaragua can only, to a very limited extent, claim them as standards of her present position as an independent and vigorous Republic. Weak in her army, devoid entirely of a marine, she possesses but little ability to defend herself from the armed aggressors or fillibusters, who seek wealth, pleasure, and repose in her inviting territory.

With a population sufficient to rouse her from the lethargy of the Past, with products capable of enabling her to assume her proper rank among vigorous nations, and with a superabundance of mineral wealth wherewith to support her dignity as a Republic, naught seems wanting save an innate spirit of Enterprise. As yet, her minerales yield gold only to strangers; her extent of public lands are unredeemed from total neglect; *Disunion*, that baneful, leprous curse, prowls through her realm, and Religion, in the absence of her first-born—Education, doubly mourns the inattention to her invocations. Lying in the path of the thriving, enterprising Republic of the United States, she must either rouse from her apathy, or she will indeed add, in a few years, but one more star to our Banner.

A wise provision in the Constitution of a State may woo the stranger to her domain, a cold reserve will chill his approach. The Plain of Leon is admirably adapted to the cultivation of sugar, and many sections to the growth of cotton. Her tobacco ranks high, her soil is generous, and to the agriculturist indeed inviting. Her mines are abundant and wealthy. Can it be that she will indulge in the apathy of the by-gone? Where the rank grass waves, crops of maize should flourish, and where the swarthy Cayman reposes, the settler would obtain his muck for vegetation. A little liberality upon the part of its Government would quickly meet an ample recompense. From San Jorge to Realejo are found haciendas, with but few exceptions, in even tolerable condition. Everywhere is a lack of enterprise and capital. A system of drainage would produce an ample supply of excellent water, and the climate would hence be improved. To an American, life in this land would pass as a pleasant dream.

To him who, reared in the mountainous districts of the United States, seeks bracing air and a life of excitement, Nicaragua offers great inducements; to the ardent Southerner, Rivas, Granada, Managua, and Leon appeal; to the enthusiast who would woo Nature, here is she prolific in charms, and to him who has dived deeply into the yawning gulfs in search of ores, I can only add, here he cannot be disappointed. With a population introduced, composed of such, the Future of this State would indeed be glorious. With the proposed Canal and her subsequently-developed resources, we could proudly acknowledge this Central Land as a kindred Republic. But as I write, her destiny is being recorded. She must awake, or sleep forever; for while she apathetically resigns herself to an inactivity neither "masterly" nor advantageous, a vigorous Republic is on the wing, whose tramp is heard on the neighboring islands as she marches to her Pacific children.

The European powers are concentrating on the eastern borders of Asia. Australia, from being a penal colony, springs magically into importance, her gold replenishing the exhausted coffers of the Eastern Hemisphere, while her agricultural resources, vast, illimitable, invite and retain the thrifty husbandman, alike with the industrious and enterprising mechanic. Japan is opening her sealed ports, and American influence has impressed its masses with our ability, courage, and advancement as a great people. China and Cochin-China are peering from behind their ancient walls, and inquiringly scan us *vis-a-vis,* while Russia, cold in climate, breaks the fetters of her serfs, and without jealousy, marks our Flag upon foreign lands and seas, and meets us openly and fairly in our national exchanges.

Spain perceives our shadow lying on the threshold of the halls of the Montezumas—on the dominions of the Incas—on the shores of the Antilles—and she feels we must eventually plow her ancient empire on this Continent. And how true the suggestion that whatever France, England, Russia, and Spain may accomplish here, our Republic must eventually become enriched thereby. The Empire of Brazil exists, 'tis true, and Portugal possesses in her transatlantic territory a treasure. Yet her minerals are undeveloped, her forests unknown, her diamond mines but imperfectly worked, and her agricultural resources certainly not in a progressive state

The soldiers of Pizarro inculcated in Peru not an idea of thrift. They marched over her soil, despoiling, murdering, blighting. The industry of her population was crushed in the germ, and the public works of the Incas, grand in conception and magnificent in design and detail, have fallen to decay, or remain in a state of semi-completion, as when the gold-shod steeds of the Conquerors knelled on the arched bridges death and devastation through the heart of their Empire. The Chilians are somewhat awakening from their past degradation, though the South Americans, generally, are but little removed from the slavish condition in which they were when the Mother of the Conquest abandoned the New World for her Hispanian shores.

In proportion as the Eastern shores of Asia become thronged with Europeans, are the resources of our Pacific States developed, and thither are drawn magnetically the Republics of the Southern Continents, who, enervated by hitherto spasmodic kite-flying in bogus minerales and short-lived speculations, seek our enterprising markets, not only desiring to acquire affinities political, but to partake of the wealth which is steadily flowing to us in honorable, orthodox, mercantile pursuits. Already are our engineers, architects, and mechanics engaged on the Southern Continent, spanning with bridges and railways the hitherto trackless wilds, and as our Territories fill up, the intercourse between North and South

America must increase. Our relations with the world at large are comparatively undisturbed, our resources are annually increasing, and the great work of peopling the Pacific shores invites our energies and capital. The traffic from our realm is not to be limited to China or Japan. The vast Tartarean region of the Amoor River, the Seas of Ochotsk and Kamschatka, the Philippines, Borneo, Sumatra, the Eastern coast of British India, Burmah, Ceylon, Siam, and the numerous groups of islands in Oceanica, may be engrossed in the account.

Let us approach the subject, prepared to invest, provided we find in its investigation a guaranty for the capital desired. California must be made an Emporium—a National Mart. Its position justifies the undertaking. Thither various routes are already tending from the Atlantic sea-board. Railway, Steamship, and Clipper Companies, are all dispatching valuable freights of travelers and goods, and all striving for advantages over their healthy and energetic competitors. Established railways are becoming connected by lateral routes, while new ones are springing annually into existence, and the two months' travel to New Orleans of a few years past, has already been reduced to about four or five days. From thence, San Francisco can be made in sixteen days *via* Tehauntepec, and thence to Shanghai in eighteen more. Fresh teas from China may therefore be upon the sale-counters in Philadelphia in thirty-eight days—now the time necessary for sailing vessels is at least four months—sometimes more.

Various surveys are traced to the Constantinople of the Americas. True, these numerous branches will merge into one Capital Trunk, leading thither-ward, and in a few years the links thus forged will form a complete chain, and our Republic will stand on the Pacific, the Banker of the world. But this great chain should be a national one. The climate through which surveys have been made possesses every advantage. Our territory would be more easily protected, and hence safer and more inviting to the native and emigrant.

From all directions of our country, the mails bring fresh news from the Mines, and add new gold washings and findings to the already extended list. In the Middle States the precious ore has been found, and from Maryland to Virginia is but a pleasant trip; then the Carolinas, Georgia, Alabama, Kentucky, Tennessee, and the States bordering on the great range of mountains, all yielding the auriferous deposit, blended in rock, or found in the generous streams. Our new-sprung Territories—some of them scarce baptized, with their earliest accents, send tidings of continuous washings. Nebraska from the Cherry and Dry Creeks, and the Platte River, gives us thrilling news; and far on the outer-basin, Frazer River, invites the enterprising and hardy.

There is a vast field in Nicaragua, open for the agriculturist and the grazier, for where there is and has been a general desire, in fact, a mania, for gold fields, the venders of the necessaries of life have accumulated all the wealth, while the miners, in the majority of instances, have either returned home almost as poor as when they left, or have ruined their constitutions in incessant toil in damp and unhealthy localities, where they amassed their "dust" at the expense of their health. The history of the gold hunters of the Conquest compares with that of those of the present age, and we should profit, by a perusal of those pages which chronicle the vices, the few virtues, and the superstitions and violences of the bygone.

The sudden enjoyment of great wealth had its natural and unwholesome effect; the means thus lightly obtained were little prized; the passion for gaming was indulged in without restraint, and the prize money which was the reward of years of toil, was oftentimes staked and lost in a single night. The Spaniard Lequizano, whose share of booty in one victory in Peru, was the image of the Sun, and who lost it in the indulgence of this national vice, gambling, has fathered the Spanish proverb, "Juéga el Sol antes que amanezca"—Play away the Sun before Sun-rise. The acquisition of fortunes, whether by a chain of successes at the gaming table, or by "streaks of luck" in mining, are seldom beneficial or lasting, for where the soldier stakes his last *réal* and loses, he consoles himself with a new conquest, and the miner turns from the monte-table a bankrupt, with the proverb, "Well! Well! Mountains never keep accounts."

The gold-bearing quartz we have traced along the routes of the Great Central Road to the Constantinople of the Americas, whose history will be written with a pen of gold at some remoter period. For the full development of our resources, and the union of the Pacific with the Atlantic, three continental lines of railway are necessary. One, starting from the west shore of Lake Superior, traversing Minnesota, Nebraska and Washington, about on the parallel of the forty-seventh degree North latitude, and terminating at Puget Sound. Another starting from St. Louis, crossing Kansas and Utah to San Francisco, in latitude thirty-eighth degree; and the third, from Memphis, Tennessee, traversing Arkansas, Texas, the southern part of New Mexico and California to San Diego, on the Pacific.

A wagon-road is even now established between San Francisco and the Mississippi, and the feasibility of one of the above indicated routes, has been thereby evinced. That road has been established within a year past, by order of Congress, for the conveyance of mails and passengers between St. Louis and Memphis, and California, and per contract, the Company stipulate to carry the letter-mails semi-weekly, each way, in four-horse post-coaches, suitable for the conveyance of passengers, and to make the trip within twenty-five days. The route selected by the Post-Office Department for this Mail Line, probably possesses superior advantages, admitting of travel the entire year, without interruption from snow or severe cold, affording a practicable stage-road the whole way, and furnishing accommodations of water, food, forage and fuel along the line. The starting-points on the Mississippi, are St. Louis and Memphis, and the two branches converge at Little Rock in Arkansas; thence the road crosses the northern portion of Texas, the southern part of Mexico, striking the head of the Gulf of California at Fort Yuma, and proceeding north-westerly across California to San Francisco. From Memphis to San Diego the way is plain.

This is a practicable Rail-Road Route, for the distance traveled by the Post-Coaches, is eighty miles per day. The trade with Asia seeks an avenue across the Continent, and this as well as travel between Europe and Asia will prefer this route, provided we forestall Great Britain in her desire to build a rail-road from Halifax through the Canadas to Victoria on the Pacific. This latter, however, would cost at least two hundred and fifty millions of dollars, and when completed, the track would be covered with snow for six months in each year, and for three or four more additional, it is said with water.

A quarter of a century past, and the summer tourist viewed a trip beyond the limits of his own State, indeed a journey;

now he seeks the Rocky Mountains, and as he roams through its grand ravines, and from some hoary pinnacle gazes far down upon the glorious lap of Nature, how grandly do the beauties of his own domain—his native land, appeal to his soul! The Alps, the Rhine, dwindle into insignificance when compared with creations in our own realm! Our continent is indeed a world in itself. On our matchless prairies, and in our unexcelled savannahs, we can sow and reap, and the harvests are sufficient to feed a world. Where find finer timber, grander streams, more majestic scenery? Where find a more enlightened nation? In her progress already, she hath proven her strength and activity.

Our Steamers sweep the Seas, our Clippers sail in the wake of no foreign and competing crafts, our mechanics are myriad, and that which they must learn they acquire but to excel in. Thirty millions strong, and at peace with mankind! Even this truism seems fabulous! We are adrift upon a Sea, and our helmsman fears not the storms beating against our Ship of State! Thirty millions of freemen, proud of their independence, untrammeled, nerved for action, look forward for the consummation of the great work leading to the Mediterranean of the Future, where the Pacific, far exceeding the Mediterranean of the Past, leads to a nation of freemen, not serfs and slaves, bigots and despots. In the days of the Conquest, Cortés and his followers looked on the Pacific as the famed Indian Ocean, studded with golden islands and teeming with the rich treasures of the East.

The Telegraph and Rail-Road will, in my opinion, advance us as a nation, in the present century, beyond the dreaming fantasies of the wildest enthusiasts, and with Protection upon our Minds as well as upon our Banner, our Victory is assured. San Francisco is already in telegraphic communication with Utah Territory. A line extends to Geneva in Carson Valley, and it will be carried to Salt Lake; there connecting Salt Lake City with our Western telegraphic limits, we shall have a working communication from San Francisco to Washington, and thence to all our Eastern Cities.

The advantages to the United States, in point of distance from Canton and Calcutta, per the proposed Nicaragua Ship Canal Route, must strike the reader. From England to Canton *via* the Canal, is fifteen thousand eight hundred miles, while by the Cape of Good Hope it is only fifteen thousand six hundred. From New York *via* the latter, to the same port, seventeen thousand one hundred, but by the former, only twelve thousand six hundred miles. From England to Calcutta *via* the Cape of Good Hope, thirteen thousand five hundred miles, and *via* the Canal, seventeen thousand four hundred. From New York to the same, by the former route, fifteen thousand miles, and per the latter, fourteen thousand.

By the best present route, Great Britain enjoys an advantage in distance to the Asiatic ports of seventeen hundred miles, while, should the Canal ever be perfected, there will be a gain in favor of the United States of three thousand miles—an average of fifteen to twenty-two days. From England to Valparaiso per the Cape of Good Hope, nine thousand one hundred and thirty miles, while New York is ten thousand three hundred and sixty; but *via* the Canal, England would be eight thousand five hundred, and New York only five thousand five hundred miles. Again: From England to Callao, by the Cape, ten thousand six hundred miles; New York per the same, twelve thousand one hundred, while by the Canal we find the distance from England only seven thousand miles, and from New York four thousand.

The Sandwich Islands from England, are fourteen thousand five hundred miles per the Cape; from New York, sixteen thousand. *Via* the Canal, the distance would be from the former, eight thousand five hundred miles, and from New York five thousand five hundred. Will our nation seize these presented advantages, and in concert with others, consummate the proposed Ship Canal, or will we concentrate capital exclusively upon our own domain, and speed the Grand Central Rail-Road, which shall connect the children now scattered from the maternal side, yet seeking protection?

CHAPTER XXXII.

HOW THE CASTILIAN CONQUEST WAS ACHIEVED—THE ROMANCE OF THE FIFTEENTH CENTURY—CAPITAL OF THE QUICHE KINGDOM—LAS CASAS IN GUATEMALA—CONFLICTING OPINIONS AMONG AUTHORS—WHOSE SHALL WE ACCEPT?—THE PAST AND PRESENT OF MEXICO—SENATOR HOUSTON'S PROPOSITION—WHAT BRANTZ MAYER SAYS—WHAT THE ABBE MOLINA SAYS—WANT OF CONFIDENCE ILLUSTRATED—NICARAGUA AS IT IS—WHAT PRESCOTT SAYS—WHAT SPAIN WAS UNDER FERDINAND AND ISABEL—WHAT SHE IS NOW—CAUSES OF A NATION'S RISE OR FALL—DESTINY OF THE UNITED STATES—ONE OF WEALTH AND UNIVERSAL REDEMPTION.

THE Conquest was achieved by the Castilians, aided by rival factions of the countries whose shores the invaders sought; the Tlascalans, who had been subdued in the onset, by Cortés, proved allies subsequently, in the hour of need, without the aid of whom, his followers must have perished, as would those of Pizarro unsustained by national reinforcements. The Aztecs and Peruvians disunited, fell victims to those, who with superior weapons, and skilled in warfare, whether in field or ambush, felt their superiority; and who kindled anew, at every advance, the smouldering fires of discord and hate.

The romantic history of the Incas and Aztecas, possesses an interest which flooding years neither erase nor dim. The question of the early independence of Guatemala, Don Domingo Juarros has especially defended with marked zeal and ability; he has adduced arguments to prove that it was never subjected to the Mexican sovoreigns, although at the same time acknowledging, "that a considerable emigration took place from Mexico at a very early period." While Cortés was engaged in his wars in the latter, civil war was raging in Guatemala, between two of the most powerful nations of the Province, the Kachiquels and Zutugils. The fame of Cortés having reached this country, the King of the Kachiquels sent deputies to him, asking his aid, and offering submission to Spain. Pedro Alvarado, with three hundred Spaniards and a large force of Mexican allies, were sent, arriving in the beginning of the year 1524, when they commenced an attack upon the Quichés, the most warlike and numerous of the thirty tribes of the kingdom. Disorganized, and disunited, the different races fell under the unrelenting sword of Castile.

The King of the Quichés, joined by other States, mustered on the Plain of Tzaccaha, two hundred and thirty-two thousand warriors, who, defended by entrenchments, and surrounded by fosses lined with poisonous stakes, were yet completely defeated in the first contest by the small army of Alvarado. The Spaniards pursued their advantage, and by the middle of the year, had subdued the entire country. The City of Utatlan, the Capital of the Quiché Kingdom, was said by Fuentes, to be indeed magnificent; and so populous, that the king was enabled to draft from it "no less than seventy-two thousand combatants to oppose the Spaniards." After a minute description of the city, he says, the Grand Palace surpassed every other edifice, and in the opinion of Torquemada, it could compete with that of Montezuma, or of the Incas.

We are compelled to forego an account in this volume of the early history of Guatemala the Mother of Nicaragua, who in the far-gone ages of the Conquest, possessed both wealth and civilization. Although Indians—and characterized by some recent authors as ignorant, cunning and deceitful—yet the most authentic accounts represent them otherwise, and as a whole much in advance of the nations surrounding them. In the variety of its languages, Guatemala presents a still more singular phenomenon than Mexico—twenty-five, according to Juarros, being still spoken. Of course the Castilian became the language in vogue. Philip II. ordered a correct history of the inhabitants while in a state of Idolatry, to be written by the resident Priests, which, if prepared, cannot be discovered. No tradition exists, which proves, or leads to the supposition that human victims were offered to Idols. Las Casas settled in Guatemala in 1530, and with meek humility, mild persuasion, and acts of kindness, won Vera Paz, which had baffled the arms of the hitherto victorious Castilians.

Shall we, in reviewing the past of Spanish America, accept the statements of Botturini, Gomara, Solis, Robertson, Bernal Diaz, Clavigero, Sahagun, Ixtlilxochitl, Torquemada, and a host of other writers who have labored in this field? Shall we reject the researches of Muñoz, who, by a royal edict, was allowed free access to the public archives, and to all libraries, public, private, and monastic? Upon what shall we predicate our knowledge of the bygone, if we accept and reject carelessly, or confine our researches only to the dim pages of a solitary tome? Upon no subject do historians more widely differ in their views and results, than upon the early histories of Mexico and South America, some, relying implicitly upon the statements of a certain author, or set of authors; others, as in the case of Prescott, principally basing their deductions upon Bernal Diaz; while Judge Wilson, and others, entirely disregarding old authorities, hold Diaz as a counterfeit personage, and his history consequently a fiction. By the former the Conquerors are held to be soldiers of the Holy Faith, glowing with religious fervor, by the latter they are considered as demons, who devastated the provinces of poor Indians. The majesty of the ancient Aztecs is denied them, and the whole career of Cortés and Pizarro, instead of being one of romantic chivalry, as depicted by Prescott, is beclouded with demoniac ferocity, and rendered, only as a great Indian war, or a succession of rapid, startling battles, waged by the expert and mailed warriors of the East against naked, ignorant tribes.

Shall we credit the historian who, regardless of established authorities, and by an evident desire to be novel in opinion, now seeks to entirely subvert our romantic associations with the Aztecs and Incas, and to establish his own arguments, proclaims Gomara, a De Foe, Bernal Diaz, a myth, De Alva, a magician, Boturini, Clavigèro, Veytia, and others, romancers, and yet what better does he proffer to sustain his sweeping charges against the array? For myself, I have not ventured beyond historic realms, my subject only in a measure being linked with the Early History of the Aztecs and Peruvians. There was a definiteness, a fixedness in the purposes of those nations, which I cannot trace with any of the Indian tribes of the early United States.

At the beginning of the Sixteenth century, before the arrival of the Castilians, the dominion of the Aztecs "reached from the Atlantic to the Pacific, across the continent. Under Ahuizotl, its arms had been carried into the farthest corners of Guatemala and Nicaragua." Their form of government, pursuits, and mode of life, differed materially from mere Indians; in fine, though in some respects similar, in the aggregate there appears to me to have been more of intellect in the Aztec in those remote ages, than has ever been discovered since amid the tribes whom modern writers assimilate, and with whom they identify them. Prescott, from a mass of manuscripts, has produced his Conquest of Mexico as perfect as the student could desire. He has carefully weighed each authority adduced, and when conflicting testimonies presented themselves, has invariably scrutinized the positions of the authors, their motives, their inducements to miscalculate and mislead, and has decided impartially.

Governments, revered by their subjects, would have withstood successfully the feeble arrays brought against them; but foes *without*, leagued with traitors *within*, accelerated the ruin of the "ill-compacted fabrics." Succeeding generations mourn successive turmoils, and the Mexican of the Present, witnesses or participates in kindred revolutions, allied to one faction or the other, who, in turns, hail with enthusiasm a Despotism or a Republic. Like the French, they have had both, and still like the former, they have saddened, sickened, and revolted under each. They refuse to be devoured by a lion, but are being gnawed piecemeal by rats.

The proposition of Senator Houston, of a Protectorate over Mexico, which was received with levity when broached, now hath its weight. Shall we interfere to protect bands of banditti from ruthlessly murdering each other upon our own confines? Have we the right to prevent continual warfare on our continent and in our midst? Must all intercourse, political and commercial, be suddenly broken, that the conflicting parties may deluge the land in blood, and yearly lessen the national revenues? Already do our claims urge Executive attention. Shall their justice be deferred and denied, and shall we supinely mark the total prostration of Mexico's prosperity, assured of her future inability to discharge our claims, if she is thus periodically revolutionized, and not demand a cessation of hostilities, or a guaranty against bankruptcy? Is it not our right to have one or the other? Shall we purchase this ulcerous demesne, and thus assume its sovereignty, or shall we occupy the territory as security for our just debt? Will foreign powers interpose, as in the question of the purchase of Cuba, and shall they dictate, even to the possessor, the propriety of disposing of its wares? Is Spain no longer independent? Is she, as well as Mexico, wards of the European powers, and shall we have the Mosquito protectorate attempted again?

Brantz Mayer, in "Mexico as it was and as it is," remarks, "Nations habituated to be ruled for centuries, cannot rule themselves in a minute." And again: "Agriculture must be cherished, and farmers made to elevate themselves in society, to become rich by their toil, and cultivated by study. The mechanical class must become ambitious of being something more than the mere servant of the capitalist's wants." And again he adds: "It has been a difficult thing to make the Mexicans believe that they possessed any other kind of wealth but money or mines." The same author also observes: "The lesson of chicanery and corruption taught to its colony by old Spain, through her injustice and oppression, became a principle of action, and duplicity was raised to the rank of virtue."

Abbé Molina in his History of Chili, remarks in relation to the valleys of the Andes: "The vegetation here is more luxuriant and vigorous, and the animals larger and stronger than in the other parts of the country; but as the people who inhabit this district are Nomades or herdsmen, and in reality cultivate nothing, it is difficult to determine with precision the degree of their fertility." The constant demand upon those, who cultivate agriculture, in time of war, in all Spanish Countries or Provinces, has been the chief drawback in the development of the naturally rich soil. In Nicaragua, the mules are taken summarily from the cart and field, and "pressed" with the driver into the ranks. The indigo plantations, upon which much labor and capital have been expended, are abandoned, and the crop and the estate left entirely at the mercy of marauders and the elements.

With the Spaniard, the farmer has no caste, save in the light of a laborer. The adventurer, who magnanimously proffers his services to the State as a soldier, is received with pomp and parade, while he who would develop the resources of the country is looked upon with distrust, or only causes a ripple upon the surface of national attention. As an illustration, I offered certain information relative to the establishment of a Mint in Granada. There being none in Nicaragua, and the currency being chiefly Costa Rican, or that of the United States, I had expected that my proposition would receive attention. "The idea," I was answered, "was good, but who should be the Director ?" I at once perceived the want of confidence prevalent, and of course discontinued my negotiations. At all times, Capital can be enlisted in Spanish districts for the development of minerales, but it is impossible to raise any wherewith to consummate an agricultural operation, predicated, certainly, upon results less fickle and unstable.

As I have observed, in the former part of this work, a grazier in the Chontales district could amass a speedy fortune; yet it is extremely difficult to find even a tolerable horse or mule, and if found, the price desired is very extravagant. Beef is scarce in the market, and the little to be had, tough and lean, yet the abundant herds lowing over the green mountains, and through the fertile vales, justify my assertion, that to an American, life would here pass as a pleasant dream, and fortune be easily accessible. No stately modern structures pierce the sky in Nicaragua, no grand aqueducts, or macadamized roads, have been constructed by the modern Aztec;

the plains are as the race of old left them; no added pyramids, palaces or temples, yet the same Sun glows on the same hills, over the same savannahs; but the present race are broken in energy, they shrink from foreign contact, they are content in gazing mournfully upon the wrecks about them, and they dream, poetically, of the Past, and sigh for the grandeur of the era of Montezuma.

Prescott, in his "Conquest of Mexico," remarks in relation to the Mexicans of the present compared with the ancient race: "The difference is not so great as between the ancient Greek and his degenerate descendant, lounging among the master-pieces of Art, which he has scarcely taste enough to admire—speaking the language of those still more imperishable monuments of literature which he has hardly capacity to comprehend." And again: "The same blood flows in his veins that flowed in theirs. But ages of tyranny have passed over him—he belongs to a conquered race." The panegyrics of Sonnini and Eaton have led us astray, no doubt, on this subject, while Thornton and De Pauw have debased the Greeks. If they, the Mexicans and Nicaraguans, may never be truly independent, may they not be subjects, or citizens, without being slaves?

The Jews, and the Catholic peasantry of Ireland, suffer moral and physical ills—they live, struggling against truth—Are they vicious? If so, is it not in self-defense? Is the

Nicaraguan accustomed to gentleness from the outside world? His Atlantic sea-board occupied by England, his town of San Juan del Norte taken from him, and even its old name *whitewashed* or *greywashed* into the very English one of Greytown. Tigre Island once summarily occupied, Buccaneers and Fillibusters invading his home, is he to be thankful for these foreign invaders, and grateful for the introduction of such elements? Dogs, oft-beaten, snap at the fingers that casually caress them, and to the journalist who abuses, the traveler who misquotes and decries, and the foe who plunders and destroys them, the Nicaraguan and Mexican are to return a *Laus Deo!* Although they are divided, dismembered, they have Hope—the future will determine whence it tends.

The flag which waved over the throne of Isabel I. is less haughty, and flaunts over a shorn territory now under the reign of Isabel II. Under the enterprising regime of the former, Spain occupied an eighth part of the known world, its inhabitants numbering seventy millions, and its dimensions comprising a space of eight hundred thousand square miles. Of this vast domain, more than two-thirds have been lost. In 1565, the Isle of Malta was given up to the Order of St. John. In 1620, the Lower Navarre and Bearne were yielded to France, and in 1649, the Rousselon. In 1640 she lost Portugal and her colonies. In 1648 she recognized the sovereignty of the Netherlands. In 1626, the English wrested from her the Barbadoes; in 1665, Jamaica; in 1704, Gibraltar; in 1718, the Luccas; in 1759, Dominica; and in 1797, Trinidad. In the seventeenth century, France took possession of Martinico, New Grenada, Guadaloupe, and the half of the Isle of San Domingo, and in 1800, Louisiana.

In the eighteenth century she yielded up Sardinia to the Duke of Savoy, and to Morocco her rights on Mazalquivir and Oran. She ceded to Princes of the House of Bourbon, Parma, Placencia, and Lucca, with other dominions in the north of Italy, and in 1759, Naples and Sicily were emancipated from her government. In 1819, Florida was sold to the United States; in 1821 she lost her half of the Isle of San Domingo; and before 1825, all the vast continent which her ancestors had acquired by chivalrous conquest, was alienated forever. Of all her past immense power, what remains? Her African possessions, the Philippines, Porto Rico, and the Isles of Cuba. The Antilles comprise nearly all of her ancient empire in the New World.

At no period in her national existence did she occupy a more haughty position than under the reign of Ferdinand and Isabella. We find, in reverting to her history, that this was truly a warlike regime; then Charles I. the era of the soldier; under Philip II. the cowl and toga; then the Bourbons, courtiers, ribboned and starred; and again the soldier in Ferdinand VII. Her succeeding eras have been devoid of enlightened diplomats, marked by no generous spirit, but rather by the vacillating policy of yore, and a settled aversion to the introduction of improvements which, encouraged by other nations, have rendered Old Castile but a third-rate power in our century. Engineers, picks, shovels, railways, steam-engines, and the various paraphernalia of material development, have now commenced the grand work of restoration, and her Future may be yet as glorious as her Past has been chivalrous and brilliant.

Unnecessary expansion weakens States as well as individuals. Nations may develop themselves too suddenly; but by amassing their energies, their wealth, and by innate cultivation, by the proper protection of national interests, they will strengthen themselves, rendering the citizen a soldier at the approach of war, a producer in the calm hours of peace and prosperity. That country which imports to flatter idle tastes, or gratify popular vanities, cannot, in the hour of peril, expect heroes in her pampered populace. When the tocsin hath sounded, she discovers, too late, that the rank and file are indeed degenerate, while the leaders are, at best, but bevies of lute-voiced orators, improvident with cologne, but averse to powder!

The well-adjusted fabric of our Republic can stand the wear and tear of bomb and expletive, and our hardy pioneers are already well-nigh on the Pacific bulwarks. Mexico profits not from the Past! Will Nicaragua? If not, her shattered wreck will strew the waters, and the coming of Montezuma will indeed remain a traditional echo—a hope—while the Anglo-Saxons, ripe with energy and intelligence, will people the arid plains, and rescue the minerales from oblivion. Were the Ship Canal through Nicaragua, and the Pacific Railroad from our East to the West completed, what would be the destiny of the United States? Her Pacific borders would resound with commerce—thrift on the mountains—wealth in the valleys—and from the fastnesses of her northwesternmost stations long trains of mules would wend, laden with gold, to barter for the silks of the Indies, the spices of the Orient, the velvets of Genoa, the embroideries of France, the wines of Spain and Portugal, the cutlery of England, and the manufactures of thorough Europe. Within the Constantinople of the Americas, the turbaned Turk would display his gems and perfumes, and the dark Asiatic his ivory and cachmeres. The mines of Mexico would here find vent, and to the Castilian, who, of yore, deemed that land alone desirable which teemed with gold and gems, our remote possessions would prove El Paraiso regained.

The intervening and neighboring domains, sooner or later, will imitate, if they do not merge. 'Tis the reason we would conquer—Step by step we shall advance, surely if slowly.—Not by violence is the great battle to be won, the prize to be gained. We shall stand upon the entire length of the Pacific shore, permanently, *moral victors*, potent, vigorous, and happy, not as blood-stained Conquerors, urged forward by rapine and false glory. Already Commerce throngs the Gulf of California—the waves of the Sea of Cortés ripple under our keels, bearing us onward to a peaceful and glorious Conquest. However high the storms may dash the warring waves, true to her purpose will our gallant Ship of State ride the billows, and anchor where the Sun smiles in his decline, upon the Mediterranean of the Occident. Where the gonfalon of Spain, as Prescott beautifully renders it, "romantic Spain, the land where the light of Chivalry lingered longest above the horizon," once waved in haughty triumph, the flags of vigorously competing nations will flaunt, as Commerce, with her votaries, sweeps steadily on, intent upon a destiny of wealth and universal redemption.

THE END.

Memoirs of the Queens of France. Written in France, carefully compiled from researches made there, commended by the press generally, and published from the Tenth London Edition. It is a truly valuable work for the reader and student of history. By Mrs. Forbes Bush. 2 vols. in one. Cloth. Price $1 75.

Memoirs of the Life of Anne Boleyn, Queen of Henry VIII. In the records of biography there is no character that more forcibly exemplifies the vanity of human ambition, or more thoroughly enlists the attention of the reader than this—the Seventh American, and from the Third London Edition. By Miss Benger. With portrait on steel. Cloth. $1 75.

Heroic Women of History. Containing the most extraordinary examples of female courage of ancient and modern times, and set before the wives, sisters, and daughters of the country, in the hope that it may make them even more renowned for resolution, fortitude, and self-sacrifice than the Spartan females of old. By Henry C. Watson. With Illustrations. Cloth. $1 75.

Public and Private History of Louis Napoleon, Emperor of the French. An impartial view of the public and private career of this extraordinary man, giving full information in regard to his most distinguished ministers, generals, relatives and favorites. By Samuel M. Schmucker, LL. D. With portraits on Steel. Cloth. $1 75.

Life and Reign of Nicholas I., Emperor of Russia. The only complete history of this great personage that has appeared in the English language, and furnishes interesting facts in connection with Russian society and government of great practical value to the attentive reader. By Samuel M. Schmucker, LL D. With Illustrations. Cloth. $1 75.

Life and Times of George Washington. A concise and condensed narrative of Washington's career, especially adapted to the popular reader, and presented as the best matter upon this immortal theme—one especially worthy the attention and admiration of every American. By Samuel M. Schmucker, LL. D. With Portrait on steel. Cloth. $1 75.

Life and Times of Alexander Hamilton. Incidents of a career that will never lose its singular power to attract and instruct, while giving impressive lessons of the brightest elements of character, surrounded and assailed by the basest. By Samuel M. Schmucker, LL. D. With Portrait on steel. Cloth. $1 75.

Life and Times of Thomas Jefferson. In which the author has presented both the merits and defects of this great representative hero in their true light, and has studiously avoided indiscriminate praise or wholesale censure. By Samuel M. Schmucker, LL. D. With Portrait. Cloth. $1 75.

Life of Benjamin Franklin. Furnishing a superior and comprehensive record of this celebrated Statesman and Philosopher—rich beyond parallel in lessons of wisdom for every age, calling and condition in life, public and private. By O. L. Holley. With Portrait on steel and Illustrations on wood. Cloth. $1 75.

Public and Private Life of Daniel Webster. The most copious and attractive collection of personal memorials concerning the great Statesman that has hitherto been published, and by one whose intimate and confidential relations with him afford a guarantee for their authenticity. By Gen. S. P. Lyman. With Illustrations. Cloth. $1 75.

Life and Times of Henry Clay. An impartial biography, presenting, by bold and simple strokes of the historic pencil, a portraiture of the illustrious theme which no one should fail to read, and no library be without. By Samuel M. Schmucker, LL. D. With Portrait on steel. Cloth. $1 75.

Life and Public Services of Stephen A. Douglas. A true and faithful exposition of the leading incidents of his brilliant career arranged so as to instruct the reader and produce the careful study which the life of so great a man deserves. By H. M. Flint. With Portrait on steel. Cloth. $1 75.

Life and Public Services of Abraham Lincoln. (In both the English and German languages.) As a record of this great man it is a most desirable work, admirably arranged for reference, with an index over each page, from which the reader can familiarize himself with the contents by glancing through it. By Frank Crosby, of the Philadelphia Bar. With Portrait on steel. Cloth. $1 75.

Life of Daniel Boone, the Great Western Hunter and Pioneer. Comprising graphic and authentic accounts of his daring, thrilling adventures, wonderful skill, coolness and sagacity under the most hazardous circumstances, with an autobiography dictated by himself. By Cecil B. Hartley. With Illustrations. Cloth. $1 75.

Life of Colonel David Crocket, the Original Humorist and Irrepressible Backwoodsman. Showing his strong will and indomitable spirit, his bear hunting, his military services, his career in Congress, and his triumphal tour through the States—written by himself; to which is added the account of his glorious death at the Alamo. With Illustrations. Cloth. $1 75.

Life of Kit Carson, the Great Western Hunter and Guide. An exciting volume of wild and romantic exploits, thrilling adventures, hair-breadth escapes, daring coolness, moral and physical courage, and invaluable services—such as rarely transpire in the history of the world. By Charles Burdett. With Illustrations. Cloth. $1 75.

Life of Captain John Smith, the Founder of Virginia. The adventures contained herein serve to denote the more noble and daring events of a period distinguished by its spirit, its courage, and its passion, and challenges the attention of the American people. By W. Gilmore Simms. With Illustrations. Price $1 75.

Life of General Francis Marion, the Celebrated P[illegible]isan Hero of the Revolution. This was one of the most distinguished [illegible]n who [illegible] on the grand theatre of war during the times that "tried men's so[illegible]s," and his bri[illegible] career has scarcely a parallel in history. By Cecil B. Har[illegible]ey. With Illustrations. Cloth. $1 75.

LIFE OF GENERAL ANDREW JACKSON, THE CELEBRATED PATRIOT AND STATESMAN. The character here shown as firm in will, clear in judgment, rapid in decision and decidedly pronounced, sprung from comparative obscurity to the highest gift within the power of the American people, and is prolific in interest. By ALEXANDER WALKER. $1 75.

LIFE AND TIMES OF GENERAL SAM HOUSTON, THE HUNTER, PATRIOT, AND STATESMAN. It reminds one of the story of Romulus—who was nurtured by the beasts of the forest till he planted the foundations of a mighty empire—and stands alone as an authentic memoir. With Maps, Portrait, and Illustrations. Cloth. $1 75.

LIVES OF THE THREE MRS. JUDSONS, THE CELEBRATED FEMALE MISSIONARIES. The domestic lives and individual labors of these three bright stars in the galaxy of American heroines, who in ministering to the souls of heathens, experienced much of persecution. By CECIL B. HARTLEY. With steel Portraits. Cloth. $1 75.

LIFE OF ELISHA KENT KANE, AND OF OTHER DISTINGUISHED AMERICAN EXPLORERS. A narrative of the discoverers who possess the strongest hold upon public interest and attention, and one of the few deeply interesting volumes of distinguished Americans of this class. By SAMUEL M. SCHMUCKER, LL. D. With Portrait on steel. Cloth. $1 75.

THE LIFE AND ADVENTURES OF PAULINE CUSHMAN, THE CELEBRATED UNION SPY AND SCOUT. Stirring details from the lips of the subject herself, whose courage, heroism, and devotion to the old flag, endeared her to the Army of the Southwest. By F. L. SARMIENTO, Esq., Member of the Philadelphia Bar. With Portrait on steel and Illustrations on wood. Cloth. $1 75.

JEFFERSON DAVIS AND STONEWALL JACKSON: THE LIFE AND PUBLIC SERVICES OF EACH. Truths from the lives of these men, both of whom served their country before the war, and afterwards threw themselves into the cause of the South with unbounded zeal—affording valuable historic facts for all, North and South. With Illustrations. Cloth. $1 75.

CORSICA, AND THE EARLY LIFE OF NAPOLEON.

Delicately drawn idyllic descriptions of the Island, yielding new light to political history, exciting much attention in Germany and England, and altogether making a book of rare character and value. Translated by HON. E. JOY MORRIS. With Portrait on steel. Cloth. $1 75.

THE HORSE AND HIS DISEASES: EMBRACING

HIS HISTORY AND VARIETIES, BREEDING AND MANAGEMENT, AND VICES. A splendid, complete, and reliable book—the work of more than fifteen years' careful study—pointing out diseases accurately, and recommending remedies that have stood the test of actual trial. To which is added "RAREY'S METHOD OF TRAINING HORSES." By ROBERT JENNINGS, V. S. With nearly one hundred Illustrations. Cloth. $1 75.

SHEEP, SWINE, AND POULTRY. Enumerating

their varieties and histories; the best modes of breeding, feeding, and managing; the diseases to which they are subject; the best remedies—and offering the best practical treatise of its kind now published. By ROBERT JENNINGS, V. S. With numerous Illustrations. Cloth. $1 75.

CATTLE AND THEIR DISEASES. Giving their

history and breeds, crossing and breeding, feeding and management; with the diseases to which they are subject, and the remedies best adapted to their cure; to which is added a list of remedies used in treating cattle. By ROBERT JENNINGS, V. S. With numerous Illustrations. Cloth. $1 75.

HORSE TRAINING MADE EASY. A new and

practical system of Teaching and Educating the Horse, including whip training and thorough instructions in regard to shoeing—full of information of a useful and well-tested character. By ROBERT JENNINGS, V. S. With numerous Illustrations. Cloth. $1 25.

600 RECEIPTS WORTH THEIR WEIGHT IN GOLD.

An unequalled variety in kind, the collection and testing of which have extended through a period of thirty years—a number of them having never before appeared in print, while all are simple, plain, and highly meritorious. By JOHN MARQUART, of Lebanon, Pa. Cloth. $1 75.

500 Employments Adapted to Women.

Throwing open to womankind productive fields of labor everywhere, and affording full opportunity to select employments best adapted to their tastes—all the result of over three years' constant care and investigation. By Miss Virginia Penny. Cloth. $1 75.

Everybody's Lawyer and Book of Forms.

The simplicity of its instructions, the comprehensiveness of its subject, and the accuracy of its details, together with its perfect arrangement, conciseness, attractiveness and cheapness make it the most desirable of all legal hand-books. By Frank Crosby, Esq. Thoroughly revised to date by S. J. Vandersloot, Esq. 608 pp. Law Style. $2 00.

The Family Doctor. Intended to guard

against diseases in the family; to furnish the proper treatment for the sick; to impart knowledge in regard to medicines, herbs, and plants; to show how to preserve a sound body and mind, and written in plain language, free from medical terms. By Prof. Henry Taylor, M. D. Profusely Illustrated. Cloth. $1 75.

The American Practical Cookery Book.

A faithful and highly useful guide, whose directions all can safely follow, making housekeeping easy, pleasant, and economical in all its departments, and based upon the personal test, throughout, of an intelligent practical housekeeper. Illustrated with Fifty Engravings. Cloth. $1 75.

Modern Cookery in all its Branches. Designed

to interest and benefit housekeepers everywhere by its plain and simple instructions in regard to the judicious preparation of food, and altogether a work of superior merit. By Miss Eliza Acton. Carefully revised by Mrs. Sarah J. Hale. With many Illustrations and a copious Index. Cloth. $1 75.

Thirty Years in the Arctic Regions. The

graphic narrative of Sir John Franklin, the most celebrated of Arctic Travellers, in which Sir John tells his own story—unsurpassed for intense and all-absorbing interest—sketching his three expeditions, and that part of the fourth now shrouded in mystery to the world. Cloth. $1 75.

EXPLORATIONS AND DISCOVERIES DURING FOUR YEARS' WANDERINGS IN THE WILDS OF SOUTHWESTERN AFRICA. Important and exciting experiences, full of wild adventure and instructive facts, which seem to possess a mysterious charm for every mind, and in which the spirit of intelligent and adventurous curiosity is everywhere prominent. By CHARLES JOHN ANDERSON. With Illustrations. Cloth. $1 75.

LIVINGSTONE'S TRAVELS AND RESEARCHES IN SOUTH AFRICA. Given in the pleasing language of Dr. Livingstone, and rich in the personal adventures and hair-breadth escapes of that most indefatigable discoverer and interesting Christian gentleman—making a work of special value. By DAVID LIVINGSTONE, LL. D., D. C. S. Profusely Illustrated. Cloth. $1 75.

TRAVELS AND DISCOVERIES IN NORTH AND CENTRAL AFRICA. Recounting an expedition undertaken under the auspices of H. B M.'s Government, exhibiting the most remarkable courage, perseverance, presence of mind, and contempt of danger and death, and immensely important as a work of information. By HENRY BARTH, Ph. D., D. C. L., etc. With Illustrations. Cloth. $1 75.

ELLIS' THREE VISITS TO MADAGASCAR. Written in Madagascar, while on a visit to the queen and people, in which is carefully described the singularly beautiful country and the manners and customs of its people, and from which an unusual amount of information is obtainable. By Rev. WILLIAM ELLIS, F. H. S. Profusely Illustrated. Cloth. $1 75.

ORIENTAL AND WESTERN SIBERIA. A Stirring narrative of seven years' explorations in Siberia, Mongolia, the Kirghes Steppes, Chinese Tartary, and part of Central Asia, revealing extraordinary facts showing much of hunger, thirst, and perilous adventure, and forming a work of rare attractiveness for every reader. By THOMAS WILLIAM ATKINSON. With numerous Illustrations. Cloth. $1 75.

HUNTING SCENES IN THE WILDS OF AFRICA. Thrilling adventures of daring hunters—Cummings, Harris, and others—among the Lions, Elephants, Giraffes, Buffaloes, and other animals—than which few, if any works, are more exciting. With numerous Illustrations. Cloth. $1 75.

HUNTING ADVENTURES IN THE NORTHERN WILDS. A tramp in the Chateaugay Woods, over hills, lakes and forest streams, at a time when millions of acres lay in a perfect wilderness, affording incidents, descriptions, and adventures of extraordinary interest. By S. H. HAMMOND With Illustrations Cloth. $1 75.

WILD NORTHERN SCENES; OR, SPORTING ADVENTURES WITH THE RIFLE AND THE ROD. Affording remarkably interesting experiences in a section where the howl of the Wolf, the scream of the Panther, and the hoarse bellow of the Moose could be heard—presenting a racy book. By S. H. HAMMOND. With Illustrations. Cloth. $1 75.

PERILS AND PLEASURES OF A HUNTER'S LIFE; OR, THE ROMANCE OF HUNTING. Replete with thrilling incidents and hair-breadth escapes, and fascinating in the extreme, while depicting the romance of hunting. By PEREGRINE HERNE. With Illustrations. Cloth. $1 75.

HUNTING SPORTS IN THE WEST. An amount of novelty and variety, of bold enterprise and noble hardihood, of heroic daring and fierce encounters, which seem to be much more entertaining by the quiet fireside than they would be to the one going through them in the forest or field. By CECIL B. HARTLEY. With numerous Illustrations. Cloth. $1 75.

FANNY HUNTER'S WESTERN ADVENTURES. Vividly portraying the stirring scenes enacted in Kansas and Missouri during a sojourn of several years on the Western Border, and fully representing social and domestic affairs in frontier life—containing curious pictures of character. With Illustrations. Cloth. $1 75.

WONDERFUL ADVENTURES, BY LAND AND SEA, OF THE SEVEN QUEER TRAVELLERS WHO MET AT AN INN. Revelations of a singular and unusually entertaining character, in which the most terrible circumstances and mysterious occurrences are faithfully and forcibly placed before the reader By JOSIAH BARNES. Cloth. $1 75.

NICARAGUA; PAST, PRESENT, AND FUTURE. Setting forth its history, the manners and customs of its inhabitants, its mines its minerals, and other productions, and throwing light upon a subject of very great importance to the masses of our people. By PETER F. STOUT, Esq., late U. S Vice-Consul. Cloth. $1 75.

FEMALE LIFE AMONG THE MORMONS; OR, MARIA WARD'S DISCLOSURES. Romantic Incidents, bordering on the marvelous, which show the evils, horrors, and abominations of the Mormon system—the degradation of its females, and the consequent vices of its society. By MARIA WARD, the Wife of a Mormon Elder. With Illustrations. 40,000 copies sold. Cloth. $1 75.

MALE LIFE AMONG THE MORMONS. Detailing sights and scenes among the Mormons, with important remarks on their moral and social economy; being a true transcript of events, viewing Mormonism from a man's standpoint, and forming a companion to the preceding volume. By AUSTIN N. WARD. Edited by MARIA WARD. With Illustrations. Cloth. $1 75.

PIONEER LIFE IN THE WEST. Describing the adventures of Boone, Kenton, Brady, Clark, the Whetzels, the Johnsons, and others, in their fierce encounters with the Indians, and making up a work of the most entertaining and instructive character for those who delight in history and adventure. With numerous Illustrations. Cloth. $1 75.

THRILLING STORIES OF THE GREAT REBELLION. Fearful adventures of soldiers, scouts, spies, and refugees; daring exploits of smugglers, guerillas, desperadoes, and others; tales of loyal and disloyal women; stories of the negro, and incidents of fun and merriment in camp and field. By Lieut. CHARLES S. GREENE, late of the U. S. Army. With Illustrations in Oil. Cloth. $1 75.

HISTORY OF THE WAR IN INDIA. FURNISHING the complete history of British India, together with interesting and thrilling details which have scarcely a parallel in the world's history, to which is added a memoir of General Sir HENRY HAVELOCK. By HENRY FREDERICK MALCOLM. Illustrated with numerous Engravings. Cloth. $1 75.

OUR BOYS. Personal experiences of the author while in the army, presenting the richest and raciest scenes of army and camp life ever published, and portraying various events in all their originality. By A. F. HILL, of the Eighth Pennsylvania Reserves. With Portrait on Steel, and characteristic Illustrations. Cloth. $1 75.

OUR CAMPAIGNS. The marches, bivouacs, battles, incidents, camp life, and history of a regiment during its three years' term of service in the war, together with a sketch of the Army of the Potomac under Generals McClellan, Burnside, Hooker, Meade, and Grant. By E. M. WOODWARD, Adj't Second Penna. Reserves. Cloth. $1 75.

MARGARET MONCRIEFFE, THE BEAUTIFUL SPY. An exciting story of Army and high life in New York, in 1776, presenting facts and historic names, and showing the mutual attachment between Aaron Burr and Margaret Moncrieffe, as well as the influence of the latter upon the former in the more important events of his life. By CHARLES BURDETT. Cloth. $1 75.

SIX NIGHTS IN A BLOCK HOUSE; OR, SKETCHES OF BORDER LIFE. Feats of hero hunters and thrilling exploits among the Indians; furnishing the names of hunters well known in western history, and showing the most exciting drama of border warfare, and, as a whole, the most intensely interesting and instructive work upon Indian life now offered the public. By HENRY C. WATSON. With 100 Engravings. Cloth. $1 75.

THRILLING ADVENTURES AMONG THE EARLY SETTLERS. A series of desperate encounters with Indians, daring exploits of Texan Rangers, incidents of guerilla warfare, fearful deeds of desperadoes and regulators of the west, and graphic delineations of hunting and trapping well worthy universal preservation. By WARREN WILDWOOD, Esq. More than 200 Engravings Cloth. $1 75.

THRILLING INCIDENTS IN AMERICAN HISTORY. Events which are among the most striking and important in our national annals, covering the Revolution, the French War the Tripolitan War, the Indian Wars, the War of 1812, and the Mexican War—all of which are of great usefulness to the student and general reader. By the author of "The Army and Navy of the United States." With Three Hundred Illustrations. Cloth. $1 75.

SCOUTING EXPEDITIONS OF THE TEXAN RANGERS. Operations which occurred during some of the prominent events of the Mexican war, together with sketches of the celebrated partisan chiefs, Hays, McCulloch, and Walker, whose courage, sagacity, and remarkable exploits should be familiar to all Americans. By SAMUEL C. REID, Jr , late of the Texan Rangers, and Member of the Louisiana Bar. With Illustrations. Cloth. $1 75.

THE BATTLE-FIELDS OF THE REVOLUTION. The most brilliant points in the history of the Revolutionary war, recounting the principal battles, sieges, and other important events—the whole interspersed with numerous characteristic anecdotes. By THOMAS Y. RHOADS. With many Illustrations. Cloth. $1 75.

THRILLING ADVENTURES AMONG THE INDIANS. In which are enumerated the most remarkable incidents of the early Indian Wars, which abound in dangers, vindictiveness, endurance, heroism, gratitude, treachery, stoicism, and revenge, and in which there is much to fascinate the reader, and store the inquiring mind. By JOHN FROST, LL. D. With more than 300 Illustrations. Cloth. $1 75.

THE HERO GIRL, AND HOW SHE BECAME A CAPTAIN IN THE ARMY. The highly dramatic story of Molly Pitcher who, having lost her husband at the battle of Monmouth, gallantly stepped forward, took his place at the cannon, and continued serving it until the battle ended—after which the rank of Captain was conferred on her by Gen. Washington. By THRACE TALMOI With Illustrations. Cloth. $1 75.

MRS. PARTINGTON'S KNITTING WORK, AND WHAT WAS DONE BY HER PLAGUY BOY IKE. In which all will see the acid and sugar, and spirit and water—forming an intellectual punch, of which all can partake without headache or heartache. Wrought by the old lady herself. With characteristic Illustrations, including a portrait of the old lady in specs, surrounded by the Partington family. Cloth. $1 75.

WAY DOWN EAST; OR, PORTRAITURES OF YANKEE LIFE. Embodying some of the raciest stories of the "Down Easter" ever published by this humorous author—containing much of genuine wit and attractive thought. By SEBA SMITH, the original Major Jack Downing. With several rich and original Illustrations. Cloth. $1 75.

www.ingramcontent.com/pod-product-compliance
Lightning Source LLC
LaVergne TN
LVHW020123110826
845151LV00001B/258

* 9 7 8 1 4 2 5 5 4 0 5 7 9 *